PB

A

Philip E. Lilienthal

BOOK

The Philip E. Lilienthal imprint
honors special books
in commemoration of a man whose work
at University of California Press from 1954 to 1979
was marked by dedication to young authors
and to high standards in the field of Asian Studies.
Friends, family, authors, and foundations have together
endowed the Lilienthal Fund, which enables UC Press
to publish under this imprint selected books
in a way that reflects the taste and judgment
of a great and beloved editor.

The publisher gratefully acknowledges the generous support of the Philip E. Lilienthal Asian Studies Endowment Fund of the University of California Press Foundation, which was established by a major gift from Sally Lilienthal.

Following the Leader

Following the Leader

*Ruling China, from Deng Xiaoping
to Xi Jinping*

David M. Lampton

UNIVERSITY OF CALIFORNIA PRESS
Berkeley · Los Angeles · London

University of California Press, one of the most
distinguished university presses in the United States,
enriches lives around the world by advancing scholarship
in the humanities, social sciences, and natural sciences. Its
activities are supported by the UC Press Foundation and
by philanthropic contributions from individuals and
institutions. For more information, visit www.ucpress.edu.

University of California Press
Berkeley and Los Angeles, California

University of California Press, Ltd.
London, England

Library of Congress Cataloging-in-Publication Data

Lampton, David M.
　Following the leader : ruling China, from Deng
Xiaoping to Xi Jinping / David M. Lampton.
　　pages　cm
　Includes bibliographical references and index.
　ISBN 978-0-520-28121-9 (cloth : alk. paper) —
　ISBN 978-0-520-95739-8 (e-book)
　　1. China—Politics and government—1976–2002.
2. China—Politics and government—21st century.
3. Political leadership—China.　4. Political culture—
China.　I. Title.
　JQ1516.L36　2013
　320.951—dc23

　　　　　　　　　　　　　　　2013032715

Manufactured in the United States of America

22　21　20　19　18　17　16　15　14
10　9　8　7　6　5　4　3　2　1

In keeping with a commitment to support
environmentally responsible and sustainable printing
practices, UC Press has printed this book on Natures
Natural, a fiber that contains 30% post-consumer waste
and meets the minimum requirements of ANSI/NISO
Z39.48-1992 (R 1997) (Permanence of Paper).

To Noah Joseph and Sadie Mae Lampton,
who will live with and shape this century's
relations with China

Contents

Illustrations and Tables

Acknowledgments

This book represents many things, not least of which is the accumulation of conversations and assistance I have received from people throughout Greater China since my residence in Hong Kong in 1972–73. I wish, therefore, to acknowledge the literally thousands of Chinese people who have given their time, shared their knowledge, and expended their energy to educate me over the years. I cannot thank them individually, but they know who they are and the gratitude I feel.

No person is an intellectual island, and the tides and waves of many great teachers and colleagues have defined my shores, not least those from Stanford University, Ohio State University, the Kettering Foundation, the National Academy of Sciences, the National Committee on United States-China Relations, and the Johns Hopkins School of Advanced International Studies (SAIS). I particularly want to thank one of my dearest and most respected colleagues, Ms. Jan Berris, vice president of the National Committee on United States-China Relations. In addition to all she has taught me about China and working with others, she made available to me her monumental collection of meeting notes that I used when writing about the early years following the epoch-changing visit to the People's Republic of China (PRC) by President Richard Nixon in 1972.

In undertaking this project I have benefited from the research assistance of several very talented PhD students at SAIS—individuals who have helped me install and utilize the data management system that has permitted me to exploit the large number of interviews that are central to this volume's architecture and informational base. In addition, they have helped me think through concepts and have undertaken fact checking: David Bulman, Lily Chen, Eric Hagt, Selina Ho, Amanda Kerrigan, and Tabitha Mallory have my sincere appreciation and admiration. To Dr. Thomas Fingar at Stanford University, I express my thanks for his comments on the entire manuscript, as well as his friendship over our careers. On the editing front, I owe an enormous personal debt to my editor of long standing, Krista Forsgren. At the University of California Press, Senior Editor Reed Malcolm has given me much-valued substantive advice over the years, not least his assistance and guidance with this volume. I also wish to thank Dore Brown, project editor, for her careful and expeditious shepherding of the manuscript through the production process. To Elisabeth Magnus I wish to express my gratitude for her superb copy editing, and Susan Stone has my thanks for preparing the index. Moreover, the staff of UC Press have been most helpful, particularly Editorial Assistant Stacy Eisenstark. Finally, to the anonymous reviewers who assessed the manuscript for the Press, I express my thanks for their suggestions for revisions and corrections that improved the manuscript.

For providing me the resources, time, and productive environment in which to execute the research and writing embodied in this volume, I express my appreciation to several individuals and organizations. Gratefully, I acknowledge the Rockefeller Foundation and its Bellagio Center for providing me a Residency at Villa Serbelloni on Lake Como in northern Italy. There I was free to do nothing but write and interact with a group of creative scholars and artists from around the world in mid-2011. I thank the Foundation and the Center's managing director, Ms. Pilar Palacia, as well as the Center's attentive and excellent staff, for affording me an unparalleled creative environment in which to work.

At SAIS, I have been blessed not only with the graduate students mentioned above but also with a school administration and other colleagues that have been most supportive of my work. I wish to particularly thank former dean Jessica Einhorn, our senior associate dean for finance and administration, Mr. Myron Kunka, and our current dean, Vali Nasr, for their moral and material support of my work. To the Johns Hopkins University and its president, Ron Daniels, and then provost Lloyd Minor, I wish to express my thanks for the ongoing research support provided as part of my designation as a Gilman Scholar. To my colleague Zhaojin Ji, I express my gratitude for her help throughout the process of producing this book. Finally, I must thank the National Bureau of Asian Research and the Woodrow Wilson International Center for Scholars for providing resources connected to the Scalapino Prize of 2010, resources that have greatly facilitated this project and others.

Turning to family, the bedrock upon which my lifetime pursuits have been built, I want to express the love and gratitude I feel for my wife, Susan, and for her support over the forty-five years of our married life. I also want to thank my mother, Mary Jane Lampton, who passed away in April 2012—she and my father, Jack W. Lampton, to whom she was married for nearly seventy-four years, gave me the example of values and hard work that I have tried to emulate. To conclude, this book is dedicated to our grandchildren, Noah Joseph and Sadie Mae Lampton. As the world evolves, may it present them with a U.S.-China relationship that makes a better twenty-first century possible.

David M. Lampton
Washington, D.C.
September, 2013

Introduction

"Mao was great because he made China unified/independent.
Deng Xiaoping opened China. And Jiang Zemin, he let the
Chinese people have a normal life. Before, when I was young,
my folks told me not to make political mistakes. Now I can
tell my kids to learn in school well and they can be million-
aires. The environment is now free, more relaxing. People
now like to go see *Titanic* [the movie], and one lady saw it
nine times and cried every time. Enjoy everyday life, this is
our new idea. Before we had to talk about contributing to the
masses. But we came to the world to enjoy our short lives. A
normal life is very important for Chinese. In the Cultural
Revolution I was a Red Guard, and my daughter was
surprised and said I had been a bandit. In my house, growing
up, before every meal, before a picture on the wall of Mao
[Zedong], we recited quotations from Mao. Now it seems
funny to have done such stupid things."

—Secretary-general of a special event, July 2003, Beijing

Based on 558 interviews with Chinese leaders, on case studies, and on
innumerable documents, this book humanizes China's extraordinary
course of development since Deng Xiaoping's 1977 return to power,
examining domestic politics, foreign relations, natural and manmade
disasters, civil-military relations, and the Chinese style of negotiating.
This volume reveals the human frustrations China's leaders feel, the
nightmares disturbing their sleep, and the sheer scale of the challenges
they face. Challenges run the gamut from meeting rising political expectations and keeping the economic juggernaut going, to providing citizens breathable air and potable water and reassuring an apprehensive
world that Beijing's growing power is not a threat. In the second decade

of the new millennium, China is in a far different political space than it was in 1977. Today, with weaker leaders, an increasingly fragmented society and bureaucracy, and empowered societal and interest groups, bringing a lagging political system into increasing harmony with a changed society is the central challenge.

China's unparalleled growth and societal change since 1977 poses a vital question: "Will the Chinese government be able to control its own internal and external behavior in the years ahead?" If not, major trouble lies ahead for China and for the world. Part of the answer to this question of whether control will continue to be maintained lies in the types of leaders China has had and will produce. What vision do China's leaders convey to their people and the world, and how might that change? How will these leaders interact with the ever more complex and pluralistic society they seek to govern? Will China's pluralism become progressively more anchored in institutions, laws, regulations, and ethical norms that are increasingly shared worldwide?

Leaders count in world affairs. Their behaviors are grounded in a complex and ever changing combination of personal and group experience, domestic economic/social/political forces, institutional structures, international regimes, external pressures, and luck. Since leaders count in explaining the behavior of states, one must inquire into the specific motivations, capacities, and perceptions of individual leaders to anticipate future behavior. General theorizing is inadequate. China's leaders face internal governance tasks of such magnitude and complexity that they will be preoccupied for a long time. Present and future PRC leaders are, and will remain, ambivalent about assuming international burdens and responsibilities that many outsiders consider essential. These leaders are torn between the attraction of gaining greater global status and protecting the PRC's growing world-wide interests and the knowledge that their country remains poor and their grip on power tenuous. As China's citizens, companies, and other organizations expand their global reach, Beijing will find it increasingly difficult to control their myriad activities.

Since the early 1970s, how have Chinese leaders at all levels evolved their thinking about governing their own nation and dealing with the outside world? To what extent is the Chinese political system different than it was when Deng Xiaoping returned to the national and international stages in July 1977—the date at which I reckon the reform era began?[1] This book allows Chinese leaders to speak for themselves.

However, this book has broader purposes than simply to humanize China's extraordinary course of development—it presents an evolutionary picture, concretely specifying changes and continuities and revealing the reality, inasmuch as possible, of working in the often frustrating Chinese system. This work is a selective history of challenges confronting contemporary PRC leaders, illustrated with case studies and individual-level data. It defines in both graphic and theoretical terms how China has changed and the future challenges this presents to its people and to the world.

"Leaders" I define here as those persons in the public, private, and social organization sectors who exert significant influence over diverse realms of policy and public discourse (political, military, social, economic, and intellectual). Leadership in China is broader in scope than simply the small number of members of the Standing Committee of the Politburo who sit at the apex of the national power hierarchy. One of the most important changes in Chinese society over the reform era has been the gradual enlargement of the scope and diversity of individuals who reasonably can be counted as leaders.

There have been both continuities and dramatic changes in the reform period with respect to how Chinese leaders view the governance of China and its role in global affairs. Understanding these continuities and changes is important to those who live *in* China and to those abroad who must live *with* China in the twenty-first century. For example, one area of continuity with significant consequences for both citizens of the PRC and the outside world is the still deeply engrained idea among the vast majority of the Chinese population that the state has a legitimate, essential, and expansive role in information management; one Chinese Academy of Social Sciences study found that more than 80 percent of those urban Chinese respondents surveyed agreed that the Internet should be managed or controlled, with nearly 85 percent of those respondents arguing that the government should be the entity to manage it.[2] On the other hand, one great change over the past four decades is that the idea of global interdependence is increasingly recognized and accepted, not only by elites but by ordinary citizens as well. The biggest change is the development of a domestic social and political system characterized by a weaker, less cohesive leadership group, a more pluralized society and bureaucracy, and subnational actors in government, society, and the economy with more resources to promote their interests. If these trends continue in the absence of (a) more legal and regulatory control, (b) more transparency and accountability, and (c) more ethical constraints, an untethered China will spell trouble for itself, its neighbors, and the international community.

HISTORICAL BACKGROUND

In the twentieth century, China had three revolutions, two of which were in the communist era: the first was the collapse of the Qing dynasty in 1911 and with it the demise of the traditional dynastic system. After a protracted transitional period of domestic and international strife in the first half of the twentieth century came the second (communist) revolution with Mao Zedong in 1949 and what soon emerged as his grotesque exercise of power, which lasted until his death on September 9, 1976. Finally, in the last two-plus decades of the twentieth century came a third revolution, albeit a more gradual, less violent phase, in the communist order itself—the reform era. Its character is illustrated by an exchange between Deng Xiaoping and CBS journalist Mike Wallace in 1986. When Wallace commented, "The China of Deng Xiaoping is different from the China of Mao Zedong. It's a new revolution that is going on here, at least you are trying to make a new revolution, it seems," Deng replied, "You are right. We too say that what we are doing now is in essence a revolution. In another sense, we are engaged in an experiment. For us, this is something new, and we have to feel our way. Since it is something new, we are bound to make mistakes. Our method is to review our experience from time to time and correct mistakes whenever we discover them, so that minor mistakes will not grow into major ones."[3]

After decades, the extremes of Mao's era appear distant, almost ephemeral, while the implications of the changes Deng Xiaoping wrought become clearer and loom larger. Though there is a certain popular nostalgia for the faux equality and simplicity of Mao's era, deep dissatisfaction with some of the unwelcome consequences of the reform era that followed his rule, and deep resentment at changes that have failed to occur, there is no significant constituency for the deprivation, brutality, social and economic control, and national dysfunction that were the central features of Chairman Mao's "order." Chinese society has changed so fundamentally since 1977 that, barring something approaching total social breakdown, the preconditions for such national tyranny no longer exist.

This book chronicles, explains, and assesses the evolution of the ongoing revolution from the death of Mao Zedong through the eras of Deng Xiaoping, Jiang Zemin, and Hu Jintao and into the era of Xi Jinping that began in the fall of 2012. Revolution is an abrupt and systematic change involving the repudiation and overthrow of the preexisting sociopolitical order. Though it can be initiated from above or below, revolution is energized by mass popular participation and characterized by new institutions and patterns of behavior. As Crane Brinton observed in *The Anatomy of Revolution,* revolutions often go through cycles of initial moderation, growing excess, popular reaction, and sometimes a new revolutionary sequence—this describes the Mao Zedong–to–Deng Xiaoping progression.[4]

In October 1949, with the ascension to power of Mao Zedong and the Chinese Communist Party (CCP), China entered its communist revolutionary phase. Chairman Mao's increasingly excessive and ever more costly experiments over the next more than quarter century set the stage for what I will term (and what Deng himself called) a second communist-era revolution beginning in July 1977, when Deng Xiaoping returned from political exile to the upper reaches of leadership and quickly emerged as China's supreme—though not entirely unconstrained—leader. In a policy sense, the first dramatic evidence of Deng's revolution was expressed in the policies of the Third Plenum of the Eleventh Central Committee in December 1978. This conclave defined the new era as concerned with socialist modernization and decentralized rural production systems and came immediately on the heels of the announcement of the establishment of formal diplomatic ties between the United States and the PRC—a bold move that marked an entirely new posture toward the outside world.[5]

Much as Mao Zedong's 1949 assumption of power marked an abrupt and enormous change in governing regime, legitimating ideology, leadership characteristics, institutions, distribution of power, socioeconomic foundations, and active support of a large percentage of the governed (in the beginning, at least), Deng Xiaoping's rise nearly three decades later marked a similar immense revolutionary transformation. In the new reform era, there was dramatic change along a number of dimensions: from Marxist/Maoist political dogma to measureable and pragmatic economic and governing performance indicators; from the planned economy to a substantially more market-driven system and all that implied; from rule by older ideologues, peasants, and heartland revolutionaries to rule by younger, more urbane, coastal, educated technocrats and others with diversified disciplinary backgrounds;[6] from an autarkic economy to a pacesetter for globalization and interdependence; from a system shut off from the outside world intellectually to an increasingly information-saturated society that sent its best and brightest abroad for study in great numbers while simultaneously dramatically expanding education at home; and from a totalistic political system to an authoritarian system with the more limited objective of keeping the CCP in power. In short, in moving from the first to the second Chinese communist-era revolution, the PRC transmogrified from a system that actively sought to shape human behavior (and thought) to one that cares principally about keeping a calm political status quo, and from a system that defined self-sufficiency and isolation as success to one that aims to keep expanding China's power and status on a global scale.

The description of the Deng-initiated changes as "revolutionary" requires one important qualification. By Deng's design, the CCP maintained its monopoly on political power and permitted virtually no non-party contestation for the commanding heights of the governing system. Over time, however, the composition of the CCP has changed considerably, becoming more reflective of the society it rules, and very limited political competition has gradually emerged at the lowest levels of the Chinese hierarchy (in villages and in urban districts). There have also been circumscribed attempts to introduce competitive and performance-based dimensions into official post selections within the CCP by using devices such as straw polls, putting forth more candidates than there are posts, and drawing on performance reports that incorporate popular input.[7] Moreover, within the political elite, over time, competition to get on the Standing Committee, the Politburo, and the Central Committee and to attain specific posts at those commanding heights has become more publicly apparent, as seen in the run-up to the Eighteenth Party Congress in the fall of 2012 and the National People's Congress (NPC) the following spring. Chongqing first party secretary Bo Xilai is a case in point: during his several years there, Bo tried to elbow his way onto the Politburo Standing Committee by constructing a populist support base fueled by resentment toward corruption, a desire for a more secure and state-centered social safety net, and a vague nostalgia for the seeming simplicity of the Mao era. The spring of 2012 saw his rapid and ignominious political demise, in part precipitated by his wife's murder of the foreign businessman Neil Heywood and subsequently his desertion by subordinates who regarded him as a sinking political ship.

The struggles to achieve more harmony between the new society and the old politics, sustainable and balanced economic growth, and strengthened legal and judicial, regulatory, and auditing institutions will drive Chinese politics in decades to come. Reform, not least political reform, is like riding a bicycle—either you keep moving forward or you fall off.

THE ROLE OF LEADERS AND SOCIAL FORCES

There are at least two contending ways to understand, and perhaps even anticipate, the behavior of nation-states. One is to apply theories and observed general patterns of state and interstate behavior to a particular situation and to anticipate that future behaviors will accord with the general pattern. So, for instance, John Mearsheimer or Paul Nitze would consider that in the circumstance of a rising power (China) gaining strength in the face of a currently dominant power (the United States), in a largely anarchic international system, it is likely that the rising power will emphasize the conversion of economic power into coercive strength, thereby striving to displace the top dog and achieve dominance, hence security, for itself.[8] In turn, this behavior by the rising state will theoretically induce the current top dog (the United States) to defensively react, thereby producing an upward spiral of competitive tensions and eventually conflict, if not war. Specific behavior is predicted from the asserted generalized pattern and theory, without much reference to the specific institutions or personalities within individual states at a given moment. The example of China's maritime behavior in Asia in the new millennium, the concerns of the PRC's neighbors, and the American response of trying to shift U.S. attention and assets toward the Pacific provides some evidence for this view.

This volume, however, is grounded differently. It seeks to understand China's institutions, sociopolitical systems, and leaders on their own terms. The focus is on discerning the goals and objectives of leaders, the institutions that constrain or facilitate their activities, and the lenses through which key individuals and groups filter information. This approach is inside-out; it is inductive. An additional perspective embraced in this volume is interdependence theory—the assertion that institutional and economic interdependence in the international system dampens impulses toward conflict. Interdependence constrains the choices facing leaders and can promote cooperation. Shanghai's city fathers, for instance, are forthright about how their city's welfare is directly tied to the economic vitality of its major export markets, especially the United States. The predominant inclination in Shanghai is to find a way to avoid conflict either across the Taiwan Strait or with America—it is simply bad for business!

No one perspective, either the deductive strategic perspective or the inductive, data-driven approach, is the sole path to understanding the PRC. Today, however, I see an understanding of China derived from big-power conflict theory to be in dangerous ascendance, not just in the United States, but in certain quarters of China as well.[9] This volume seeks to inform our understanding of China by populating our visions of the PRC in the early twenty-first century with real people, speaking in their own voices about their country, its current circumstances, and its future. I seek to convey a vision of Chinese leaders and society that is not only more authentic than the vision deduced purely from cross-national theory and generalization but also more predictive of future Chinese behavior—more human. The diplomat George Kennan, speaking to his biographer John Lewis Gaddis, expresses a similar approach to understanding another nation's (in this case the Soviet Union's) behavior and distinguishes it from that of his longtime Cold War associate Paul Nitze:

> [Paul Nitze] has the characteristic view of the military planner. . . . Who is the possible opponent against whom you're supposed to plan a war? What do we assume on his part? We assume that he wishes us everything evil. We don't inquire why he should wish this. But, to be safe, we assume that he wants to do anything evil to us that he can do. And secondly, then, when we are faced with uncertainties about his military strength, about his capabilities, we take the worst case as the basis for our examination. These things, I suspect, enter into Paul's views.
>   And you see, then, that one of the differences is that he [Nitze] is dealing with a fictitious and inhuman Soviet elite, whereas I am dealing with what I suspect to be, and think is likely to be, the real one.[10]

Inductive though my basic approach here is, this book reaches a central, theoretical conclusion and makes a prediction. The conclusion is that the Chinese polity has fundamentally changed since July 1977 when Deng returned to power—leaders have become weaker, society stronger, and both leadership and society more pluralized. The prediction is that it will be difficult to maintain social and political stability without further, dramatic changes in political and governing structures and processes, as well as further evolution of China's political culture. China has undergone enormous change, but only further enormous change can preserve stability well into the twenty-first century.

THE INFORMATION BASE: STRENGTHS, LIMITATIONS, AND RESPONSIBILITIES

Though official, other documentary, and statistical data are critical materials upon which this volume draws, its foundation is a set of 558 interviews conducted between 1971 and 2013. The vast majority of these interviews (93 percent) were conducted by me personally, but I have also utilized interviews conducted by a few colleagues, most prominently Ms. Jan Berris, vice president of the National Committee on United States-China Relations. In very few cases, I have included in the data set U.S. government transcripts of high-level meetings and discussions and interviews by journalists, particularly from the 1971–77 period, a time when China was just opening to the United States and before I was regularly traveling to the PRC.[11] Overall, 70 percent of my interviews were conducted with PRC respondents (not including Hong Kong), and 19 percent with respondents from Taiwan (the Republic of China or ROC), with the remainder including "others" (including Hong Kong) who fell outside these two areas, as explained in greater detail in the Appendix.

Throughout my career, starting as an assistant professor at the Ohio State University and then becoming president of the National Committee on United States-China Relations in New York and founding director of the China programs at the American Enterprise Institute and the Nixon Center (which later became the Center for the National Interest) before returning to academe to become Hyman Professor and director of China Studies at the School of Advanced International Studies, I have taken nearly verbatim notes of most meetings, conversations, and formal interviews with people from Greater China and surrounding jurisdictions. The notes are from one-on-one and group meetings with leaders at all levels that took place during protracted periods of fieldwork in China (1982), Taiwan (1978), and Hong Kong (1972–73) as well as during shorter research stints, and from innumerable policy-oriented delegations and dialogues in which I have participated over the years since the mid-1970s.

The encounters occurred in a variety of settings, often circumstances in which I had a mixture of academic, bureaucratic, and policy purposes. These varied and often intertwined objectives meant that I was involved in building continuing, long-term relationships—some spanning decades. This has given me a feeling for individuals and their constraints and has provided me with a sense of change rather than just variation across personalities, but with this insight come possible blind spots and an empathy that not only can clarify but also can cloud judgment. Accompanying such association and access must come a sense of responsibility to one's informants.

A significant fraction of interviews were conducted exclusively in Chinese, or in circumstances where the interviewee spoke in Chinese followed by consecutive interpretation into English (often by Chinese government interpreters). When consecutive interpretation is used, as it often was, the bilingual listener has two passes at the information being conveyed, first in the speaker's native language and then in the note taker's mother tongue. This increases the reliability of what is recorded and how it is interpreted. With senior PRC academics, policy analysts, and think tank researchers, the interviews usually were conducted in English, given their relative language proficiency. This circumstance also meant that interpreters and note takers often were not present to officially record the conversation and disturb the intimacy of the setting. The overwhelming bulk of interviews were conducted in China, Taiwan, and the United States. Initially, in the 1970s and early 1980s especially, conversations conducted in the United States were relatively less constrained for the Chinese interlocutor, but it has seemed to me that over time PRC Chinese have felt less reticent to express their thoughts on the ground in China as well.

The 558 interviews in this data set are not all of the conversations I have documented during the forty-plus years covered in this book, but they are those conversations for which I have high-quality materials and that I believe to be most significant. Each document in my data set usually provides an introductory "Note" that sets the stage for the conversation, provides some biographic information about the subject as well as our possible prior interaction(s), and describes the setting (physical and political) that created the context of that particular conversation. Each interview has been entered into a Microsoft Access data management system that permits the researcher to search using key words as well as "fields" such as date of interview; interviewee name; political jurisdiction in which the interview occurred; interviewee gender; status; rank; and domain. More details of the data management system and all terms are provided in the Appendix.

Interviews are searchable by the "political jurisdiction in which the interview occurred," meaning that throughout my career I have adopted a "Greater China" perspective. While the dominant focus has been the PRC, I have never lost sight of the importance of Taiwan, Hong Kong, Macau, and the Chinese diaspora (especially the Chinese communities throughout Southeast Asia). These communities outside the administrative control of the PRC are vital sources of ideas, talent, marketing networks, capital, and sometimes political support for China, not to mention the sources of policy, security, and other challenges for Beijing. These jurisdictions should be factored into any comprehensive picture of the PRC's governance, development, and international behavior, even though their populations are not large in comparison.

An "interview," by my definition here, is often, in fact, a group meeting, with the thoughts and views of more than one individual respondent expressed during the course of the discussion, including the views of one or more foreign guests.[12] I do not know how many different persons have their views reflected in the entire data set, but it is far more than 558. For instance, in one 1971 interview with Premier Zhou Enlai, two notorious members of the Gang of Four (Yao Wenyuan and Zhang Chunqiao) were present and expressed their frighteningly vacuous views. Parenthetically, the American visitors in that session did not generally acquit themselves very well either.[13] Reading the words of this conversation more than forty years later, one would have had no inkling that today's China or, indeed, today's Sino-U.S. relationship would emerge. In other interviews, subordinates of the "principal" leader sometimes briefly contributed to the conversation, though subordinates seldom spoke; of the senior leaders I have met over the years, Premier (and subsequently general secretary) Zhao Ziyang was the most amenable to participation by subordinates.

The convention I have employed in quoting from these interviews is as follows: given that most interviews are characterized in their introductory "Note" as "near verbatim, with exact words in quotation marks," in the chapters that follow, where a passage is set off as a block quotation, I put double quotation marks only around the exact words within it (in a few instances, around the entire quotation to indicate that the entirety is exactly worded). Where a quotation is run into an ongoing paragraph or sentence, I put double quotation marks around the start of the "near-verbatim" portion and single quotation marks around the exact words within (which may be the entirety). With respect to the romanization of personal Chinese names, I use the spellings that the respondents use if they have a preferred romanization about which I know. In the absence of such a preference, I use Pinyin in most cases, with the exception of Taiwan. With place names I also use the locally preferred romanization.

THE PLAN OF THIS BOOK

This book is divided into four sections—a beginning, two major sections in the middle, and a conclusion.

I. Chapter 1 paints a broad picture of the changes and continuities characterizing the evolution of Chinese governance, leadership, and elite perspectives on relations with the outside world from 1971 to 2013. This overview pays particular attention to the strategic thrusts of Deng Xiaoping's reform policy in the years immediately following his return to power in 1977 and the results of these policies from the perspective of the twenty-first century.

II. Part 1 (chapters 2 through 4), entitled "China, a Wide-Angle View," deals with system change and continuity from 1971 to 2013 across wide swaths of China's bureaucracy, society, and geography. Chapters 2 and 3 in this section focus on China's governance and leadership and the policy-making system because one of the thoughts suffusing much analysis of contemporary China is that there has been economic change but virtually no political system change. The truth is much more complex. There have been important areas of both change and continuity in China's governance, leadership, and policy-making system. In chapter 4 I discuss continuity and change in China's view of, and behavior in, the world.

III. Part 2 (chapters 5 through 7), entitled "China, an Up-Close View," takes a more fine-grained look at aspects of China's governance and dealings with the outside world. The chapters "Nightmares," "Soldiers and Civilians" (on civil-military relations), and "Negotiation Chinese Style" make the Chinese system come alive along specific dimensions of particular interest to policy makers, scholars and students, and general readers.

IV. The final chapter, "Conclusion: Driving beyond the Headlights," assesses China's trajectory, both internally and globally, in light of the many considerations that I have raised in the volume. I conclude with assessments of what this path will require of China's people and the rest of the world, not least the United States, in the years ahead.

CHAPTER I

Evolution in the Revolution

Crossing the river by feeling for stones.

—A phrase popularly attributed to Deng Xiaoping and emblematic of China's pragmatic approach to reform since 1977

First of all we must recognize the huge gap between China and the rest of the world in the area of science and technology. We cannot fool anyone because you can't visit our country without seeing how backward we are. We can only fool ourselves by saying that we are not backward.

—Deng Xiaoping, October 23, 1977

I accompanied Deng [Xiaoping] in 1992 [on his Southern Journey—*nanxun*], and one day he met officials and said that historically [China] was poor for thousands of years—we need development as soon as possible. This is our task. Cities like Guangzhou need a fast growth rate. If [the growth rate of GDP] is below 10 percent [per year], we cannot handle the problems and it brings lots of difficulties.

—Mayor of Guangzhou Li Ziliu, "Remarks," June 9, 1994

Beginning in 1979, Chinese have experienced great transformations in their lives. Of course future difficulties will be inevitable. But as we Chinese often say, the most important thing is that "we've broken the ice and the ship has begun to sail."

—Professor Li Shenzhi, "The History and Future of Sino-American Relations"

The core interest is regime survival and regime security. "Opening and reform were not to improve China, it is to improve the survival of the party; it is a by-product of the improvement. For its own survival [the party] has to bring benefits to the people, as the Kuomintang [in Taiwan] did before 1987."

—Remarks of a senior academic, August 1, 2011

In 1977, the question for China was simple: Could the nation and the state become stronger and more prosperous? More than thirty-five years later, the original question is almost laughable, and now the question is: Can a much stronger China control itself, become more just, and contribute to global stability and development?

Deng Xiaoping's second communist-era revolution cannot be as precisely dated as the first, which officially started on the day that the PRC was founded, October 1, 1949, and which I choose to end in mid-1977, when Deng Xiaoping reappeared after his second Cultural Revolution–era exile. From the vantage point of the twenty-first century, the revolution we associate with Deng and his reform-minded colleagues represents the accumulation of initial key strategic decisions concentrated in the eight years following his return. Some consequences of these early decisions were anticipated, others were not, and still others have yet to be fully revealed. These outcomes have included

- Vastly improved material circumstances for the Chinese people and an enormously expanded, relatively positive role for China in the world
- Growing economic and social inequality and market failures resulting from the spread of market mechanisms in the absence of effective regulatory and tax institutions, the absence of land rights in rural areas, and the presence of corruption on a very large scale
- The explosion of China's accumulated capital, the abrupt expansion of international financial and trade roles, and the global imbalances to which all of this has given rise

- A staggering pace of urbanization and a swiftly growing middle class that is gradually becoming a force for participatory political change[1]
- Economic growth that is testing the still blurry outer limits of environmental sustainability, as well as the capacity to keep military strength within bounds that China's neighbors can accept

Thus, while Deng Xiaoping pushed the stone of "his" revolution down the mountain, its precise route, effects, rate of movement, and final resting place have been and will continue to be shaped by a myriad of forces, many of which will prove to have been beyond initial intentions, expectations, or control.

This scene-setting chapter first describes the seven principal strategic decisions made at the outset of the Deng era and then examines some of the resulting transformations. In subsequent chapters we examine how Chinese leaders at various levels and in different areas of responsibility have understood important continuities and discontinuities since 1977 and how they have sought to shape the developing circumstances in which they find themselves and their nation.

BACKGROUND

Following Chairman Mao Zedong's death on September 9, 1976, there was a brief interregnum in which Mao's nominal successor, Hua Guofeng, and a cohort of revolutionary elders around him were rooting out the key leftist Cultural Revolution holdovers, stabilizing the economic and political situation, and deciding what role, if any, the still-exiled Deng Xiaoping would play moving forward.[2] On July 17, 1977, the issue of Deng was officially announced as settled by the Third Plenary Session of the Tenth Party Congress: he was reinstated to all the positions from which he had been ousted in April 1976 (vice-chairman of the Central Committee, vice-chairman of the party's Central Military Commission [CMC], chief of the general staff of the People's Liberation Army [PLA], vice-premier of the State Council, and, of course, member of the Central Committee and the Politburo Standing Committee). Little more than a year earlier a failing Mao Zedong had yet again turned on Deng in the aftermath of unrest in Beijing that had been sparked by Premier Zhou Enlai's death in January 1976—unrest that the Cultural Revolution leftist contenders for power in the fast-approaching post-Mao era correctly judged was aimed at them, and for which they found it expedient to blame Deng.[3]

Upon returning to his duties in the summer of 1977, Deng initially focused on science and technology and education policy. However, he rapidly accumulated influence and started to make a series of policy pronouncements establishing the overall direction and dimensions of change that he foresaw. By 1982, Deng had completed easing Mao's weak successor Hua Guofeng out of power, though as a sign of things to come he did not humiliate him. Unlike Chairman Mao, Deng left his vanquished opponent with a shred of dignity by letting him recede gracefully into the background, thereby lowering the temperature of elite politics considerably.[4] After this, though never as omnipotent as Mao, Deng became China's uncontested principal leader, or its primus inter pares, by a considerable margin. Between 1977 and 1985, Deng identified and initiated the principal strategic policy departures associated with the second Chinese communist-era revolution.

Below, we examine these directions and the transformations to which these policy changes have given rise. China's point of departure in comparative economic and social perspective at this moment is illustrated in table 1, which shows the situation in 1980 according to World Bank figures. China's then nearly 25 percent of global population accounted for somewhere around 2 percent of global GDP. The PRC at that time accounted for less than 1 percent of global trade. The urban population was less than one-fifth of China's total, and nearly half of the overall population had not completed a primary school education. At the time, except for health indicators that the Maoist system did drive up (bringing great human benefit to China's people), the PRC was behind India in several categories of societal performance, including percentage of population living in urban areas. Tiny Hong Kong accounted for a larger share of world trade than mammoth mainland China. And even Italy's population had two times more of the global share of GDP than did China's.

The point is clear—the China that Deng inherited was poor, *very* poor, albeit able to pin down large contingents of the Soviet military along a vast common border. Most of the outside world did not foresee the day when Chinese modernization would give birth to a far different actor on the world stage, a result of the initial strategic decisions made and implemented by Deng and his colleagues. Yet by retrospectively talking about "strategic decisions" one runs the risk of imposing an order on the process that, at the time, did not exist; in his day, Deng's

TABLE I CHINA'S COMPARATIVE STARTING POINT, 1980

	GDP (PPP), % of world	GDP per capita, PPP (constant 2005 $)	Share of world trade (%)	Hospital beds (per 1,000 people)	Life expectancy (years)	Infant mortality rate (per 1,000 births)	Urban population (% of total)	Adult population with primary education (% of total)
China	2.0	524	0.9	2.2	66.0	46.1	19.6	54.6
India	2.3	895	0.6	0.8	55.1	103.2	23.1	28.4
Hong Kong	0.3	13,945	1.1	4.0	74.7	NA	91.5	72.0
Italy	4.1	18,837	4.4	9.6	73.9	14.1	66.6	84.1
Korea	0.8	5,544	1.0	1.7	65.8	17.0	56.7	86.0
Japan	7.8	17,570	6.3	13.7	76.1	7.4	59.6	89.4
USA	22.1	25,531	12.2	6.0	73.7	12.5	73.7	97.4

NOTE: Data for this table are all for 1980 and come from the World Bank's World Development Indicators (http://data.worldbank.org/indicator), except for education data, last column, which are taken from Barro-Lee Educational Attainment Data Set (2011), www.barrolee.com.

push was above all experimental, opportunistic, reactive, and relent-less—essentially seeking those places where the population wanted to run in the direction he desired to take China.

THE MAJOR STRATEGIC DECISIONS

Between 1977 and 1985, Deng and his allies created and immediately began to feverishly implement strategic policy initiatives that fall into seven fundamental categories. Not all of these initiatives were entirely new, and from today's perspective, they have not all proven to be equally successful or even mutually consistent. While their overall success has been considerable, some have had enormous downsides, others have not yet been taken to their logical conclusions, and still others remain difficult to assess.

These seven categories of decisions or policy tendencies are not listed in presumed order of importance, nor can one necessarily point to one "decision" having been made at one precise time. All of them were clearly articulated by Deng, with some being signaled as early as 1974 but most being promulgated between 1977 and 1985. While the major-ity of these policy tendencies pertained to domestic initiatives, two were international in focus, and all had enormous domestic and international impact.[5]

Strategic Category 1: From War and Revolution to Peace and Development

A governing necessity in China has always been to first define the era in which the nation finds itself. Defining the era helps establish goals and priorities and provides the parameters for messages going out from the center to tens of millions of party and state cadres and to a citizenry whose population was closing in on one billion by the time Deng returned to power. Mao defined his era as one of "War and Revolution." By way of contrast, Deng clearly defined his era as one of "Peace and Development."[6]

Deng and his colleagues were fortunate that history developed as it did in his early years of taking the helm, making his description of a new era credible.[7] This new focus helped establish the generally peace-ful and economically oriented regional environment that he needed and from which most other players in the region and the world benefited. Much that was helpful was happening in the years in which Deng's policies took shape:

- The United States had recently exited Vietnam.
- Taiwan was in a relatively open phase under Chiang Kai-shek's son and successor, Chiang Ching-kuo.
- Globalization of trade and manufacturing was gaining momentum.
- The dynamic East Asian economies of Japan, South Korea, Singapore, and Taiwan were taking off, in search of opportunities for surplus capital and sites for the low-wage components of the production chain as their labor and land costs rose.

With the costs of international shipping dropping, and the U.S. economy moving up the value chain, China had opportunities and Washington was willing to cooperate. Although the Soviet Union was (and would remain) a threat well into the 1980s, with new "friends" China no longer had to confront Moscow alone, and economics quickly became the game throughout the country and in much of Asia.

Deng was ready to learn from others and participate in the global economy, as he told a group of American visitors in October 1977, less than three months after his return to power: "We must, for instance, learn from advanced countries something that the Gang [of Four] had called slavish imitation. . . . One must have enough confidence in one's own ability to take in other things. By self-reliance we should also absorb from advanced countries."[8] In a single sentence he turned Mao's concept of "self-reliance" on its head.

This calculation on Deng's part was fundamental to nearly all of the other policy thrusts. Had he and his colleagues not judged that the international environment was relatively benign, and would remain so for a considerable period, it would have been difficult for him to keep military expenditures very low in terms of absolute *renminbi,* as a percentage of the PRC's GDP, and as a percentage of the Chinese budget for the first dozen years of reform. This enabled him to focus scarce resources on domestic investment and reduced the anxiety level of most of China's neighbors, thereby further relaxing the regional environment. Had Beijing faced the threat it faced in the 1960s from both America and the Soviet Union simultaneously, the military would have played suffocating domestic, economic, and political roles. Because of his own military credentials, Deng *could* talk about the need to constrain military expenditures—postponing increases until the domestic economy was far stronger (see figure 1). Having been a major military figure, Deng was able to constrain the armed forces in

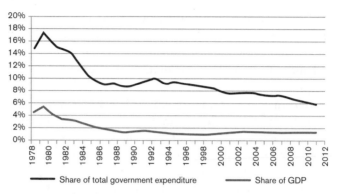

FIGURE I. Budgeted national defense expenditure, 1978–2011.

a way that his civilian successors without such stature would one day find more difficult.[9]

Strategic Category 2: Pragmatic Experimentalism

Deng's revolution was as much a state of mind as it was a specific set of policies. That state of mind was "Let's see what works to produce economic growth," by permitting different regions and levels of the system to develop responses to problems, and then popularizing successful policies—allowing these to spread from the grassroots up. Lower-level leaders want many things from superiors (money and resources being central), but often the most valued thing that the top can give the bottom is policy leeway. Deng provided this type of freedom: he often encouraged local initiative and hung back without committing himself. Only when success was assured did he weigh in definitively, encouraging successful models to be tried elsewhere. In one 1979 conversation Deng put it this way to a group of U.S. governors: "The most important method we have accepted is since China is so big, we are carrying out decentralization, including giving large powers and decision making to enterprises. Only in this way can they naturally find the right way. . . . During the past two years, [we have] carried out experiments and in this respect all have proved successful. This has been confirmed and now this will be made part of the system."[10] While Mao could also be described as an experimentalist, his experiments were always to serve ideological aims, and they usually ended with an enforced uniformity in the name of giving the initiative to the "masses." Deng allowed for diversity, although he sometimes then had to try to recapture at least partial central control when deviations became too great and the loss of central authority too extreme in key areas such as central revenues.

Strategic Category 3: Material Incentives, Markets, and State-Society Balance

Political leaders have different predispositions with respect to which tools of power they find most effective or congenial. The available instruments of power are coercion, material reward (remuneration), and ideological (normative) persuasion.[11] Mao was a believer in the first (coercion) and the last (ideology), with a distinct bias against material incentives. Mao would consider the latter only if China was in a severe economic crisis, as was the case in the immediate post-Liberation period from 1949 to 1953 and in the aftermath of the Great Leap Forward in 1960. Because he emphasized coercion and ideology, Mao needed a strong state and party that could create and wield such instruments.

In contrast, Deng relied principally on remunerative power, employing coercion only when the political system was threatened, as in 1979 with the Democracy Wall movement and again a decade later with the Tiananmen demonstrations. Deng wanted a strong state, but one that was far less intrusive in its relation to society—using material incentives, as opposed to direct administrative control and mass mobilization, as often as possible. Some of his policies, most notably those in agriculture, were almost self-implementing because they so closely aligned with the interests and inclinations of those applying them and because people were so relieved simply to be freed from policies that had proven catastrophic. In speaking to a group of visiting Americans in 1979, Deng could not have been clearer: "[It is] impossible to give play to personal enthusiasm and initiative without linking it to incentives. During the past ten years [1969–79], it has been proved that all those enterprises which had decision powers—the workers themselves increased income and have given more profit to the state. Not only in factories but in the countryside as well."[12] In a fall 1977 conversation in which he seemed worn and wary shortly after his return to power, Deng said: "As for wages, over the past decade there were no raises of wages. In 1974 there was a proposal to raise some wages, but the Gang of Four opposed it. Again the same thing happened in 1975, and now we are working again on raising wages."[13] Deng believed that higher pay produced more work and that more work produced more benefits for both the workers and the state. Mao was a zero-sum type of political leader, while Deng was a win-win leader, except when it came to keeping the CCP in its solitary leading role.

With respect to markets, Deng was persuaded of their power and efficiency in the wake of the Great Leap Forward in the early 1960s when he worked hard to bring China back from starvation.[14] The first big initiative Deng embraced upon his last return in the late 1970s was to restore production incentives to rural households and reopen moribund rural markets. From there, he and his colleagues methodically introduced markets on an ever broader front, moving sequentially to raw materials and labor markets. Much has been accomplished to further open markets in the intervening years, but full interest-rate liberalization and land market development, along with reduction of selective monopolies and subsidization by the state, are areas where change remains incomplete.

Deng's introduction of markets was economically crucial and had far-reaching political implications. By taking many economic decisions out of the hands of central state planners and bureaucrats, Deng unleashed an evolving process in which the state-society balance was gradually altered. It has been liberating to the degree that individuals have gained more control over their economic lives. To the degree that tyrannical lower-level officials have been able to capture some or most of the power relinquished by the center, it has been disappointing: in some cases it seems that one group of tyrants has simply been replaced by another. Markets have consequences for equality, equity, and social justice that have been progressively harder to contain within the confines of a rigid political system, though Deng's successors have thus far proven remarkably adaptable.

Strategic Category 4: Population

One of Deng Xiaoping's earliest preoccupations was with the sheer size of China's population—he felt he had to stop it from growing. In an October 1979 conversation with U.S. governors, Deng put it simply: "The most outstanding characteristic is that the population of the country is too large. Even if by upgrading production to the level [of more advanced countries,] . . . producing lots of steel, various kinds of industrial products and food grains, the average per capita GNP still won't be very high compared to the rest of the world."[15]

Deng was adamant that the PRC's population was too big: each year's added increment of population expansion would eat up a large fraction of gains.[16] He was thinking about political legitimacy, which in the early 1980s required a rapid increase of the per capita income of his people. A growing population worked against this because even a low birth rate added many people in absolute terms. Deng's basic measure of progress was per capita income, and the more "capitas," the harder it would be to achieve success. Perhaps Deng also feared that the peace and prosperity his policies would bring would generate a fertility boom that would make raising per capita welfare even harder. Whatever his precise logic, he rejected Mao Zedong's populist notion that the more people China had the stronger it was. In retrospect, Deng clearly was not thinking about longer-term demographic issues such as gender imbalance or an inverted age pyramid.

This was Deng's thinking and the origin of the one-child policy of the late 1970s. This policy was implemented in many ways throughout the PRC and changed over time but soon became synonymous with coercion throughout the world with its initial indiscriminate enforcement across social and economic groups and many instances of forced sterilization and/or forced abortion. As Deng said in 1977, "It is difficult to get zero [population] growth. Much effort must be made in the countryside to overcome the desire of all Chinese for huge families."[17]

Strategic Category 5: Capable Personnel for the Economy and Polity

For Deng Xiaoping, the Cultural Revolution produced a personal loss of power, humiliation, exile, and grief,[18] but for China the movement led to a lost decade in which China's youth had little to no formal education. Scientific research was at a standstill outside military-related areas. Deng told a group of U.S. governors in 1979, "As you know, we have suffered a gap of ten years when we didn't produce skilled or scientific personnel. We have lost a generation. . . . So, in this respect, we are going to learn from advanced countries, not only technological knowledge but management skills."[19] In almost every conversation with visitors, whether it was President Carter's science adviser Frank Press in 1978, U.S. university presidents in 1979, or Robert McNamara of the World Bank in 1980, Deng pressed for substantial educational assistance. In July 1978, Deng and Frank Press agreed to an exchange of PRC and American students, with the number of the former limited only by their capacity to be admitted to U.S. institutions of higher education and to obtain the necessary financial support. One of the World Bank's first initiatives in the PRC was to help modernize key educational institutions and link them to the outside world. In 1978, there were 50 Chinese students in the first contingent coming to the United States; by 1984, this number had reached 14,000; by the 2010–11 academic year China had 157,558 students enrolled in U.S. colleges, universities, and other educational settings; and by the academic year 2011–12, the number had jumped another 23 percent, to 194,029 students.[20]

In terms of the domestic tertiary education system, upon his return to power, Deng immediately reopened schools and began rigorous testing and admissions regimes; the number of college and university undergraduates expanded from 165,000 in 1978 to 950,000 in 2000, then vaulted to 5.3 million in 2009.[21] Further expansion of all forms of tertiary education is occurring rapidly in the 2010s.[22] By 2011, only five other countries had "more universities than China in the top-ranked 500 universities of the world, compared to twelve [countries] just eight years ago."[23]

Deng was just as deeply concerned about the educational deficiencies of literally tens of millions of party, state, and military cadres who were old and set in their ways, uneducated as well as untrained, and politically dogmatic—"ossified" was his preferred characterization. Mao's promotion criteria had prioritized political reliability over technical capacity—"better red than expert." In 1979, about a year following the pathbreaking Third Plenum of the Eleventh Central Committee that constituted the launch of the initial stages of reform, Deng said: "The line and principles adopted for the modernization program are correct, but the problem—and it is a serious one—is lack of trained personnel necessary to carry them out."[24] Daringly for the era, he went on to praise capitalism, saying: "We say that capitalist society is bad, but it doesn't hesitate to discover and utilize talent. . . . The seniority system represents a force of habit and is backward."[25] He immediately began to establish midcareer training schools, set retirement ages, and make entry into government service progressively more competitive and skill based, rather than a mere political litmus test.

Strategic Category 6: Preservation of the Communist Party's Monopoly of Power

With all of the policy loosening in the social, intellectual, and economic realms that Deng was promoting between 1978 and 1979, citizens predictably began to explore the limits of political space—and quickly ran up against them. The years 1978–79 saw a personal challenge to Deng and some of his policies in the person of Wei Jingsheng (and others) who argued that there would not be economic and societal modernization without the emergence of political democracy, or, as Wei himself put it: "We want to be the masters of our own destiny. We need no gods or emperors and we don't believe in saviors of any kind. We want to be masters of our universe, not the modernizing tools of dictators with personal ambitions."[26] This movement, known as Minzhu Qiang, or Democracy Wall, snowballed in the early months of 1979 and was further fueled by China's sub-par performance in the brief military conflict—"the counterattack waged in self-defense"—with Vietnam in February-March of that same year. This "punitive" military campaign came in the immediate wake of Deng's postnormalization visit to the United States, when President Carter advised against a military strike against Vietnam but clearly was not prepared to do much to seek to prevent it or to sanction China afterward.

Deng pressed for an end to the Democracy Wall movement (which had spread beyond Beijing to other parts of the country) by articulating and imposing "the Four Cardinal Principles," the core of which was (and remains): "We must uphold the leadership of the Communist Party."[27] Deng observed this principle repeatedly throughout his career: his involvement in the antirightist campaign of the latter part of the 1950s, the repression of the Democracy Wall movement in 1978–79, and subsequently the June 4, 1989, Tiananmen crackdown.

The internal contradiction within Deng's overall program was apparent then and became progressively more glaring as time wore on—the social pluralization and empowerment of subgroups that his economic, educational, social, and foreign policy initiatives promoted worked against the ongoing CCP political monopoly. Deng felt that economic progress, and the Chinese people's tragic experiences with instability throughout the twentieth century, not least in the communist era itself, would combine to provide a breathing spell during which he could put his foot on the brake of political liberalization while depressing the economic accelerator. As he said to a group of visitors from the United States in 1979, "As to the so-called Democracy Wall or the demonstrations and sit-ins, etc., this can't represent the genuine feeling of our people."[28] I think that he truly believed this. And while he was correct that there would be a breathing spell—a period during which satisfying participatory political demands could be deferred because economic progress and social stability were priorities for all citizens—he left his successors with a ticking time bomb. The questions are, how much longer will this breathing spell last? How much counterproductive repression may be needed to prolong it? If a political explosion in the indefinite future is to be avoided, does a smoother course to a more participatory and responsive future system need to be charted? This issue is at the forefront of the challenges facing China's fifth-generation leaders, not least Xi Jinping, in the second decade of the twenty-first century.

Strategic Category 7: From Autarky to Comparative Advantage and Interdependence

Mao Zedong believed that trade carried a high risk of dependence and that the PRC would be secure and independent only when it was as self-sufficient as possible. In contrast, Deng understood—perhaps from having seen the trading nations of Europe up close as a student in the 1920s, and from observing the successes of the dragon economies around China in the 1970s and 1980s—that trade was essential to the wealth and power of a nation. He believed in the mutually beneficial effects of trade. From the earliest days of his return to power in 1977, Deng planned to enmesh China in the international economic system in at least three ways outlined below, two of which were successful beyond what he probably imagined.

The unsuccessful effort was his initial presumption that China had sufficient energy resources (coal and anticipated oil reserves) to export to earn foreign exchange that could, in turn, buy technology. As it turned out, in 1993 China became a net oil importer because of the combination of faster-than-expected growth in domestic energy demand and smaller-than-hoped-for energy discoveries. This fact obviated Deng's initial energy-based development strategy. Nonetheless, in the earliest stage of reform, Deng was hopeful that by trading the PRC's energy for the West's technology he could jump-start the economy. His hopes, and perhaps some uncertainty, come through in his words to visiting directors of the National Committee on U.S.-China Relations in October 1977.[29] "We are planning to export more oil products. We have very large oil deposits. Basically, we can solve the exploration problems ourselves. Our main imported technology will be in the oil industry. The Japanese told us that Americans had told them that China has fifty billion tons in reserve. How do you know? I asked Bush [George Herbert Walker Bush] of the CIA. 'Did you get it [the figure] from the sky?' He said, 'Maybe.'"[30]

What proved to be a wildly successful effort to enter the international division of labor, however, began in 1978, as reform-minded Vice-Premier Li Lanqing subsequently recounted in his memoir *Breaking Through*.[31] This economic push involved making China a destination for foreign direct investment (FDI) and employing capital from abroad to construct manufacturing and assembly platforms in selected coastal areas with favorable conditions to produce exports, thereby earning foreign exchange. This would soon involve developing Special Economic Zones (SEZs) in Fujian and Guangdong provinces (Shantou, Xiamen, Shenzhen, and Zhuhai), and the development of an interesting (democratic) governance experiment in Shekou. The economic and administrative policies associated with the four SEZs spread geographically in the 1980s—the opening of Shanghai in the early 1990s being a notable landmark along the way.

Parenthetically, Xi Jinping, who became CCP general secretary in late 2012, grew up in the midst of these developments and at that time was just leaving school and working in Beijing in the State Council and then the Central Military Commission. Xi Jinping's father, Xi Zhongxun, whom I met twice, was Deng's close colleague and, in his role as second secretary of the Guangdong Party Committee, developed and promoted an avant-garde "Report on a Tentative Plan for Building Foreign Trade Bases and Urban Development in Bao'an and Zhuhai Counties."[32] In December 1978, this plan was adopted by Beijing, and Xi Zhongxun was named first party secretary of Guangdong Province, with Yang Shangkun (later president of the PRC) as his deputy; on January 23, 1979, part of Bao'an County became Shenzhen, the most famous of the SEZs. With all of this, Xi Zhongxun was laying a cornerstone for the edifice of Deng's legacy. In the fierce battles over adopting and implementing this set of then controversial economic policies, Deng said, "The central authorities do not have the money, but we can give you some policies to allow you to do it on your own and blaze a new trail."[33]

The other successful effort was to start to closely cooperate with the World Bank and other Bretton Woods institutions. Robert S. McNamara, president of the World Bank (April 1968–June 1981), describes Deng's enthusiastic acceptance of financial assistance and, perhaps more importantly, the Bank's advice. As Robert McNamara put it in a 1991 interview with the World Bank History Project:

> When I went to China in April of 1980 and met with Deng Xiaoping. . . .
> My purpose was in negotiating the reentry of the People's Republic into the
> Bank, which they'd begun the year before. Accomplishing that with Deng

Xiaoping, I then said to him—we'd started out; we'd agreed on reentry—
"What is it you wish?" I said, "I guess there's no need to ask you, (A), do
you want us to help you?" He had told me he was just beginning. . . . And I
said, "Well, number two, do you want us to help you in developing macroeconomic policies?"

He said, "Yes."

"Do you want us to assist in financing the adjustment process?"

"Yes."

"Do you want us to have an office in Beijing?"

"Yes."[34]

At a meeting with Chinese researchers some years later, McNamara
evaluated Deng's leadership in the early years of reform, saying:

"Twenty-five years ago [as president of the World Bank] I spoke with Deng
Xiaoping about his objectives. They were to quadruple the Chinese GDP by
2000 and to expand the welfare of his people. People in the U.S. don't understand this accomplishment. He accomplished clear objectives. The one-child
policy. He required senior executives to assume responsibility for moving
toward the objectives. Deng Xiaoping required all senior people in his cabinet to read the summary volume of the eight volume World Bank assessment
that had been made of the Chinese economy. And officials all know the main
social welfare indicators on poverty reduction nationwide over time. His
priorities were the military in the last place. He provided incentives. The
result was eight percent growth in agriculture—unheard of."[35]

THE PRINCIPAL TRANSFORMATIONS

We now fast-forward from clusters of decisions made between 1977
and 1985 to the resulting transformations that we can observe in the
second decade of the twenty-first century. This approach sacrifices
chronological detail for the clarity that this contrast provides. In the
chapters to follow, however, we will capture the detail by examining
various dimensions of China—through both wide-angle and up-close
lenses—from the perspective of a diversity of Chinese leaders over time.
Here, though, we paint a picture of the broad circumstances that China's leaders confront more than three decades after the initial policy
decisions described above. Table 2 demonstrates how far China had
come by 2010 using the same measures as employed in table 1. In a
comparison of tables 1 and 2, particularly notable are China's increased
share of global GDP, the dramatic increase in the PRC's share of world
trade, gains in basic health indicators, the degree of urbanization, and
progress in the educational system.

TABLE 2 COMPARATIVE INDICATORS OF CHINA'S CIRCUMSTANCES IN 2010

	GDP (PPP), % of world	GDP per capita, PPP (constant 2005 $)	Share of world trade (%)	Hospital beds (per 1,000 people)	Life expectancy (years)	Infant mortality rate (per 1,000 births)	Urban population (% of total)	Adult population with primary education (% of total)
China	13.5	6,810	7.8	4.1	73.3	16.6	44.0	84.4
India	5.6	3,240	1.9	0.9	64.1	50.3	29.8	65.4
Hong Kong	0.4	41,871	2.6	NA	82.7	NA	100.0	85.7
Italy	2.4	26,713	3.3	3.7	81.4	3.4	68.2	93.1
Korea	2.0	27,027	2.5	12.3	80.3	4.5	81.7	96.1
Japan	5.8	30,920	4.0	13.8	82.9	2.4	66.6	95.9
USA	19.5	42,551	11.3	3.1	78.7	6.8	82.0	98.9

NOTE: Data for this table are for 2010 and come from the World Bank's World Development Indicators (http://data.worldbank.org/indicator), except for the education data, last column, which are taken from the Barro-Lee Educational Attainment Data Set (2011), www.barrolee.com.

With regard to qualitative change over the 1977–2013 period, four broad areas of contrast are particularly illuminating: political, economic, societal, and global.

Political Changes

There have been major political changes in China since 1977, though not of the type considered significant by many Westerners. These changes hold both the promise of further positive change and the certainty of major challenges, indeed dangers, ahead.

The Basis of Legitimacy

Mao Zedong, and to a considerable extent Deng Xiaoping, had political legitimacy rooted in their personal histories and the authoritarian political culture from which they sprang. They were leaders who sank deep roots into the three fundamental bases of power in China: the party/bureaucracy, the military, and the core geographic regions of the country. They possessed diversified and deep bases of power.[36] Current Chinese leaders do not have such compelling revolutionary histories or such strongly diversified power bases, and they preside over an increasingly knowledgeable, networked, and urban population. Thus leaders today depend more heavily upon performance-based legitimacy—with their performance measured by economic growth, social stability, and expanding opportunity for citizens. All Chinese leaders today speak about the importance of "public opinion," and they are busy measuring it. For example, one district party secretary in Shanghai in 2007 told me: "'In the Tang dynasty we didn't care about people's views, now we listen. Every day I read *Time, USA Today,* and the Internet. Actually, this is the biggest change in governance, in governing philosophy.'"[37]

Mao Zedong presided over policies that starved millions and, so far as I am aware, never went to the rural areas to show a shred of compassion, much less to acknowledge his mistakes. He went to the countryside to mobilize but never to apologize once his grandiose initiatives had gone awry. Today, when natural disasters strike, such as the May 12, 2008, Wenchuan earthquake in Sichuan Province, the Chinese premier and other senior officials are there, with TV hookups carrying images within hours and social media and cellular communications conveying information even faster. Similarly, in the earliest days of the Hu Jintao–

Wen Jiabao era in late 2002/early 2003, SARS hit first southern China and thereafter rapidly spread to other parts of the country and abroad. The holdover health minister and local officials had ignored, and then minimized, the escalating disaster. The new Hu-Wen leadership fired the minister of public health, Zhang Wenkang, in April 2003, thereby establishing some accountability. This move boosted the new leadership's legitimacy and sped Jiang Zemin's move toward the sidelines of power in 2003–4.

While this certainly does not constitute democracy, it is what political scientists have called responsive authoritarianism.

Ambitions of the State, Preemptive Accommodation, and Repression

One of the most significant transformations in the post-Mao era has been the withdrawal of the state from enormous swaths of everyday life. The ambitions of the state for control have contracted since 1977, although there are no legal or constitutional guarantees that this situation will persist and, in certain domains such as cyberspace, control has become possible where it was not previously. If you ask what Mao sought to regulate in his day, even if he was unable to accomplish it, the answer is, "Everything." Today, the party-state principally seeks to protect its monopoly of power against any organized opposition—and this it has done to remarkable effect, thus far.

Beyond that arena of protection, however, enormous areas of human endeavor have been politically deregulated: personal income decisions; lifetime career planning and personal mobility; freedom of expression, as long as it is not antisystem in an organized way; and the ability to go abroad. Even the right to express oneself in print has expanded, with the system shifting from crude prepublication censorship to postpublication punishment if views stray too far—a standard that oscillates, with punishments ranging from admonishment to imprisonment.

The challenge now is, having partially freed so much of human life from the Maoist straitjacket, how can the CCP keep threats to its monopoly of power from reaching critical mass, particularly in the era of universally available social media? The party has sought to do so by preemptive accommodation and repression: identify the popular grievance as early as possible, meet reasonable demands, prevent disparate social groups from linking up, and arrest the leaders who are prominent in organizing protest if it becomes too public or too threatening. While clearly not democratic, this approach is not totalitarian either.

Types of Leadership

Though this topic will be addressed in considerable detail in chapter 2, the type of leader one finds in China today is very different from Mao, or even Deng. James MacGregor Burns has described three ideal types of leader: transformational, transactional, and power wielder.[38] All politicians have elements of each in their makeup, but leaders are distinguished by their dominant proclivity, by their goals, and by the instruments of power with which they feel most comfortable and effective.

Transformational leaders establish spiritual or ideological connections with their followers, and their sway over citizens is based on, and aimed at, establishing entirely new social and political orders. Such leaders often lead revolutions (Mao Zedong or the Taiping Rebellion's Hong Xiuquan, for example) or address grave systemic crises in more established orders (i.e., Franklin D. Roosevelt).[39] These leaders thrive, not on the thin gruel of system maintenance, but rather on major crises and systemic change. Transactional leaders, by way of contrast, function more as the lubricant of the political mechanism of an established order—reducing friction, building coalitions, finding incremental ways through political problems, cutting pragmatic deals, and performing system maintenance tasks (the "great triangulator" Bill Clinton may be the prototype here, or Jiang Zemin). Power wielders are distinguished by their devotion to maintaining personal power; the means by which they do so, or the policies pursued, are evaluated only in terms of their ability to prevail personally (Iraq's Saddam Hussein comes to mind).

Various types of leaders have different vulnerabilities—a particular set of dangers awaits the transactional leaders who are now dominant in the PRC. Events can quickly alter the public view of them from essential, pragmatic problem solvers to weak, indecisive, and inadequate persons. Transactional leaders must keep solving problems and building workable coalitions; when they are unable to do so their utility is at an end. Elections are a regularized way to get a new team in democracies when the old team is tired out, but authoritarian regimes are saddled with less predictable, often more disruptive means.

Not only have Chinese leaders changed dramatically in terms of their type, moving from transformational toward transactional since 1976, but they also have become more educated, considerably younger, and more diverse in professional and geographic origins. Cheng Li's examination of 538 of the so-called "fifth-generation" leaders, who were predominantly born in the 1950s, finds a gradual increase in the number of non–Communist Party officials at the vice-governor and vice-minister levels and above; some diversification in birthplace away from the eastern seaboard; increasing diversity in academic and professional study and subsequent functional specialization (away from engineering and the hard sciences); ever higher levels of education, with 73 percent of fifth-generation leaders having postgraduate degrees (though of widely varying quality); and more experience studying abroad.[40]

All this change is pushing the system into uncharted political territory. While Deng set his country on a radically different course, it was a course that would require huge and continuous changes for a protracted period. Will his increasingly transactional and less muscular successors prove able to produce the transformations that are required? Less dominant leaders now face a stronger society.

Economic Changes

Changes in the political system affect, and are affected by, economic transformations. Several economic changes have been particularly important in China: (1) transformations from a planned to a market economy; (2) a shift from stifling state ownership to substantial non-state control; (3) a rise in state-corporation power that is not as responsive to central control and is now capable of pursuing its own interests, one of which is to maintain its monopolies in key sectors of the economy; (4) a shift from agriculture toward manufacturing and services; (5) development of regulatory institutions, however imperfect; and, (6) a change from autarky to interdependence.

Changes in Economic Structure

With regard to ownership over time, in 1977 peasants were still in communes and industrial activity was almost entirely in the state-owned sector. In contrast, by 2009, state-owned enterprises (SOEs) accounted for only 11.5 percent of gross national output, only 8.1 percent of profits, and a mere 10 percent of industrial employment—while consuming a disproportionate 31 percent of investment. On the other hand, what the World Bank calls "pure private firms" accounted for 29.6 percent of gross national output, 28 percent of profits, and 33.7 percent of the industrial labor force, while getting only 21 percent of total investment.[41] A number of conclusions can be drawn from these figures, but three stand out. First, the efficiency of investment in the private sector has been stunning compared to that in the SOE sector. Second, there has been ongoing discrimination against the private sector in credit allocation—a major source of systemic inefficiency. And third, further movement toward a genuinely competitive private sector would unleash enormous additional growth.

Turning to the structure of the Chinese economy, in 1978, 28 percent of GDP came from primary industry (mostly agriculture), about 48 percent from secondary industry (manufacturing), and a very low 24 percent from tertiary enterprises (services). By 2008, primary industry as a share of GDP had dropped to 11 percent, secondary industry remained about the same at 48 percent, and tertiary industry had grown to 40 percent (reaching 43 percent by mid-2012).[42] There is still enormous growth potential in further boosting the service sector's share of GDP, particularly in health care and education.

Building a Regulatory Structure

Once the decision to utilize markets was made in the late 1970s, diverse economic actors increasingly needed to be regulated. In the planned economy, regulatory functions were handled (to the degree they were handled at all) by fiat and the relevant functional bureaucracy. Under the new conditions of an evolving market economy, special-purpose agencies had to be created from the ground up to regulate increasingly dynamic markets and an ever greater number of economic players, many of whom were beyond easy reach. Even state-owned enterprises, once energized by profit, required independent regulation. Regulatory and administrative law had to be developed. When I first went to the PRC in October 1976, I examined the pharmaceutical regulatory apparatus: it was basically nonexistent at the national level, and what masqueraded as one at the provincial level was ineffective. I asked one official how many drug products had ever been recalled for safety or quality reasons. His answer? None.[43]

Greater economic dynamism has meant that regulators are continually behind the ever evolving, ever more creative market-driven actors. Since the 1990s, on an ongoing basis, the PRC has seen the emergence of securities regulators; banking regulators, including the emergence of a more effective central bank; food and drug regulatory agencies; environmental regulatory bodies; and nuclear power regulators such as the National Nuclear Safety Administration, just to name a few. Barry Naughton points to the particular economic and social importance of the 1990s development of regulatory bodies, laws, and regimes as they related to the fiscal and tax system, the banking and financial system, corporate governance, and foreign trade and the external sector—not least membership in the World Trade Organization and all that this implied.[44] It is not easy to develop a force of skilled regulators, provide them the investigatory tools and legal remedies to be effective, keep them from getting co-opted by the industries they are supposed to regulate, and keep party officials from shielding their pet projects and pecuniary interests. Corruption is just one danger.

In this race between market innovation and public-interest regulation in the PRC, young, untested, compromised, or nonexistent regulatory authorities have often lost, as seen in many areas, such as

- Scandals involving tainted drugs and food products, some of which have found their way into the global supply chain
- Environmental disasters with international effects, notably petrochemical spills
- Infrastructure failures such as bridge collapses
- Unsafe toys and manufactured goods
- Bogus securities
- Violations of domestic and foreign intellectual property rights
- Fraudulent credentials and scholarly work—rampant in academic settings
- Shocking inattention to safety in coal mines and other workplaces, even among subcontractors making components and assembling products for iconic Western brands such as Apple[45]

From Autarky to Interdependence

Mao was committed to "self-reliance" (*zili gengsheng*) and inflicted enormous costs on the Chinese people to avoid dependence on others, particularly after his negative experience with Moscow in the 1950s. This experience also initially clouded Deng's thinking, as shown by his telling a group of American visitors in 1977: "Another aspect of self-reliance is to rely upon our own savings and not borrow money from others. We once had to borrow a great deal from the Soviet Union, and we built up a debt with them. Later, the Soviet Union tried to control us through our debts. They wanted to make us into an Eastern European satellite country. So we fell out with them."[46]

By 1980, however, Deng had overcome whatever compunctions he had (and whatever domestic opposition he faced) concerning indebtedness to foreigners and was ready to move ahead with the World Bank, though he remained very concerned that Beijing always be assured of its repayment capacity. In 1982, China had 0 percent of GDP in World Bank loans; by 1993 China peaked out at a World Bank loan to GDP ratio of 2.2 percent. Then, by virtue of the PRC's growing domestic capacities, by 2010 this ratio had declined to a mere 0.37 percent of GDP.[47] Another sign of China's willingness to rely on the international financial system in ways unimaginable to Mao is that in September 2008 China surpassed Japan as the largest foreign holder of U.S. Treasuries and by June 2012 held $1.1643 trillion in Treasury securities.[48] With regard to external debt, *China's net external debt is negative* (China is a net creditor), though Beijing did have large external debt amounting to $695 billion at the end of 2011, or 9.52 percent of GDP, much of this being trade financing.[49]

China's willingness to accept interdependence is found in other critical areas, such as key foodstuffs, most notably soy. A cardinal rule of governance in China from its earliest recorded history has been "*Yang min*," or "Feed the people." For Mao, this injunction meant domestically producing all the food—particularly grain—that the PRC needed, irrespective of the efficiency of so doing (as opposed to buying grain and other foodstuffs from more efficient producers in Australia, Canada, Brazil, or the United States). For Mao, depending on foreigners for food was equivalent to having the hands of your enemies around your nation's throat. By 2004, however, China had become a net food importer, with an 80 percent dependence on soya, a relatively high dependence on vegetable oil and edible sugar, and a variable dependence on wheat.[50]

A similar pattern exists with respect to energy. In 1993, China became a net petroleum importer—and has never looked back, becoming a larger oil importer than the United States in December 2012. More recently the PRC has also become a major player as an importer in the global coal market. Kevin Tu and Sabine Johnson-Reiser explain: "The country's [PRC] dependence on other nations' coal exports is growing. . . . With 182 million tons (Mt) of coal sourced from overseas suppliers in 2011, China has overtaken Japan as the world's top coal importer."[51]

Another important aspect of interdependency is that as many as forty-five million Chinese workers nationwide (2007) were employed in the export sector, or about 6 percent of the active mainland workforce.[52] In Shanghai, exports constitute a significant fraction of the city's GDP, as mentioned to me by then Shanghai mayor Xu Kuangdi in 1998: "We have seventeen thousand foreign-invested ventures [in Shanghai]. Thirty-five percent of our exports [from Shanghai] are from foreign-invested firms. One-third of Shanghai's GDP is from foreign-invested ventures."[53] In Jiangsu, in a 2007 meeting with then provincial first secretary Li Yuanchao, later head of the party's Organization Department, Politburo member, and vice president, a colleague of his pointed out that his province's 8,600 U.S.-invested projects accounted for 80 percent of his province's exports to America.[54]

Concisely, since the late 1970s, China has accepted interdependence, which has great bearing on economic growth, political stability, and consequently regime survival. Local finances often depend on taxes from enterprises connected to the international trade system, and customs revenues are a significant fraction of the central government's revenues. Customs revenue in 2011 reached 1.61 trillion *yuan* ($256 billion). PRC government fiscal revenue in 2011 hit 10.37 trillion *yuan* ($1.64 trillion). So customs accounted for 15.5 percent of total government revenue.[55]

Finally, although much of what was discussed above is positive in its implications, there have been problematic economic dimensions as well. Among them is a web of explicit and implicit market-distorting subsidies, rebates, and other arrangements, not the least of which is the low interest rate, resulting in a low price for capital. Also, certain "pillar" industries (such as steel and the auto- and electronics-related sectors) are targeted for special attention and protection, contributing to misallocation of capital domestically and the lack of a level playing field for foreign firms. Finally, the economy remains substantially overweighted toward investment and exports, starving essential domestic areas (such as health, education, and social safety net systems) of appropriate attention and, in the process, inundating the world with exports that contribute to unsustainable imbalances given America's insufficient national savings rate.

Societal Changes

Dramatic societal changes have occurred in China between 1977 and 2013, including breathtaking urbanization, the rise of a middle class, striking demographic developments, and social and bureaucratic pluralization. Much of this change has been positive, but there have been enormous downsides as well—ranging from ecological destruction to mounting corruption, growing inequality, and an increasingly lopsided demographic structure. One of the most important consequences of these societal shifts has been the emergence of less dominant leaders and a stronger society, as is discussed in the following chapter.

Urbanization

In 1978, China's population was 18 percent urban; in 2011, China's urban population exceeded its rural population for the first time in history;[56] and by 2030, the urban population is expected to reach 68 percent of the national total, according to the Chinese Academy of Social Sciences.[57] That is to say, in the 2013–30 period, China is predicted to add to its urban population an additional number of persons about 80 percent the size of the United States in 2011. Urbanization has driven the growth of China's middle class, which, according to the Organisation for Economic Co-operation and Development, was 157 million persons, or about 12 percent of total population, in 2010.[58] The World Bank predicts that the size of China's urban middle class is likely to double in the 2011–21 period.[59] This shift, in turn, drives rising consumption levels (a 1 percent increase in urban population increases consumption by 1.6 percent) and creates ever larger demands for water, energy, and other resources.[60]

The growth of China's middle class, however, has left many behind—the Gini coefficient for income inequality (a statistical measure of inequality where "1" is perfect income inequality and "0" is perfect income equality) has increased from below 0.3 in 1980 at the start of the Deng era to close to 0.45 by 2009, reflecting a yawning urban-to-rural income ratio of 4.1 to 1 in 2007.[61] Martin Whyte, in his book *Myth of the Social Volcano*, tells us that as important as these distributive inequalities may be, they are not, at least at this moment in China's development, the social volcano most likely to erupt.[62] Rather, what is potentially most explosive concerns a whole array of procedural injustices in which individuals and social groups feel unfairly treated. One important procedural injustice is that the household registration (*hukou*) system confers substantial benefits on those registered in urban areas and discriminates greatly against citizens with rural registration—it is extremely difficult to have one's rural registration converted to urban status, even if migrants have worked in a city for years.

Population

The combined effects of urbanization, rising education and income levels, and greater opportunities for women help account for what has been a dramatic multidecade decline in China's total fertility rate—a decline that began well before Deng's one-child policy was launched, as noted above. The decline in total fertility (in conjunction with the one-child policy) has had a number of effects, including a rapidly aging population; a soon-to-be-declining proportion of working-age people; and severe gender imbalance—with a sex-at-birth ratio of about 118 boys for every 100 girls in 2010.[63]

The sustained fertility decline and very low birth rate (calculated to be about 1.44 children per woman in the Sixth Census of 2010) have enabled China to raise per capita GDP faster than otherwise would have been the case because for a prolonged period the PRC has had a relatively high percentage of working-age people, as Deng presumably envisioned in the late 1970s when he launched the one-child policy. However, this short-run gain must be judged against some of the long-run costs. Comparing the circumstances of Japan and China, Yi Fuxian explains: "Japan grew rich before it aged, while China has aged before growing rich. The average per capita GDP in Japan is now over US$40,000, while the figure in China is merely US$4,000. By the year 2013, China's total working population, aged between 15 and 64, will hit its peak and turn downhill."[64]

Social and Organizational Pluralization

Chinese society and government are becoming more complex, with increasing income and educational stratification; more numerous bureaucratic organizations (e.g., regulatory agencies); increasingly active and capable large-scale economic actors in both the state and nonstate sectors; more professional associations and connections with global epistemic communities; more groups and organizations with their own, independent resources; a rapidly growing body of social organizations; and more foreign involvement of all sorts. With respect to the number of "social organizations" (or *shehui tuanti,* roughly equivalent to what we call the "third sector" or nongovernmental organizations, in the United States), in 1988 the reported number was 4,446, and by 2010 this figure had grown about a hundredfold, to 445,631.[65]

This, in turn, means there are more varied interest groups in China, many of which are developing the capability to articulate their own, often parochial concerns. One example is the episodic ability of the military to proceed along avenues that have broad impact without sufficient coordination with other organizations or, sometimes, the knowledge of the senior civilian leadership itself (see chapter 6). Policy making is becoming more arduous. Simultaneously, Chinese leaders are becoming weaker in relationship to society and the organizations atop which they sit. As they become relatively weaker, they have to build coalitions, not force obedience. Can less dominant, transactional leaders effectively address the unfinished agenda of Deng's reforms? Can they deal with the problems and seize the opportunities those reforms have presented, challenges largely unforeseen thirty-five years ago when Deng started this whole second revolution of the communist era—a growing middle class and global warming among them? This brings us to China's global role.

Global Role

The political, economic, and social changes recounted above have substantially transformed China's world role since 1977. The China asking for help in the late 1970s and 1980s is now dispensing foreign aid in ever greater quantities in 2013, with its foreign aid growing 29.4 percent annually in the 2004–9 period.[66] The China asking to rejoin the World Bank in 1980 and borrowing substantially into the new millennium is now the China that is gaining a bigger say in running the organization and related Bretton Woods institutions. The China that was starving its military of resources from the late 1970s until 1990 is today putting considerably more effort into the modernization of its armed forces. Debtor China now is creditor China, and the PRC not only seeks FDI but is becoming a sought-after investor by countries from Argentina to the United States and Zambia.[67] "If China follows the pattern of other emerging nations," Daniel Rosen and Thilo Hanemann tell us, "more than $1 trillion in direct Chinese investment will flow worldwide by 2020, a significant share of which will be destined for advanced markets such as the United States."[68] Three dimensions of change in China's global role call for particular attention: power projection, foreign entanglement, and pride and confidence.

Power Projection

Power projection refers to a nation's capacity to reach increasing distances beyond its air, sea, and land boundaries in order to bring power to bear on distant objects. Comprehensive national power projection is the capacity to bring all forms of power (coercive, economic, and ideational) to bear on an increasingly global scale.

Outside observers pay particular attention to the capacity to project military strength. Though still limited compared to those of the United States, the PRC's capacities in these regards have grown markedly from the mid-1990s, and include

- Five successful manned space launches from 2003 through mid-2013, carrying a total of twelve *taikonauts,* including two women
- Progress in the arms manufacturing and aeronautics industries[69]
- The shooting down of an aging satellite in 2007
- The PLA navy's participation in Gulf of Aden antipiracy operations, announced in late 2008 and conducted thereafter
- Testing of anti–ballistic missile capacity in 2010
- Demonstration of initial stealth aircraft capacity in January 2011
- Sea launch of China's first aircraft carrier in 2011
- Ongoing development of more robust nuclear submarine and submarine-launched missile capability
- Increasingly sophisticated cyber capabilities
- Demonstrated ability to evacuate nearly thirty-six thousand Chinese citizens and other nationals from conflict-torn Libya in 2011[70]

Thus PLA modernization has come a long way in three decades but still has a long way to go. It should also be noted that a substantial fraction of power projection capacity acquisition has been aimed at making credible Beijing's ability to back up its Taiwan policy, securing the PRC's maritime lifelines, backing up its claims to South and East China Sea territory, making credible its nuclear deterrent, and protecting its citizens abroad on an ever more extensive basis.

Power projection is more than military might—it is also the capacity to exert economic and intellectual strength from great distances. Above we noted the PRC's expanding capacities in the realms of economic and financial strength. In terms of communications, cultural exchange, and diplomatic muscle, Beijing's strengths are greater than ever before—building regional and global telecommunications and broadcasting systems, hosting ever more foreign students in China (50,000 in the year 2000, rising to 265,090 in 2010, with plans for 500,000 by 2020), and building ever larger foreign service and foreign assistance establishments.[71]

In short, China has moved from being a regional power to a global presence. This is quite remarkable, given that at the time of Mao's death the PRC could hardly move militarily, economically, or intellectually to any significant distance beyond its borders.

Foreign Entanglement

In his first inaugural address in March 1801, Thomas Jefferson enjoined his American compatriots to have "honest friendship with all nations, entangling alliances with none." An analogous staple of Chinese foreign policy since 1954 has been the "Five Principles of Peaceful Coexistence," principles that boil down to noninterference in the internal affairs of other countries. Just as Jefferson's principles eventually gave way to the necessities of growing power, expanding interests, and mounting fears of vulnerability with the advent of modern warfare, the luxury of sitting on the sidelines is proving infeasible for Beijing. One Chinese general's remarks in 2011 summed it up for me: "'Because of China's growing comprehensive national power and because our national interests are expanding, we need the military to protect our interests.'"[72]

China's increasingly global reach and its involvements, however, are not principally military in character. China, for example, as the biggest foreign holder of American Treasury debt, is hostage to American fiscal and monetary policy—subjects about which Beijing now feels entitled to offer Washington advice. When Chinese citizens are trapped in states that are descending into chaos, Beijing must become involved in extracting its nationals, as was the case in Libya in 2011. Noninvolvement and noninterference are less frequently an option for a globalizing China. To simply see the PRC's increasing involvement as a portent of aggressive intent is to forget the far more pervasive and legitimate motivations: to take advantage of global economic opportunities and to protect the lives, property, and interests of an entrepreneurial population spreading across the earth.

Pride, Nationalism, and a Sense of National Efficacy

The transformations documented above have given China's leaders and people a greater sense of global efficacy and provided the resources to become more involved and effective on the world stage. China's growing global involvement has also created a sense among Chinese leaders and citizens that they should and can help shape external developments to protect and advance PRC interests. A Pew poll in mid-2011 reported that 63 percent of Chinese people believed that the PRC "has already replaced the U.S." as the world's leading superpower or "will eventually" do so.[73]

The world is responding, first by acknowledging Chinese power, indeed, often exaggerating it. According to a Gallup poll, in February 2009 more Americans thought China was the "leading economic power in the world today" (39 percent) than thought the United States was (37 percent).[74] And for their part, many Chinese feel empowered listening to what the outside world says about Beijing's ascendancy. As one Chinese foreign policy analyst commented on the overall sense of PRC citizens about China's position in the world: "You [the United States] need our cooperation to save your auto industry; our World Bank voting share is up; so China will have a larger say in trade and financial issues. 'Money talks.' 'Invest more in Africa and finally China will bypass the United States.'"[75]

As we will delineate in the chapters that follow, China has enormous challenges that it still needs to overcome before it can prudently act on the sense of empowerment expressed above. The biggest challenge will be adapting its political system to the new society to which Deng's second communist-era revolution has given birth, and the subject to which we turn in the next chapter.

China has come far since Deng Xiaoping's initial conversations in the late 1970s with Western interlocutors. With clear strategic decisions and impressive implementation, China in 2013 is in a radically different position—domestically and internationally—than anyone (Chinese or Westerner) could have forecast in 1977.

Below we examine how Chinese leaders at all levels have looked at the challenges they have confronted to date and those that lie ahead. How have the Chinese themselves understood the problems of domestic governance and international affairs in the 1977–2013 period, and what can that tell us about what the world can expect in the decades ahead?

As far as the PRC has come since 1977, it still has a very long and uncertain road ahead. Deng made key strategic decisions, he pushed them forward, and though he was not a transformational leader like

Mao Zedong, his policies, as Ezra Vogel has said, have transformed China.[76] Looking ahead from 2013, the main issue is: Can China's "fifth generation" of largely transactional leaders make the tough choices that are the consequences of Deng's reforms? And, having made the choices, can they effectively implement them? Political instability is conceivable, perhaps likely, although its scale, duration, and consequences are uncertain. The biggest challenge facing the PRC is whether it can control itself at home and abroad with less dominant leaders *and* a much more pluralized and empowered bureaucracy and society.

PART ONE

China, a Wide-Angle View

CHAPTER 2

Governance and Leadership

"This vast country, it isn't easy, but it is hopeful."

—Deng Xiaoping in a meeting with governors from the United
States, October 17, 1979

"My bureau's work is 'dealing with contradictions.'"

—Bureau director, Ministry of Urban and Rural Construction and
Environmental Protection, November 10, 1982

"History in China is different. Since the Tang dynasty
[618 CE–907 CE] we've had a central government."

—Yang Xizong, governor of Sichuan, December 1983

"As for myself, regardless of international reports about me,
all those who have contacted me can come to the conclusion
that I am not an authoritarian person—not a dictator. Why?
The elements of Western capitalist education I received
carry considerable weight in my brain. I studied the history
of capitalist revolution in Europe, the Declaration of
Independence, the Gettysburg Address—all elements of
Western culture. So I am among those Chinese who know a
considerable amount about the West."

—President Jiang Zemin, Zhongnanhai, Beijing, June 14, 1996

Governance and leadership in today's China reflect an alloy of continuities and discontinuities. The continuities are seen to greater and lesser
extents in political culture, institutional practice and structure, resource
constraints, and the problems that governing such a populated and
expansive land entails. Since 1977 the discontinuities are seen in the

facts that individual Chinese leaders have become less dominant in the overall system, society and the bureaucracy have become increasingly pluralized (fragmented), and many actors at all levels of the system have become empowered to act in their own interests—they have information, human resources, and money. China's central leaders have the old pretenses of control but face new problems born of reform and change in politics, society, and the economy.

How will a political system with presumptions of centralized control, a strongman leadership tradition, and an overloaded decision-making structure deal with the realities of weaker leaders, an increasingly balkanized society, and more empowered players at all levels? Will a China struggling to control itself be a cooperative actor in an interconnected world?

THE BIG PICTURE: CONTINUITY AND CHANGE

Continuities

Governance and leadership in China have had considerable continuity throughout the reform era starting in 1977. Indeed, aspects of contemporary governance and leadership have resonance with China's traditional dynastic system and a deeply engrained political culture characterized by leaders who are deeply anxious about their grip on such a huge and diverse population and territory. As C.H. Tung, Hong Kong's first chief executive in the postcolonial period, has remarked, "'[Chinese] leaders, from their earliest days, are taught to expect that dangers lurk around every corner. Be cautious!'"[1]

The basic wisdom about governing China has been voiced by Yao Yilin, one of China's most prominent (and politically conservative) economic leaders: "China was so big that it was very difficult for things to go completely bad or go completely well, and hence leaders had to simply manage big problems as well as possible and not go to extremes in either actions or analysis."[2] Herbert Simon called this "satisficing"—less jargonistically, this is the search for "good enough," or *chabuduo* in Chinese.

It is striking how enduring the tasks of governing China have been over time, tasks that boil down to achieving growth and maintaining social and political stability. Central to achieving stabilization has always been "feeding the people" (*yang min*); maintaining revenue flows to the central state; communicating policy expectations effectively down the very deep hierarchies; monitoring the implementation of central directives and having adequate internal intelligence to warn of pending instability locally or nationally; and securing China's historically elastic boundaries from threats both near and far, often from non-Han peoples with populations spilling across far-flung frontiers. In a 1979 meeting, Vice-Premier Li Xiannian (later president), who presumably had the experiences of the Great Leap Forward and the Cultural Revolution fresh in his mind, revealed his underlying worry by stating his minimalist governance objective: "[I] can't guarantee results but I'll 'guarantee no starvation.'"[3]

Chinese citizens and leaders have persistently believed that the centralized state plays a decisive role in achieving these objectives. For Americans, government is a danger; for Chinese, government ought to be the solution. In January 2000, Vice-Premier Qian Qichen expressed the view that East Asian governments could not achieve progress without strong government.[4] Chinese political discourse revolves around what the government can and should accomplish and how it can do so effectively. This is a far cry from American beliefs on limiting government and enlarging the private and individual sectors. One senior PRC academic explained in 1999, "'In America government is accountable to the people. In China, the people are accountable to the government.'"[5]

China scholar Lily Chen illustrates these concepts in a Chinese idiom:

> In the older Chinese governance tradition, officials, especially local governors, are called *fumu guan*, or parent officials. Local governors in ancient China were called *mushou*, which means that they will guard the mass or the herd of people for the emperor. This implies that these local officials have rights over their herd, just as the parents, knowing and having the best interests over their children, have rights over their children, including education, training, and discipline. This concept of *fumu guan* is somewhat inherited after 1949. . . . The antithesis of this concept, I think, is "taxpayer," a concept Chinese borrowed from the West, implying that the mass, the people, have a right to know what the officials have done with their tax money, and therefore implying a sense of democracy and representativeness of government officials.[6]

Thinking on Chinese governance has always stressed the importance of political leadership. Leaders are not weather vanes sensing popular will whose job is to understand what the people want and deliver it, though some impulses in this direction are evident in today's China. Rather, the core task of political leadership is to understand, define, and act upon society's enduring interests; when the populace does not understand its own underlying interests, the leader is supposed to educate, persuade, and perhaps even change popular inclinations. In a discourse deeply resonant with the Confucian tradition, the leader's legitimacy resides less in being representative than in being far-seeing, wise, and educated; exercising "humane authority" (*ren zheng*); and contributing to the shared goal of "national revitalization" (*minzu fuxin*). This has some similarities to the trusteeship vision of political leadership in Western political discourse, a tradition in which leaders implement their vision of the citizenry's actual interests, not their momentary wants. Elections are an opportunity for the public to ratify or reject the leader's understandings, but in the interim it is the leader's job to arrive at an informed understanding of the popular interest, to pursue it, and to educate the public.

The supreme leader throughout the communist era, and in earlier times, has been the one who simultaneously sits at the apex of the military, executive, and party hierarchies (what I term the "systemically central hierarchies") that run from Beijing down through the bureaucratic layers to relatively low, albeit variable, levels of Chinese society. The concepts of rule of law and checks and balances have played a far smaller role in either limiting the leader or empowering the citizen in China than in the West.

Beyond this idealized role of the leader and the state in China lies the enduring reality that its leaders are overloaded—China is underinstitutionalized and overcentralized. The combination of its geographic expanse, its massive population, its centralized character, and the expectation that senior leaders are indispensable agents of dispute resolution across an infinite range of issues means that at any given moment much in China actually is beyond the awareness or control of the center (*zhongyang*). Governing China is like "Whac-A-Mole," the arcade game in which the player has a mallet to try to pound multiple pop-up moles back into their holes—while attention is devoted to "whacking" challenges in one direction, new ones appear in several other directions simultaneously. Because multiple initiatives must be undertaken simultaneously, it often is difficult for the political center to know how implementation is going or how one policy may affect other initiatives—much less ensure reasonable congruence between initial central intention and eventual local outcomes. The center's pretense of control is considerable, but in reality the writ of Beijing is often quite limited: one mallet is insufficient. An admittedly bizarre example makes the point. When one U.S. congressman challenged Premier Wen Jiabao in a meeting to explain why a professor at Peking University had been fired for political reasons, the premier seemed almost incredulous that he would be asked about such a thing: "Perhaps we [meaning the questioner] need to change our approach; we can see China's special characteristic is lots of people—1.3 billion people. [What you are describing is a] small problem. I don't know the person you spoke of, but as premier, I have 1.3 billion people on my mind."[7]

Chinese leaders are at the top of an inverted funnel that directs the most nettlesome problems upward for resolution. Subordinates, some representing functional bureaucracies and others territorial administrations, are interdependent but often unable to resolve differences among themselves. Consequently, the contesting parties seek out authoritative superiors who can either mediate or enforce a resolution of the dispute. These senior officials find themselves with crushing travel and meeting schedules, literally jumping from resolving one conflict to another. As the bureau director cited in an epigraph at the opening of this chapter said, the job of China's leaders is "dealing with contradictions." Since China began opening up to the world in the late 1970s, domestic issues have become increasingly complex and intertwined with global considerations, requiring the attention of top leaders even more often. Chinese leaders are drinking from a fire hose, with all interested parties besieging them. As the director of a major State Council Office put it, "The higher you get, the colder it becomes."[8] Another very senior former figure in the State Council described the often informal pathways through which the elite are lobbied: it is "'like reporting in the Qing dynasty, when advisers gave slips of paper to the emperor.'"[9]

In the Chinese lexicon of governance, *xietiao* means "to coordinate," or, more loosely translated, "to resolve conflicts among bureaucracies, localities, organizations, and others." *Xietiao* is the job of the "supreme leader," vice-premiers, state councilors, and everyone in a position of political authority. This task of leadership and governance has remained much the same throughout the entire period, from the beginning of Deng's reform in 1977 to the present. Often coercion does not work, and one day's bureaucratic truce is a mere pause during which the various forces regroup for future struggles. To a Westerner, this combination of centralization, leadership dominance, and imperfect implementation, all running on a bargaining treadmill, seems like a system with all the downsides of authoritarianism without any of its presumed benefits of efficiency and focus. In China, it has been this way for a very long time.

Changes

Continuities notwithstanding, there have been dramatic changes in Chinese governance and leadership in the post-Mao reform period, and changing domestic and global conditions portend more profound future developments.[10]

One obvious change is apparent from a comparison of the psychological circumstances of both leaders and ordinary citizens from the early 1970s to the present. In 1971, fear and high anxiety were evident in all realms of society, from ordinary citizens to low-level officials, and even in the demeanor of members of the upper echelons of the party (who almost uniformly chain-smoked). Owing to the uninterrupted stream of post-1949 mass and political rectification movements, not least the Great Proletarian Cultural Revolution, by the 1970s there was an all-pervasive anxiety that anyone at any moment could run afoul of the ideological and personal whims of Mao Zedong and the machinations of his acolytes. When speaking with a group of American university students in mid-1971, for instance, Premier Zhou Enlai paid attention to the Chairman's young leftist lapdogs that were in the room, watching him carefully and listening.[11] As one of the participants in that meeting, Susan Shirk, put it in public remarks years later, "There was lots of tension in the room. Yao [Wen-yuan] and Zhang [Chunqiao] sat there, Mao's palace clique, [they] sat there looking contemptuous, clearly there to watch Zhou."[12] Zhou's concern was justified, for a couple of years later the "Criticize Lin [Biao], Criticize Confucius" (*Pi Lin, Pi Kong*) campaign was launched by the Left, aimed in no small measure at the premier.

In this same context, in 1974, shortly after returning from his first of two Cultural Revolution–era exiles, in a meeting with a group of American university presidents, Deng Xiaoping exhibited caution. He spoke meticulously and hewed closely to Mao's words, knowing that his political enemies might yet again turn Mao against him, as did occur in the spring of 1976.[13] In this conversation he contradicted what he would say quite soon after Mao's September 1976 death and the purge of the "Gang of Four," parroting Mao's thinking that a large population was China's strength: "We have seen our population grow by 60 percent in the last 20 years, but our grains increased 140 percent. Even if the population should increase by another 50 to 60 percent, we would still have enough to eat, plus a bit of surplus."[14] In an October 23, 1977, meeting with then vice-premier Deng Xiaoping shortly after he had returned from his second Cultural Revolution–era exile, Professor Lucian Pye described the scene: "Deng was very low-keyed during the whole discussion. He seemed tired and almost bored, with very little sense of fire, very little enthusiasm. It was as though he had to go through a ritual performance."[15] This state of affairs (overwhelming intimidation) was brought home to me during a 1976 meeting with Dr. Zhou Peiyuan, a theoretical physicist at Peking University who had worked with Einstein at Princeton earlier in his career. This gray-haired eminence was the nominal university leader, but the ignorant head of the university's "Revolutionary Committee" did the talking, and Professor Zhou's head was lowered.

Today, Chinese leaders at all levels generally speak with relative openness, and ordinary citizens are often caustic in their assessment of leaders, policies, and the elite's not infrequent peccadilloes and idiosyncrasies. Citizens have little capacity to organize for political change, but they can express dissatisfaction and pursue a broad range of personal and family interests. The Internet and social media have become petri dishes growing and nurturing a broad range of dissatisfaction and commentary.

Beyond the political atmosphere and self-expression, several factors have moved Chinese governance and leadership into an *entirely different political space* from that of 1977. First, there has been a *dramatic change in the type of leaders China has recruited* at very senior levels and their power in relationship to a pluralizing society—a topic raised in the preceding chapter and elaborated on here. China is moving from the transformational and charismatic leadership of Mao Zedong and the strongman leadership of Deng Xiaoping to a more transactional, system-maintenance type of leader. China has moved from a strongman system to a collective system of leadership, albeit one with fissures. One very senior policy adviser described the contemporary leadership picture as "a mosaic of China . . . a rainbow coalition."[16] I would say governance by committee.

Second, there has been *pluralization of both Chinese society and the governing bureaucracy,* reflecting economic growth, specialization and professionalization, urbanization, scientific development, and globalization. For example, the as-yet-incomplete move from classic state-owned enterprises (SOEs) to something more nearly approximating Western-style corporations is creating powerful economic actors that are only partially responsive to party-state directives, either domestically or as they act abroad. Enormous swaths of the globalizing Chinese economy are growing up outside, or tenuously connected to, the state structure. For example, more than 70 percent of Chinese ships fishing far from China's shores were privately owned in 2012, according to scholar Tabitha Mallory. One implication of this substantial privatization of fishing is that preventing overfishing in the global commons, even if the PRC government were committed to that objective, has become much more difficult.[17]

In Beijing, the Ministry of Foreign Affairs building is overshadowed (literally) by the towering headquarters of two of China's three major oil companies. In the same neighborhood is the huge headquarters of Polytechnologies, which is, among other things, a global arms merchant. One could interpret this location as a metaphorical sign that the Foreign Ministry controls these actors. Personnel in the foreign affairs system, however, portray this physical reality as a manifestation of the ministry's weakening control over the PRC's external links and behavior, and the growing influence of economic interests, asking themselves—Who is surrounding whom? Social, bureaucratic, and economic pluralization has made decision making, effective policy implementation, and monitoring of outcomes—whether domestically or overseas—increasingly difficult.

Finally, *resources (human, financial, and informational) are progressively becoming less a monopoly of the central party-state.* China's leaders know they must mobilize increasingly diffuse resources to solve ever more problems. Yet they generally fear empowering social groups (*shehui tuanti*) to assist, anxious that latitude given to such groups to address crucial challenges could morph into the pursuit of unsanctioned activities and could boomerang on the regime itself. Nonetheless, the number of social organizations is growing rapidly because of the initiative of an increasingly self-motivated and empowered citizenry determined to address the problems it confronts and the recognition of leaders that they and their bureaucratic instruments cannot alone meet all the challenges.

Resources and the capacity to act are devolving to a broader range of societal actors. Financial resources also have been diffused to the lower levels of government, thereby empowering them to act independently of the center. By 2010, for instance, over 50 percent of government science and technology expenditures were made by local governments,[18] and 71.7 percent of the entire national R&D funding that same year came from "business."[19] Thus authority has moved toward parts of the economy with unclear linkages to the center (business) and to lower

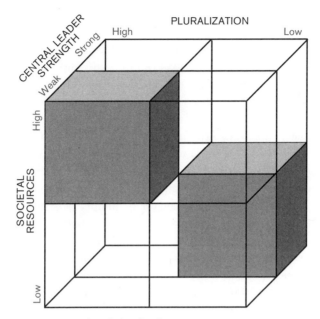

FIGURE 2. Untethered pluralization.

levels of the territorial hierarchy (local government). With respect to "business," for example, talk about the development of an incipient venture-capital industry and the need for "business-government" partnerships is commonplace these days. With respect to local government, one former battle-hardened veteran of the State Council said, "When local governments are richer they try to expand their control."[20]

In short, a once dominant center increasingly faces more potent localities, economic actors, and social groupings that possess greater financial resources, human talent, and information. These various forces have given rise to *untethered pluralism*—a stronger society and bureaucratic activism at all levels, uninhibited by an established rule of law, adequate oversight, sufficient regulatory structures, or, in many cases, ethical norms.

Figure 2 graphically illustrates the changes that have moved the Chinese system from one political space into another. From 1977 to 2013 the PRC has moved from a political space characterized by strong leaders, a relatively homogeneous society, and weak subordinate levels of society and government (lower, right rear box) to a political space characterized by less dominant top leaders, a more fragmented government and society, and increasingly empowered subordinate organizations and social groups (upper, left front box). In one generation China has moved itself from one corner of political space to the completely opposite corner.

A system characterized by weaker central leadership, ever more pluralism, and an increasingly empowered society, organizations, and individuals requires a far stronger rule of law and conflict-reducing mechanisms (courts and legislatures), as well as effective regulation, transparency, and accountability, not to mention the restraint on individuals provided by strong ethical norms. What is needed is the gradual construction of an altered political system and a broadened rationale for legitimacy. As a department director put it: "Stakeholders are relevant these days."[21] Absent these changes, China is in for a bumpy, perhaps tumultuous, period ahead. Such turbulence would spill into the wider world in very unwelcome ways.

Concisely, governing China has become progressively more difficult. Two examples provide concrete evidence of what it means on the ground when we observe that China has moved into an era of less dominant leaders, more pluralized society and bureaucracy, and more empowered subnational groups. The first illustrative case is that of a development corporation (Wanda Group) that was able to secure approvals from local authorities in Mianyang, Sichuan Province, to build two skyscrapers a short distance from the runways of the local airport (was bribery involved, or just poor planning?). Then, when the Civil Aviation Administration of China and the military (which regulate flight operations and control air space, respectively) both entreated the company to halt construction, Wanda Group ignored them and continued to construct and sell apartments, while the airport had to curtail night operations because of safety considerations at the cost of US$31,000 per day.[22]

In another case, Zheng Yanxiong, party secretary of Wukan City in Guangdong Province, put the difficulties of governing China like this: "There's only one group of people who really experience added hardships year after year. Who are they? Cadres, that's who. Me included. . . . Your powers decline every day, and you have fewer and fewer methods at your disposal—but your responsibility grows bigger and bigger every day. Ordinary people want more and more every day. They grow smarter every day, and they are harder and harder to control. Today's government officials are having a hard time."[23] Then, in the tradition of U.S. politicians, Zheng went after the mass media—"If you can trust in outside media, then pigs can climb trees."[24]

We now take a deeper look at the leadership, bureaucratic, and societal changes of the 1977–2013 period that together have pushed China into its new political space.

LEADERSHIP

Defining Leadership

China's leaders have ruled a vast and diverse territory for thousands of years and have systematically thought about the leader's tasks since the pre-Qin era (before 221 BCE).[25] Much of what outsiders view as China's Leninist governing style since the communist revolution in 1949 also has deep resonance with Chinese approaches to rule throughout history—not least the Confucian and Legalist traditions, which are, themselves, in some tension with one another.

Chinese political philosophy has placed central importance on the nature and character of the leader—the quality of that person's strategic thinking and the competence and character of the people with whom the leader surrounds him- or (rarely) herself. A great leader should possess the quality of "humane authority" (*ren zheng*) and is to take the "kingly way" (*wang dao*).[26] "Humane authority is founded on the superior moral power of the ruler himself."[27] In this view the welfare of the people directly depends on the wisdom, capacities, and compassion of the leader, as well as those who work next to him. At the same time, there is the Machiavellian recognition that a leader must also hold a knife, discreetly sheathed, not infrequently drawn, and sometimes used to make an example of lesser threats to preempt the appearance of bigger ones—"kill the chicken to scare the monkey" (*sha ji jing hou*).

As former mayor of Shanghai Wang Daohan put it in 1997, "'The starting point for Chinese understanding is the overall interest of the whole Chinese people.'"[28] It is the leader's job to discern the people's interests, to adopt policies that serve those interests, to select officials, and to effectively organize implementation. As time passes, the context changes, interests and policies evolve, and the wise leader adapts. But the central point is: the leader plays a decisive role in defining societal interests. "The interest of the people" is not simply the equilibrium that results from the clash of individual and group interests, as we often think of political life in the West. Even in contemporary democratic Taiwan, these presumptions about leadership have resonance. As a ministerial-level official in Taipei stated in 2011: "'The right vision is the key thing; leaders have the responsibility to implement policies in the interests of the people. This is their highest task.'"[29]

Chinese political philosophy speaks of the fundamental constraint on "the prince" being a basic acceptance by the people: the ruler is a boat; the people the sea; the boat floats atop the sea; if the sea becomes rough, the boat can capsize. Or, as Premier Wen Jiabao put it at a 2007 press conference, "Every cadre and leading official should know that 'while water can carry a boat, it can also overturn it.'"[30] Despite this clear understanding, in China there is an absence of policy grounded in popular will and representation. Historically, the main political task in Western democratic systems has been constraining leaders; in China it has been empowering them. The Chinese leader must be wise in assessing desirable goals, the people's interests, and what is objectively achievable given that he has fewer institutional constraints. As Zhou Enlai put it to former U.S. ambassador to the United Nations Charles Yost late one evening in June 1973, "There is a Chinese saying that a wise ruler does not make laws that he knows will be ignored."[31] The ruler makes the laws, but wisely, because widespread noncompliance strips away legitimacy and nurtures rebellion.

The Chinese leader traditionally has played a dominant role in designating a successor, though this has moved toward a more collective process in recent leadership transitions. In a remarkable meeting with Jiang Zemin during the latter days of November 2002 when he was relinquishing his posts as party general secretary and president, Jiang explained that Mao Zedong and Deng Xiaoping had each chosen the wrong successor more than once but that he, Jiang Zemin, had gotten it right the first time with Hu Jintao. He also indicated he would remain on as chairman of the Central Military Commission (CMC). Jiang framed his decision to remain CMC chairman (until 2004, as it turned out) as essentially his own to make. The fact that he publicly described the succession process in these terms with colleagues and foreigners present demonstrates something significant about shared conceptions of leadership.

> I want to talk about how I handled the transition in leadership. . . . "Our great leader" [Jiang said this in English] Mao Zedong had a number of successors—Liu Shaoqi, then Lin Biao, Wang Hongwen, and Hua Guofeng lastly. Hua was a good guy, but he later had the theory of the two whatevers [whatever Mao said is right, and whatever Mao said is to be done]. . . . As for the late Deng Xiaoping, his first intention was Hu Yaobang [as a successor]. Then he was not the right guy, and Zhao Ziyang was not the right guy.

And actually, I succeeded Deng thirteen years ago. Here I would not talk about my achievements, and some problems, but what is important is the stable situation [China has enjoyed] over thirteen years. . . . This time, before the Party Congress, I did a lot of thinking about this succession, [and] I concluded that only one of seven members of the Politburo Standing Committee could stay. Hu Jintao stays, the others resign. . . . This reminds me of Shakespeare's *As You Like It*. "The world is but a stage and all we are players, and they each have their entrances and their exits." So, it is with great pleasure that I handed over to Hu Jintao, and I would be pleased if he does better than me.[32]

The Chinese leader occupies a far different space than the leader does in American political discourse and practice. In nonwartime conditions, Americans view constraining leaders and empowering citizens as a central mission, while Chinese traditionally have seen a weak, burdened leader as a threat to be guarded against. A central component of Chinese political culture is the fear of *luan* or chaos, the fear of being rudderless and vulnerable in a predatory world. For Chinese people, their country has big problems and needs larger-than-life leaders to foster stability. What Chinese people expect from their leaders, and what Chinese leaders expect from one another, is based on this need.

Much of the PRC's conflict with the West over the proper role of government and political rights derives from this concept. Though rights consciousness is growing in China's society and may explode with the combination of popular frustration, globalization, urbanization, rising material security, a younger, wired generation coming of age, and simply the yearning for dignity, it also is true that China still has a deeply embedded political culture in which the people have seen themselves more as "subjects" than as "citizens"— still expecting to be acted upon rather than actively participating in governance. Even as China is rapidly urbanizing, in 2013 still just under half of the population remained rural. In the countryside, the expectation for leaders to act in a traditional, paternalistic, and authoritarian manner remains.

The Diversity and Evolution of Leadership

The above notwithstanding, over the reform era, leaders have changed from the traditional strongman variety toward more norm-constrained figures who are primus inter pares within a collective group. These new leaders are more incremental in their approach and transactional, focusing on system maintenance rather than on precipitous social transformation.

Despite their similarities, Chinese leaders are also diverse, reflecting the full range of personalities that one finds in every human society—running the gamut from ambitious and gregarious to retiring, from serious to humorous, from strategic thinkers to narrow tacticians, and from those who work best in back rooms to those that feel most at home out in the field talking to citizens.[33] Some are thugs and others are compassionate.

Deng Xiaoping didn't talk much, was remote, listened carefully to those he trusted, didn't rely on think tanks, and was generally noncommittal until he uttered a few clear words that constituted a decision—often punctuated with a wad of spit into a spittoon. As senior Chinese policy advisers put it in 1998, "Deng Xiaoping always had a big strategic picture in his mind and didn't need to consult with anyone except his bridge partners."[34] More intimately, Deng showed considerable devotion to those he loved, unlike Mao, for whom kinship seemed to be nearly a death sentence. Deng's daughter, Xiao Rong, recalls the touching vignette of a Deng disconsolate over the death of his first wife Zhang Xiyuan, who had died in the wake of childbirth in 1930: he visited and protected her remains for years thereafter until they could be properly buried in 1969.[35]

Premier Zhao Ziyang had a lively, inquiring mind and a winning smile and liked to be surrounded by bright young people. He believed in expert advice and listened. He was data driven.[36] General secretary and president Jiang Zemin relied on advisers and used theatrics and unpredictable discourse that ran off on tangents to defuse situations and divert attention until, circling like a bird of prey, he dived in on his point. He used humor to soften disagreements. Premier Zhu Rongji's style was to constantly ask probing questions and make observations. He possessed a nonstop, inquiring mind like a steel trap. He could criticize an errant subordinate one moment and in the next disarm an audience with his humor. The people closest to him were fiercely loyal. He was devoted to traditional Chinese music. Premier Wen Jiabao always looked nervous, twitching in the face, but he didn't waste time before getting to the point, all the while conveying humanity. He liked to quote poetry and, like Zhao Ziyang, was data and fact driven. NPC head Wu Bangguo was quite simply the fastest-talking person I have ever met at a very senior level in the PRC.

At local levels, Chinese leaders are similarly distinctive in their personalities. Take former mayor of Dalian Bo Xilai, for example—he was so hyperkinetic and anxious to attract foreign direct investment and modernize his city (which he did with great success) that he once simultaneously hosted two separate banquets for two separate delegations (one Japanese and one American) and careened between rooms the whole evening. When Bo became first party secretary in Chongqing in November 2007, he quickly unleashed a thuggish "strike the black" (*da hei*) anticorruption campaign on the city, reminding many observers of his brutal behavior as a Red Guard youth in the Cultural Revolution. In March 2012 he was removed from office in Chongqing and the Politburo as his wife stood implicated (and in August of that year was convicted) in the murder of a British national, while associates were accused of involvement in financial and other improprieties. In summer 2013, Bo was convicted of corruption and abuse of power.

In Shanghai, Mayor Wang Daohan loved books, and a later Shanghai mayor, Xu Kuangdi, went into raptures over Mozart. Shanghai party secretary Chen Liangyu (sacked for corruption in 2006) told visitors with pride that his father had studied in Chicago—"Actually, the United States is not alien; my father studied at Chicago in 1949—one year and two months in the United States. He spent longer in the U.S. than my eight months in England."[37] Thus clearly China's system does not produce only gray, bureaucratic technocrats. Caricatures of leaders can mislead. In group conversations with Premier Li Peng, for instance, I found him a careful listener, directly responding to questions, and not visibly concerned with softening his answers out of concern for the sensitivities of his listeners.

In the evolution of Chinese leaders from Mao Zedong to Xi Jinping, the kinds of individuals the Chinese political system is "selecting for" (to use a biological term) has changed. One obvious way this has unfolded is seen in the average age of Politburo members. In 1982 the average age of the Politburo was seventy-two, and in 2007 it was sixty-two.[38] In the Eighteenth Politburo selected in late 2012, the average age of Politburo members dropped marginally to "slightly over 61."[39] Indeed, in his October 20, 1971, meeting with Henry Kissinger, Premier Zhou Enlai remarked to a member of Kissinger's delegation, Dwight Chapin: "Mr. Chapin, you seem quite young." When Chapin responded, "I am thirty," Zhou commented, "So I admire you greatly. In this aspect, we Chinese still have to catch up with you Americans because you dare to use young people."[40] Beyond age, education, and similar indicators, one can describe the fundamental evolution of China's leadership over the reform era by considering two typologies: one articulated by Max Weber and the other by James MacGregor Burns.[41]

Chinese Leadership through a Weberian Lens

Max Weber categorized the bases upon which leadership exercises authority and holds power (legitimacy): *traditional authority* is the right to rule rooted in custom; *charismatic authority* is rule anchored in the character of, and devotion to, the leader; and *legal-rational authority* is a legitimacy in which authority is grounded in constitutional and legal norms.[42] Societies evolve from conferring leadership on traditional and charismatic grounds toward conferring it on the basis of legal-constitutional norms and regularized processes. As a society urbanizes and grows more complex, and as educational levels and societal expectations for participation and predictability grow, so does the tendency to anchor legitimacy in legal-rational authority. In cases of social breakdown, law, norms, and bureaucratic procedure can falter and older means of establishing authority (custom and devotion) can reassert themselves, causing political decay.

It was precisely the process of institutionalization, regularization, bureaucratization, and constraint on leadership that Mao Zedong resisted in the last decade-plus of his life. Being pushed into the "second line of leadership" in the late 1950s, he fought against this change throughout the chaotic Cultural Revolution decade (1966–76), a period during which he strove to reassert his charismatic, traditional authority. Premier Wen Jiabao was referring to this possibility of political decay when, at a 2012 press conference, he said: "Reform has reached a critical stage. Without the success of political reform, economic reforms cannot be carried out. The results that we have achieved may be lost. A historical tragedy like the Cultural Revolution may occur again."[43]

In the transitions from Mao Zedong to Deng Xiaoping, then to Jiang Zemin, Hu Jintao, and finally Xi Jinping, there has been a progression that echoes Weber's expectations. Mao and Deng were each legitimated with a distinct mix of "traditional" and "charismatic" authority, in no small part owing to their exceptional life histories—Mao was in many respects an emperor masquerading as a new type of leader, and Deng exerted great influence simply holding the title of honorary chairman of the China Bridge (as in cards) Association at the end of his life. Jiang Zemin and Hu Jintao both were designated as serial successors appointed by Deng Xiaoping himself (notwithstanding Jiang Zemin's claim of credit above). In the case of Hu Jintao, Deng Xiaoping's influence extended beyond the grave.

Only in the case of Xi Jinping was a leader's elevation to the top position the product of a collective political process less subject to his predecessor's decisive influence, though age and rotational norms already had begun to develop in the preceding successions of Jiang Zemin and Hu Jintao. This development of norms and reduced patron influence in leadership turnover does not mean that China has yet adopted a fully legal-rational system, but Xi Jinping has acquired power on a very different basis of legitimacy than his predecessors. Xi's authority rests on a selection process that involved many in a "selectorate" (upper reaches of the CCP). What the selectorate has conferred, the selectorate can withdraw. The norms governing selection are increasingly known to the wider public, and increasingly there are performance measures and opinion polling within the party that move beyond subjective assessments. The norms governing leadership selection (intraparty consultation, predictable rotation, term and age limits, and performance measurement with public input) are not equivalent to law and constitutionalism but may be a way station on the road there. These gradually solidifying norms are incomplete and reversible, but they mark a dramatic change from Mao's system, in which the Chairman, like Saturn in Goya's painting *Saturn Devouring His Son,* could singlehandedly mobilize "the street" against the Communist Party he had built, in no small part over his concern with succession.

Although Deng did not possess the unbridled and quixotically exercised power that Mao did, when it came to strategic decisions, once he had listened to respected colleagues, Deng would weigh in authoritatively and decisively. The scale and consequences of these decisions were often enormous. As Cheng Li put it, Deng "felt no need to consult think tanks when making decisions. . . . Indeed, his most significant decisions . . . have all been attributed to Deng's visionary thinking and political courage."[44] A notable illustration of Deng's dominance was his May 17, 1989, decision to declare martial law and deploy troops in Beijing—a choice made in consultation with an extraconstitutional cabal of older comrades, most of whom held no formal posts. Later in the same day, Deng's fateful decision was presented by Premier Li Peng to the Politburo Standing Committee as a fait accompli, and the Standing Committee (the body presumed to decide such things) was simply told how to proceed. Li informed the nominal head of the party, Zhao Ziyang, and his Standing Committee colleagues that "the decision on martial law . . . was made by Comrade [Deng] Xiaoping at this morning's meeting. I support Comrade Xiaoping's views on martial law. I believe that the topic for the present meeting is not whether martial law should or should not be imposed but, rather, what steps to use in carrying it out."[45] Professor Ezra Vogel reports that earlier in the day, at the meeting where Deng announced his decision, "When some in the room expressed worries that foreigners would react negatively to any use of force, Deng replied that swift action was required and 'Westerners would forget.'"[46]

In addition to this decision, several other pivotal choices by Deng come to mind, including his decision to suppress the 1979 Democracy Wall movement, mentioned in chapter 1. Deng explained to visiting Americans at the time, "As to the so-called Democracy Wall or the demonstrations and sit-ins, etc., this can't represent the genuine feeling of our people."[47] In another example of resolute decision making, the one-child policy, Deng was absolutely convinced that the PRC's per capita income could not be sufficiently raised without limiting the birth of mouths to feed, as also explained in chapter 1.[48] It seemed self-evident to Deng that individual choice should take a back seat to collective needs and the imperative of economic growth, and that to move in this intrusive direction was within his discretion.

Turning to the issue of Taiwan, while his successors hesitated to be seen as weak on an issue with so much combustible nationalism surrounding it, Deng was sufficiently secure to be ambivalent, perhaps even relaxed about the issue—certainly willing to defer conflict over the issue to the indefinite future. A very senior Taiwanese academic summarized Deng's conversation with him in the late 1980s, describing Deng's seemingly flexible thoughts on the island: "I talked with Deng Xiaoping, Zhao Ziyang, and Jiang Zemin, and conversations with Deng were the most useful. In 1987 Deng asked, 'You grew up in Taiwan?' [and wanted to know] why the DPP wanted independence. [I replied,] because [Taiwan was] a colony, the KMT was very corrupt, and [Taiwanese were] not treated very well. Deng said, 'Yeah, looks like [we should] leave cross-Strait [relations] to the next generation,' and he started eating."[49]

Fast-forwarding to China's three early twenty-first-century leaders who followed Deng (Jiang Zemin, Hu Jintao, and Xi Jinping), it is inconceivable that they—given the characteristics they embody as leaders— could have initiated policies as intrusive as the one-child policy was in the late 1970s, for example. The foundations for legitimacy have gradually shifted, and the strength that this legitimacy confers on Deng's successors has steadily diminished their capacity to initiate, much less sustain, highly disruptive, intrusive, and capricious society-wide policies. As one senior Chinese academic put it in 2011, "We have moved from a strongman leadership, through Deng Xiaoping to Jiang Zemin, who could still be called 'core leaders,' to the current situation with Hu Jintao and his presumed successor, who cannot be called 'core leaders' 'but merely first among equals.'"[50] The PRC has gone from leaders who had personal and experiential credibility to leaders who are constrained by collective decision making, by term limits, by evolving norms, by the boundaries of the permissible partially defined by "public opinion," and, in part, by their own technocratic and relatively educated characters. In 2002, a senior Chinese diplomat put it as follows: "'Mao and Deng could decide, Jiang and the current leaders must consult.'"[51]

In late 2012 and into 2013, the contrast between an empowered Deng and more constrained successors was again on dramatic display. In the 1970s, in order to proceed with normalization and build ties with Japan, Deng agreed with Tokyo to simply shelve the nationalism-laden issue of sovereignty over the Diaoyu/Senkaku Islands to the northeast of Taiwan in the East China Sea. In late 2012 and into 2013, in the context of the transition from Hu Jintao to Xi Jinping, China's new leader felt obliged to be much more assertive in the face of Japanese "nationalization" of the islands. Beyond having new capabilities at their disposal, China's twenty-first-century leaders do not have the political clout Deng enjoyed.

Chinese Leadership through the Lens of James MacGregor Burns

The political scientist James MacGregor Burns provides another vantage point from which to view the PRC's leadership evolution by looking at the leader's *goals:* there are leaders whose objectives include enormous change, while others see themselves in system-maintenance roles. These are *transformational* and *transactional* leaders, respectively. Burns also identifies a third type, the *power wielder*—the leader seeking power as an end, not as a means to other ends.

On the transformational-to-transactional continuum, Deng Xiaoping would be placed far toward the transformational end of the scale, albeit transformational in a far different way than Mao Zedong. Mao sought to change China by changing its people and fundamental societal organization—the desired direction of change often being contrary to the citizenry's natural impulses. This led the Chairman to attempt to build and use coercive educational, peer-group, and organizational instruments to create what the outside world called the "new Maoist man." He also was a ruthless power wielder.[52]

Deng Xiaoping, though also a leader with transformational goals, found his modus operandi in working with the nature of his people as he found them—people with an irrepressible urge for self-improvement, particularly materially, and a patriotic impulse to elevate China's global status. Mao sought to remake China by remaking its people and used coercion and ideology to do so. Deng's affinity for employing material incentives could not have been clearer than when he told American visitors in late 1979: "One thing is correct. [It is] Impossible to give play to personal enthusiasm and initiative without linking it to incentives."[53] Deng was going to move China up economically, and the place to start was with human acquisitiveness. One vice-minister described China's condition at the onset of reform and Deng's approach this way: "[With] the planned economy, there was not fast growth, and during the Great Proletarian Cultural Revolution [China] went to the brink of bankruptcy. 'Yes, Chinese were equals, Chinese were equally poor.' Deng [Xiaoping] will be remembered 'as the greatest man of contemporary China.' Deng said: 'Poverty is not socialism. Economic development is the priority of priorities.' 'He brought back the entrepreneurship that runs in the blood of the Chinese.'"[54]

Deng's other steps were to radically open China to foreign knowledge, encourage many of China's young people to go abroad (an attitude influenced by his own formative experience in France), and let comparative advantage, trade, and education work their magic. He was going to work with (not against) the forces of human nature to change China.

In Deng's successor, Jiang Zemin, we see a leader who was midway on Burns's transformative-transactional continuum. Jiang succeeded Deng after having "tested" best (as former Shanghai mayor Wang Daohan put it),[55] because he was viewed as capable and nonthreatening to both the forces within the party wanting reform to move forward and those wary of reform. In the initial period of his tenure as general secretary of the CCP (1989–92), Jiang trod carefully between these two contending impulses, but in 1992 Deng's "Southern Tour" rekindled reform and helped (or forced) Jiang to jump off the fence on the side of rapid reform, where he stayed until his retirement from the CMC in 2004. In 1994, the year Deng's personal office was closed out of consideration of his age and infirmities, Jiang appeared to truly step out on his own from under the shadow of Deng Xiaoping. One senior Chinese person who interacted with Jiang put the difference between working with Jiang and Deng as follows: "Deng was there, it was not easy to reach him. So think tanks had only indirect influence. Deng was much more remote. Very few people could approach him. Jiang is more willing to [meet] more different people. When we spoke to Jiang last October he took notes, worked very hard."[56]

Jiang articulated and promoted great change in China along several key dimensions. He drove forward China's accession to the World Trade Organization (2001), whereupon the PRC's trade with the world exploded, rising from 4 percent of total global trade in 2001 to 9.9 percent by 2011.[57] China's global two-way trade from 2001 to 2011 totaled roughly $20 trillion, seven times greater than the prior decade.[58] He oversaw and supported China's vigorous move into space, which was capped with its first manned space mission (2003). He articulated, for the first time, that the CCP needed to bring more creative and skilled people into its membership ranks (in February 2000 he first enunciated his policy of the "Three Represents"); thereafter, party membership jumped from 64.5 million in 2000 to 82.6 million in 2011, a 28 percent increase.[59] Between 1993 and 1999, Jiang, and his indispensable colleague Premier Zhu Rongji, put some twenty-five million state-owned enterprise (SOE) workers out of work in the quest for efficiency and transformation of the PRC's industrial base.[60] During his thirteen-year rule, China's economy grew at an average annual rate of 9.7 percent (real/constant price GDP growth).[61]

Notwithstanding all of the above, Jiang was more transactional than transformational by virtue of both his character and his circumstances. He sought balance between forces. He was an engineer, so he was practical and oriented toward making things work, as Jiang's conversation with an American group, including former U.S. congressman Barber B. Conable Jr., demonstrates:

> Shanghai, Mr. Conable was there in 1988. I was mayor, and I told him about my job; difficult; seven million people in the city center—eleven million overall. In the summer, it is a major problem to get rid of watermelon rinds; they are everywhere—a big garbage problem. When in 1981 I went to Chicago and people asked what I wanted to visit, I said I'd like to know about garbage. Chicago has these difficult problems but does a good job in garbage relative to Shanghai. "It must be very difficult for Americans to conceive of handling this [China's] population."[62]

President Jiang concluded this meeting by observing that building bridges in Shanghai was complicated too because the usual linear and horizontal approaches for bridges would cover many hectares and displace excessive numbers of residents. He then pointed to an innovative solution his municipal administration had adopted: "How to build a bridge in Shanghai is a big problem. Construction took two years. [We] saved land with corkscrew approaches. I am proud." By "corkscrew approaches," Jiang meant road approaches to the bridge that were not linear but rather built in an upward spiral fashion to minimize their footprint.[63] In a society as complex as China is becoming, governance is about trade-offs. China's leaders have less opportunity to think about transformation because they are preoccupied with more circumscribed decisions and the cost of mistakes is great.

This brings us to Hu Jintao and Wen Jiabao. Both of these leaders were much closer to the transactional than to the transformational end of the continuum. This, in part, accounts for the widespread domestic and international perception that reform in China had slowed compared to the growth and change under Deng and Jiang. A senior Chinese diplomat presciently foretold this on the eve of Hu Jintao's assumption of power in the summer of 2002: "Another trend will be toward collective [jiti] leadership, rather than supreme leaders. Future leaderships will be collective, more democratic, they will seek consensus rather than make arbitrary decisions. But the downside is that they will enjoy lesser amounts of authority. It will be more difficult for them to make bold decisions when bold decisions are needed. Such a leadership will be more careful, more committed to social progress."[64] Xi Jinping's evolution remains to be seen.

This brings us to the second dimension of the political space into which the Chinese polity has moved in the reform era: pluralization.

THE PLURALIZATION OF CHINESE BUREAUCRACY AND SOCIETY

Background

Even before Mao's death in September 1976, Western analysts were intent on specifying bureaucratic, regional, class, occupational, and other politically salient divisions that they presumed existed in the PRC—believing that politics in China, as most everywhere else, was about reconciling or energizing political cleavages to achieve goals. The Cultural Revolution revealed that there were deep divisions in the Chinese polity, yet it was difficult to see their contours. The reigning ideologically driven assertion during the Mao era was that there was only one interest: "the interest of the Chinese masses." "The masses" became the reified repository of solidarity, indeed purity. The job of governance was to repress recalcitrant forces, to educate the Chinese masses as to their true interests so they would embrace them, and, in the case of bureaucracy, to simplify it, putting functional organs under political, not expert, guidance. Governance was not about reconciling differences, it was about eliminating them.

Consider, for example, a July 19, 1971, meeting with American students in the Great Hall of the People. There a naturally cosmopolitan, but then guarded, Premier Zhou Enlai reflected the times. The setting was surreal, as he was watched closely by leftist critics Yao Wenyuan and Zhang Chunqiao:

> You have entered the Red Guard period. We will have to ask these two comrades [Yao Wenyuan and Zhang Chunqiao] to tell you something about the Red Guard movement. The Red Guards called themselves members of the "service committee," or members of the "general service committee." It is also a Red Guard trend of thought that they don't like to be called "minister" or "section head" or "director." They like to think that's all bureaucratic and therefore we must do away with the bureaucratic structure and call ourselves "service personnel" of the people. . . . I heard that you were asking why people weren't wearing the colorful cloth produced in textile mills. It is because it is the custom today to live simply and therefore people like to wear simple clothes, and also as a symbol of discipline. In order to provide a symbol of learning from the PLA, people like to wear army uniforms. And the style of simplicity is also in opposition to bourgeois degradation. . . . So we welcome very much this spiritual help from you [the students to whom he was talking]. It is "rectifying wrong ideas." That is Chairman Mao's wording. It is not brainwashing, it is rectifying erroneous ideas. I haven't thought of a way to wash one's brain yet. In a certain way I would like to have my brain washed because I have old ideas in my mind. I have already passed 73, how can it be said that I have no old ideas in my head, because I came over from the old society? . . . And if any of you have taken tape-recorders with you, you can also record the talk here if you want. Since we are meeting with you, of course we will speak freely. Maybe I will say something wrong here, or perhaps these other two comrades might say something wrong, or the interpreter might interpret wrong. . . . So if you are going to show your recordings when you get back to the United States, you must make a statement at the beginning and say there are bound to be some wrong statements in this recording. . . . Of course we stand on the position of the proletariat, and you of course are clear about that. As for our views we do our utmost to see that they are in accordance with Marxism-Leninism-Mao Tse-tung [Mao Zedong] Thought.[65]

In the more than forty years between 1971 and 2013, China's leaders and citizens have moved from denying societal and governmental conflicts to explaining governance challenges in terms of the conflicts. While pathways for the expression of interests remain limited and opaque and elites are often unresponsive, China's rulers now try to resolve interest conflicts, repressing them only when perceived threat is high.

Embracing Pluralization

During the reform era, particularly after Deng Xiaoping, China has developed a responsive authoritarianism that explicitly balances (through representation at the highest reaches of the CCP) major geographic, functional, factional, and policy interests.[66] There is an attempt to co-opt as much conflict as possible, accommodate the rank and file of groups, and impose high personal costs on the ringleaders of movements that assume an organized, antisystem coloration.

Pluralism in China is everywhere. It is present in the conflicting ambitions of powerful individuals and evident within and among China's bureaucracies, economic sectors, localities, and social groups. As one official put it, "'My view is the battlefield of interests.'"[67] In the bureaucracy, "small leading groups" (*lingdao xiaozu*) are forums in which supraministerial officials resolve fights among squabbling ministerial-level or other subordinate organizations and localities. Vice-premiers and state councilors spend much of their time resolving disputes. Provinces and industrial and commercial associations seek to push their interests using "representative offices" in Beijing to cultivate good relations with key decision makers in relevant bureaucracies. This model is duplicated by counties in their provincial capitals. Big cities (e.g., Shanghai) set up their own promotion offices that search for business and political support nationally. As one Chinese diplomat explained to me, however, these offices "don't lobby the [National People's] Congress, they lobby the executive. In China now they lobby less for money and more for favorable policy."[68] As one office director in a central government science and technology-related ministry put it, "'Stakeholders are relevant these days'" in terms of competing for R&D money.[69] While considerable lobbying efforts are directed at executive agencies to obtain administrative and policy leeway, as noted above, lobbying is also increasingly directed toward local and national legislatures.

Chinese in and out of government have become more open in describing this process. Former vice-premier Li Lanqing vented his frustration with the bureaucratic fights it was his fate to continually referee. Li recounts one meeting in which he mediated a catfight between three contending foreign trade corporations, each claiming the exclusive right to trade in designed textiles ("drawnwork"):

> The man from Chinatex claimed that drawnwork was a textile product and the man from CNACIEC contended that it was a handicraft. The leader of China Tushu argued that ramie was a native product and went so far as to declare that anything that flew in the sky, grew on the ground, or was raised by man was either native produce or an animal product and was therefore well within his company's business domain. He fell just short of saying that all commodities on earth should be left to their management. . . . When I announced the verdict, I knew it was only a temporary "armistice agreement," rather than a thorough settlement of the issue.[70]

One already can see the adaptation of local-level officials to a new mode of politics. When an American group met with the secretary of the Minhang District Party Committee (of Shanghai), this impeccably dressed, young, self-assured local official described the direction in which local governance was moving: "'In Shanghai, now in Minhang [District], there is a different way of governing. There is a different culture, a different language. We have developed so fast, it is a question of development. I spend four hours each day on the Internet, monitoring complaints, etc. The next generation will be more like this. This is a fundamental change—we have better feedback.'"[71]

This brings us to the third dimension of the new political space in which the Chinese polity finds itself: more empowered localities, organizations, and individuals.

EMPOWERED SOCIETY, DIFFUSION OF RESOURCES

The Chinese polity is also transforming because society and subordinate levels of government are becoming more empowered (as we will see in detail in chapter 3). Lower levels of society and government have more resources and information than in the past, as well as a greater capacity to be mutually aware. More often, intellectuals, policy entrepreneurs, and commercialized mass media are becoming the substance of "public opinion," which leaders increasingly invoke to bolster their legitimacy. The inability of China's central authorities to address all the problems needing attention and resources forces them to rely upon subordinate organizations within and outside government, organizations and levels of society with their own interests and resources.

Public Opinion

For Mao Zedong, "public opinion" (or the "will of the masses") was not an independent restraint on his policy; it was something that was his prerogative to define, invoke, and mobilize. Perhaps under the extreme conditions of the Great Leap Forward and its aftermath (1959–62), public desperation constituted a constraint, accounting for Mao's retreat to the second line of leadership in 1959 (when he gave up the presidency to Liu Shaoqi). But this was unusual. Although local cadres could not remain entirely unresponsive to the communities in which they had to live—except perhaps during mass mobilizations—generally speaking, "public opinion" was not a day-to-day consideration in policy at the center.

For Deng Xiaoping, in contrast, the principal motivating force behind his reform efforts was his fear that the CCP was close to losing legitimacy because of the preceding two decades of chaos and deprivation. The turbulent sea was close to capsizing the boat. The reform and opening-up policies had their raison d'être in "public opinion." Further, Deng's strategy of reform was grounded in identifying those areas of change with the greatest intrinsic public support, then using success in these domains to build momentum for further change where there was more resistance and inertia within the government, the party, and portions of society.[72] Deng's reform strategy was anchored in his correct reading of public opinion, but he went in the direction of public thinking only when it comported with his own analysis.

By the new millennium, however, China's leaders invoked "public opinion" to explain both foreign and domestic policy choices to a greater extent than ever before. Though absence is not itself proof, a computer search of all the interview transcripts used for this book for the phrase "public opinion" reveals virtually no instances in the 1970s and 1980s, very modest use of the term in the 1990s, and a relative explosion in references to the term in the 2000–2013 period.[73] Further, in the last two decades the PRC has built a very large apparatus to measure public opinion (in 2008 there were 51,000 firms conducting polling of various sorts, with 1,500 firms specializing in it),[74] and survey data concerning party leaders began to play a role in assessing cadre fitness for promotion and election within the party itself. One of these pollsters explained:

> As to the role of public opinion in society, I work mostly for companies, some for profit, but more and more of my business is from government, and

[they] "can feel the pressure of public opinion." After Deng [Xiaoping] there has been no superman [strongman], so public opinion has become a kind of "civil society." So many issues, often environmental, in Shifang, Ningbo, so now [there is] giving into public opinion, so they [central leaders] want local leaders to make no trouble, so officials have to have two voices. Leaders are using public assessment. In the United States polling is used for elections, but in China a major use is to monitor government performance. Businesswise [for me], this is good news—more and more business [for my firm].[75]

While clearly not democracy, these developments represent recognition that greater responsiveness to public views is now required.

In the post-2000 period, "public opinion" regularly has been invoked by Chinese diplomats and economic negotiators in explaining policy vis-à-vis Taiwan, Japan, the United States, the exchange rate, and maritime disputes, as well as strictly domestic actions, whether tax policy (e.g., agricultural and gas taxes) or the decision to cancel some planned industrial and infrastructure projects because of public opposition, as the pollster quoted above intimated.[76] For instance, in 2009–10 PRC external behavior became "more assertive" in the eyes of many of China's neighbors and powers at a greater distance, including the United States. This, in turn, led China's neighbors and the United States to respond by initiating a "rebalancing" (or "pivot") policy in Asia to increase solidarity in the face of what was perceived to be this worrisome Chinese shift.

Niu Xinchun, an analyst at the China Institutes of Contemporary International Relations, explained that Beijing's more assertive posture had been a response to the domestic insecurity of Chinese leaders after dealing with the public anger at how the United States and the West tried to push China around in the run-up to the Beijing 2008 Olympic games and with respect to other issues. At the same time, Niu explained, the Chinese public was proud of the nation's achievements, including space launches and the PRC's strong performance in the global financial crisis. The insecurity of leaders who needed public support, along with a more self-confident and assertive public, was Niu's explanation for Beijing's tougher posture in 2009 and 2010. "This increasing national self-confidence [by the public] and a sense of its [the Chinese leadership's] own political vulnerability pressured the country to adopt a stronger foreign policy, even while the space to do so was narrowing."[77] By 2012, the public had seized on another provocative issue that it perceived China's leaders were being "soft" on—the island disputes with Japan in the East China Sea and with Vietnam and the Philippines in the South China Sea.

A very senior official in the foreign affairs system summed it up this way—"'There is a profound social transition here. Watch the TV talk shows. The perceptions of people in the big cities are changing very rapidly. The emphasis is on freedom, rule of law, human rights, individual freedom, international practice—this is a very profound change. Eventually this will affect foreign policy and domestic policy.'"[78]

Resources: Money, Talent, Social Organizations, and Information

At the outset of Deng Xiaoping's reform era, the impulse was to decentralize resources in order to spur incentives and put resources where decisions could be made more intelligently. While there have been ebbs and flows in the balance between centralization and decentralization, for the most part resources of all kinds have accumulated at lower levels. The percentage of total state revenues spent at the central level has gone from 54.3 percent in 1980 to 17.8 percent in 2010, while that spent at the local level has gone from 45.7 percent in 1980 to 82.2 percent in 2010.[79] Similarly, the percentage of total industrial output from the state-owned sector has dropped from 78 percent in 1978 to 11 percent in 2009.[80] The share of industrial output from the private sector was negligible at the onset of reform, and by 2009 was 41 percent.[81]

Money is the most fungible type of power, and it has been pushed down the hierarchy, as have various other forms of power. The accumulation of money, resources, and discretion at lower levels of bureaucracy or society, however, does not in turn mean that either political or economic freedom is the undiluted result. Empowered corrupt local officials, crime syndicates, some military leaders, and rogue entrepreneurs engage in behavior that is in the interests of neither the center nor local citizens.[82]

There are many ways one could express the change occurring in the area of human resources, but the clearest way is to look at higher education enrollments and study abroad. In 1977–78 (the first post–Cultural Revolution year of higher education enrollment), the number of Chinese higher education students matriculated domestically was 402,000.[83] By 2010, that number had risen to 6.62 million.[84] Chinese students sent abroad from the 1978–79 academic year to 2009 totaled about 1.62 million, 37 percent of whom went to the United States.[85] In the academic year 2010–11, the number of Chinese students in the United States alone was 157,558,[86] jumping to 194,029 the following academic year. Moreover, large numbers of students who studied abroad were, and are, returning to China after their studies—roughly 497,000 had done so by the end of 2009.[87] The point is that China is generating rapidly increasing quantities of human capital and is achieving larger return rates from the students it sends abroad. This talent goes into the government but also increasingly empowers social and commercial organizations that are not entirely state dominated. As this occurs, the state-society balance gradually shifts—in favor of society.

What exactly is the power of social organizations in China, notwithstanding the very real limitations placed on nongovernmental groups and their activities? Even if the state manages to keep them somewhat leashed, each and every day these entities grow in number and capability, making them potentially more able to secure autonomy. The state's need for nongovernmental organizations (NGOs) stems fundamentally from its incapacity to meet the mounting needs of society. As the district party secretary in Shanghai's Minhang District cited above stated, "'China's [central] government is not strong; we need to transfer some functions to NGOs, but it takes time.'"[88] As one example of what is possible, NGO head Ma Jun in Beijing has been able to have his organization, the Institute of Public and Environmental Affairs, collect data on factory waste disposal practices and water contamination statistics (the water pollution database and China Water Pollution Map), publicize bad practices and "violators," and thereby bring government, public, and market power to bear on them to alter behavior. As Ma explained in an interview with *Yale Journal of International Affairs,* "This helps create public pressure on companies. . . . Some of them are quite keen to get their names off the list."[89]

Information is a key resource in political development. Ian Bremmer describes development in terms of the "J Curve," where nations often begin in a stable, low-information milieu, move through an unstable transition of increasing information availability, and eventually arrive at a new equilibrium characterized by high-information ("open") societies. A PLA general put the impact of the Internet on policy making in the PRC starkly in a 2010 conversation about U.S. weapons sales to Taiwan and a possible Beijing response: "'Decisions are being driven by "Netizens." . . . If they are sold [weapons to Taiwan], I don't know what the response [will be]. Chinese leaders cannot make this decision—Netizens will make that decision.'"[90] Another Chinese general framed it this way: "'The Internet, Twitter 2.0, and the next generation of smart phones can be encrypted and be data terminals: and this is a whole new mode of communication.' The Chinese government changed its view of Internet war. . . . We have 340 million Internet users. Six hundred million cell phones, [we are] number one in websites. 'China has to manage; in ancient China the people can float the boat or capsize the boat. Water can be channeled but it cannot be blocked, even by a mountain.'"[91]

The Internet and its addictive social networking tools, combined with globalization and the awareness and interdependence that have come with it, have given birth to what Zbigniew Brzezinski has called a "global political awakening."[92] This is deeply affecting China's governance, as is urbanization—a process that increases education and income levels, raises popular expectations, and creates high population densities just as citizens are becoming more politically aware. Urbanization is made more potent by new communications technologies. As one senior Chinese economist put it, "'In the city, people breathe the fresh air of freedom.'"[93] All this accounts for the central government's gargantuan efforts to both harness the benefits of the Internet and insulate itself from its most destabilizing effects through the simultaneous construction of the cyber "Great Firewall" and e-government.

One of the first manifestations of this "awakening" has been a tidal wave of pride stemming from China's move up the global power hierarchy, which has amplified latent nationalism, a force that Chinese leaders must channel and assuage. This pride has always been both a threat to and a boon for the regime. One of the greatest threats that these new means of communication and organization represent is the capacity of the Chinese people to organize out of sight of internal security. The first dramatic instance of this was unveiled to the elite in April 1999 when the spiritual organization the Falungong managed to gather several thousand followers outside Zhongnanhai, the leadership compound in central Beijing, without the regime being aware of the effort until it had materialized. The idea of "flash mobs" makes China's leaders extremely anxious.

The cliché that since 1977 China has experienced economic reform but not political reform has a surface plausibility that obscures a deeper, more important truth—today's Chinese polity is very different, in three key ways, from the one Deng Xiaoping encountered when he returned to power: (1) China's leaders have become progressively less dominant, weaker relative to each other and in relationship to society; (2) the pluralization of Chinese society and governing structures has become pronounced; and (3) the leadership is confronting a society with ever more resources. Taken collectively, these developments have put China in an entirely new political space. As a first party secretary and concurrently mayor in one of China's most important cities put it, "'Many people have shown an interest in political reform. But it has taken place quietly and out of view.'"[94]

These several developments could combine to produce alternative futures for the PRC, and China may not be too far from some of these major forks in the road. Scenario one: there could be political retrogression. In this scenario, economic and political insecurity could create the conditions for the reassertion of a more centralized, authoritarian system that—while resonating with the past—would ultimately fail to meet the needs of a transforming society, much less the world's need for a cooperative partner in China. A second possibility is that, in the face of disorder and decay, a charismatic, more transformational leader could appear who would establish a new order, perhaps democratic but just as likely not. Both of these first two possible paths would almost certainly entail a long and painful transition period. A third scenario is that China's current pluralization might become increasingly embedded in rule of law, regulatory structures, and shared ethical values. As such, governance might become increasingly participatory and cooperative in character. A final possibility is that China would continue to pluralize but would fail to build the regulatory institutions and culture of civic responsibility required for responsible governance at home and constructive behavior abroad—this could lead to an increasingly uncontrolled China. All of these scenarios are possible; the third path is preferred, and the fourth is to be avoided and feared.

China's greatest governance and leadership challenges are figuring out how to tame mounting social pluralism and direct it constructively and cooperatively. This requires developing a set of legitimating ideas that move beyond growth, materialism, and global status and building a set of institutions that can manage this pluralism—institutions anchored in popular support that transcends simple economic-oriented performance-based legitimacy. There needs to be a transition toward reform-based legitimacy. As one senior PRC scholar argued in 2010: "With respect to our political system, 'the problem is not legitimacy, it is that Chinese don't even understand their own political system. Our CPPCC [Chinese People's Political Consultative Conference] is not the U.S. Senate; our NPC is not the U.S. House; our democratic parties are not opposition parties. We can say what our institutions are not, but we cannot say what they are.'"[95]

CHAPTER 3

Policy Making

The allocations among ministries are "complicated" [*fuza*], and there are "lots of discussions." Allocations to ministries are based upon two considerations: (1) national policies and state priorities and (2) specific projects. "There are many contradictions," and the SPC [State Planning Commission] is the one supposed to resolve them. . . . Every ministry and province demands that the SPC give it more investment and resources, and this is a key contradiction, and this is more of a problem than in the 1950s. The national budget revenue is about 100 billion *yuan* per year. Every province and municipality wants allocations that they consider small, [but] that when added up are a huge sum. The SPC is the one that is to rationalize this and avoid a deficit.

—Conversation with commissioner, State Planning Commission, Beijing, November 10, 1982

China intends to observe international rules [such as those of WTO] and practice for its own interests. Why is it in our interests? (1) Because it will help our own decision processes. Differences between ministries and provinces, [they] have different views; they have to be sorted out; it is imperative to have a set of rules, and this will help Chinese integrate into the world. If one spokesman for one ministry at a meeting [is able to say], "WTO rules require . . . ," that ministry will prevail in the internal debate. (2) It will help China enforce its laws. Reform has created a certain chaos in internal projects, so just international rules/practice helps enforce laws. Local government "can't afford to create international difficulties and bear the responsibility."

—Senior Chinese trade negotiator, remarks in Washington, D.C., June 11, 1997

At each stage of the seemingly endless process of making policy in China, there are struggles—over resources, over power, over ego. The great achievement of the Deng era was that these struggles were waged with far less brutality than in Mao's time and resulted in far larger gains for the vast majority of Chinese citizens. How Deng and his successors fashioned a more productive policy process is an important, complex story, as is understanding the shortcomings of today's policy-making process in the PRC.

Effective nation-states possess a coherent and stable identity, accepted and effective institutions, and a balance between what society demands of the system and what its institutions provide; identity, institutions, and participation collectively constitute the body politic. Making policy is a tough, core function of the body politic. It involves defining problems, establishing priorities, specifying options, building coalitions capable of adopting policies, and making sure that the edicts from the top find reasonable reflection at society's working levels. As Shanghai's former mayor Wang Daohan put it to Brent Scowcroft in 1997, "When we look at specific problems, [we must distinguish between] the important and not important, the urgent and not urgent, the easy and the hard."[1]

The PRC's policy-making performance since 1977 is difficult to succinctly summarize, but in the second decade of the new millennium it occurs in the context of a system that has become progressively more fragmented, with less dominant leaders and greatly empowered subgroups. On the one hand, post-Mao policy has produced remarkable outcomes: high-speed growth for well over three decades, a massive rural-to-urban transition, and growth of a significant middle class, and the country has moved from the fringe of global interactions to a central place in world affairs. In the late 1970s and 1980s, a combination of creativity and pragmatism born of desperation and risk taking fueled vigorous experimentation and reform. The Communist Party's own legitimacy crisis in the wake of June 4, 1989, followed by the collapse of the Eastern Bloc and then the implosion of the Soviet Union itself, provided impetus for further reform in the 1990s.

On the other hand, the successes of policies adopted at the dawn of the reform era have had enormous consequences (both negative and positive) that must be addressed in the far different circumstances of present-day China. Some of the largest beneficiaries of initial reform have become resistant to further change that might reduce their gains. Leaders must now define and adopt policies to rekindle reform in circumstances where localities, SOEs, interest groups, and individuals have great incentive and capacity to resist change. As one party boss of a major Chinese university put it in the spring of 2012, "'The problem with state-owned enterprises [SOEs] is no longer efficiency, it is monopoly,'"[2] meaning that at the onset of reform state enterprises were woefully inefficient and that now they are more efficient but are bent on preventing the emergence of new competitors.

At the most profound level, the successes of Deng's economic growth model and approach to governance are beginning to reach their limits. The high-investment, export-heavy economic model of growth must now give way to a system driven by intensive, value-added innovation, which in turn requires liberating ever higher levels of intellectual creativity. The political apparatus must also give up its considerable control over the financial system. A growth model with no environmental values now must become more sustainable. The China from which not much was expected in foreign affairs leadership on the global stage must now meet the growing demands of an expectant international system. Making these fundamental changes will not be easy. One principal reason has to do with the character of China's policy-making treadmill.

Policy making is far more complex and arduous than it was during Deng Xiaoping's time (not to speak of Mao's) for a number of reasons. First, individual leaders can no longer dominate, with respect to either domestic or foreign policy. Second, government bureaucracies have gained the capacity to articulate their own interests, and their internal organizational structure has become increasingly complex—with bureaus, for instance, sometimes working against their own parent ministries. Third, local governments have been delegated a broader range of authority and have more resources at their command. According to a joint World Bank–Development Research Center study of 2012, "China is among the most decentralized countries in the world when it comes to government expenditures, but government revenues are highly centralized."[3] This gives rise to a huge number of fudging strategies adopted by local leaders—strategies rich in corruption, deception, and off-the books accounting legerdemain. Fourth, many new actors have appeared in the policy process, including the mass media, policy entrepreneurs, businesspersons, social organizations, and even civil and military criminal networks. Fifth, the enduring problem of a vertically segmented ("stove-piped") governmental system, with inadequate horizontal mechanisms of coordination, remains a grave challenge. Sixth, there are serious problems of transparency and accountability throughout the system, including corporate governance. All of these policy-making challenges occur in the context of myriad complex issues cascading down upon already overloaded leaders.

EVOLVING VIEWS OF THE POLICY PROCESS

In the 1950s and early 1960s, Chairman Mao's near-totalitarian system and the West's negligible access to it led Richard L. ("Dixie") Walker, in his book *China under Communism,* to provide a memorable organization chart of the PRC system as he and most other Western analysts in the early days of Mao's regime understood it (figure 3).[4]

This was a top-down structure with an all-seeing "eyeball" (literally) watching and controlling the actions of all functional systems and geographic levels: the eyeball was the CCP and its various instruments, and arrows indicating lines of authority ran principally in one direction—from the Politburo down. The citizen was linked to the system by party cadres, perpetual mass campaigns, and indoctrination. A year later, Carl J. Friedrich and Zbigniew K. Brzezinski, in their classic *Totalitarian Dictatorship and Autocracy,* gave the following account of "all autocratic regimes," writing, "The distinguishing feature is that the ruler is not accountable to anyone else for what he does. He is the *autos* who himself wields power; that is to say, makes the decisions and reaps the results."[5]

The essence of the vision of Chinese communism (and other communist systems such as the USSR) that Walker and Friedrich/Brzezinski presented was a structure dominated by one person, with policy being faithfully implemented in a system with a presumably high degree of compliance with directives that was assured by the use of heavy doses of propaganda and coercion. Within the party, ideology was presumed to be widely shared, particularly in the ruling group. This was a low-friction system in which the gears of policy making were well oiled, subordinates did what they were told, and there was a near monopoly of resources (money, coercion, and life opportunity) by the elite, if not the *autos* himself. Even in the 1950s this view obscured a far more complex reality, but it was a first approximation of how the communist authoritarian system operated.

Two developments in the 1960s and the 1970s in China, however, forced a more complex understanding of the system. The first development was the appearance of unmistakable conflict within the Communist Party, not to mention between elements of society and the party. In hindsight, this conflict was evident from the regime's earliest days, but

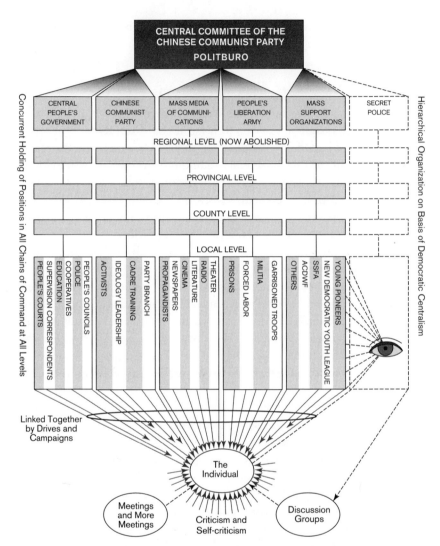

FIGURE 3. Walker's model of chains of command in communist China. From Richard L. Walker, *China Under Communism: The First Five Years* (New Haven: Yale University Press, 1955), p. 27. According to Walker, "This graph attempts to convey in rough form how the decisions and control emanating from the communist leaders in Peking make themselves felt by the individual Chinese. The arrows indicate supervision, pressure, and control."

it became increasingly apparent with Chairman Mao's forced retreat to the "second line of leadership" in 1959 in the aftermath of the Great Leap Forward. Mao's involuntary withdrawal was followed by his blatant attempts to claw back power in the 1960s, which burst forth into the Cultural Revolution decade (1966–76), when the Chairman unleashed the Red Guards—the "revolutionary masses," sometimes little more than street mobs—to attack the party he had built. The Red Guards themselves became conflicting factions (as did groups within the party itself) and fell to turning on one another—from street fighting to employment of heavy weapons pilfered from military arsenals. Then, to deal with the chaos this created, Mao frantically sought to restore order by summoning the PLA, which in turn forced him to exert himself to regain power from elements of the military now reluctant to give up their newfound authority. The Chairman then found himself locked in conflict with part of the military, a battle in which his victory was marked by the death of his chosen successor, Defense Minister Lin Biao, in September 1971 in a mysterious plane crash. Thereafter, from the early 1970s until Mao's death in September 1976, as the Chairman's health deteriorated there was a faintly visible, but fierce, battle between the party's Left and Right over who would steer China in its fast-approaching post-Mao future. Deng Xiaoping's final return to power in mid-1977 following Mao's demise marked the definitive abandonment of the Chairman's self-defined era of "War and Revolution" and the adoption of Deng's era of "Peace and Development."

The Cultural Revolution and its aftermath shattered the facade of domestic unity in the PRC and Western analysts' image of the simple top-down policy process that had accompanied it. Shattering one vision of a polity and its policy-making process, however, is quite different from developing a shared, empirically grounded alternative understanding. Outside observers could see that, in the words of Michel Oksenberg, China was a "convulsive society," but what were the specific lines of organizational and social division animating politics? In what arenas were conflicts resolved? How important were networks of individuals ("factions") compared to institutions, substantive policy rifts, and policy process in generating conflict? How did vertical functional hierarchies and horizontal territorial systems interact? And what would an increasingly marketized and globalized economy as well as population mean for the system's future operation?

Growing access to China by foreign scholars, businesspeople, students, journalists, diplomats, and others was critical to reconceptualizing Chinese politics and the policy process. Speaking to Chinese citizens and officials became increasingly possible from the mid-1970s, and the number of interviews I was able to conduct doubled every decade from then into the second decade of the new millennium—an unobtrusive indicator of the rate at which China became more open (see Appendix). Further, the restoration of old and development of new statistical systems, think tanks, research organizations, and university-based research centers in the PRC occurred from the late 1970s on and provided a wealth of information and contacts. This knowledge was supplemented by data from increasingly transparent and capable Chinese ministries and multilateral institutions that the PRC was joining and that required detailed statistics from members (e.g., the World Bank) as the price of admission. Further, there was the progressive development of increasingly profit-driven (but still constrained) mass media in China that, over time, found it to be in their economic interest to report on what people were actually interested in. Cumulatively, these developments have provided the means to evolve new understandings of China and its policy process.

In the second half of the 1980s and in the 1990s, one vision of the policy-making system emerged from the torrent of information that was becoming available—a concept that I termed a "bargaining system" in 1987 and that Kenneth Lieberthal, Michel Oksenberg, and I in various cooperative and separate writings thereafter developed as the "fragmented authoritarian" framework.[6] In developing this vision we built on the work of many others, including A. Doak Barnett's *The Making of Foreign Policy in China*.[7] This vision of the Chinese policy-making system diverged from the presumption of tight central control born of the 1950s and early 1960s and also diverged from the factional conflict model developed to account for the intense conflict of the Cultural Revolution decade.[8] The key propositions of the "fragmented authoritarian approach" are as follows:

1. *The Chinese system is a complex grid.* Running vertically from society's top to various levels near the bottom are three vertical bureaucratic systems: the party, the state, and the military. These three functional vertical systems (the *tiao* or "legs") intersect with the multitude of horizontal territorial administrations (the *kuai* or "lumps") of the system—provinces, special districts, municipalities of various ranks, counties, and townships, with hundreds of thousands of villages below. The resulting grid thus has tens of thousands of nodes where the territorial and functional systems intersect. At every intersection are multiple

officials who must cooperate if problems are to be averted. These nodes are ground zero for politics in China.

The CCP, one of the three vertical, systemic hierarchies, is the most important because it interpenetrates the other vertical and horizontal systems. The principal instrument of party control is the appointment of officials in the state and military hierarchies and the territorial administrations; the party also appoints principal leaders in state-dominated corporations.

2. *Governance, policy-making, and implementation problems stem from so many nodes operating in a diverse, populous, and far-flung country.* All officials must continually sort out to whom they will be most responsive—the vertical hierarchy or the territorial system at their level—or themselves. As the Chinese officials put it, "They have too many mothers-in-law" (*po po duo*).

3. *Many officials in the territorial system hold ranks equivalent to those of officials in the vertical systems.* These bureaucratic equals need one another's cooperation but cannot command it. For example, ministers (in the vertical system) and governors (in the territorial system) are of equal rank, so they often find themselves at loggerheads, and ways must be found to reconcile their conflicts. Consequently, there is a rich array of leadership positions, dispute resolution groups, and arenas throughout the governing structure, some ad hoc and others permanent, that are tasked with resolving conflicts among territorial units, between territorial and functional units, and among leaders in the same hierarchy at different levels. I call these individuals and institutions "cross-system integrators." They include the Politburo Standing Committee, the Politburo, the Premier's Office, vice-premiers, state councilors, the State Planning Commission in an earlier era and today's National Development and Reform Commission, leading small groups, ad hoc committees, and special-purpose standing bodies (such as flood control committees who decide in a hydrological crisis which communities will be inundated and which spared), to mention just a few. This repertoire of conflict-resolving mechanisms is duplicated one way or another at all system levels.

4. *Most disputes are addressed in an environment in which financial resources are insufficient.* Consequently, the budgetary incrementalism that Aaron Wildavsky described in his classic *The Politics of the Budgetary Process* prevails.[9] In the absence of crisis, there is a tendency to change financial allocation shares only gradually and at the margins—the Chinese call this *qie kuai*, "to cut up the lump" (of money) according to fixed percentages.

5. Politicians and bureaucrats in China have just three means by which to make decisions and coordinate behavior. (1) They can build a command, hierarchical system in which the lines of authority are clear and effective. (2) They can develop markets or bargain with one another so that decisions are diffused throughout the system and are based on mutual accommodation. (3) They can create preference counting (voting) systems.[10]

While China has plenty of hierarchical systems, there are so many levels and structures within the system that lines of authority are easily blurred. Turning to the preference counting option, because of the non-competitive ethos of the Communist Party, voting systems in China, while used at low levels and for polling purposes, have been avoided, though I expect they will gain currency as time passes.[11] Thus, if hierarchy isn't working well and voting is unacceptable, in a setting in which law, independent judicial institutions, and sound administrative regulation are weak, the system falls back on bargaining and markets. So in China the name of the game is "Let's make a deal!" This enables the system to make decisions but also fosters corruption, inconsistency, and very often gridlock.

6. When neither bargaining nor command is sufficient to produce an agreement at lower levels, disputes are kicked up the hierarchy to cross-system integrators. Given the tens of thousands of nodes in the system, superiors are usually overwhelmed with the sheer number of conflicts they are called upon to resolve.

In the more than twenty years since the fragmented authoritarian framework came into focus it has become evident to me that this approach helps illuminate not only the more open areas of the Chinese polity (economic and technical issues) but also the more closed and coercive recesses of the Chinese system—(such as the PLA, as we see in chapter 6). This analytic approach reveals a China that can now accurately be described as pluralistic, even though individuals and groups operate without the protection of clear constitutional and legal rights. In what he calls "fragmented authoritarianism 2.0," Andrew Mertha describes new players in this increasingly plural policy process—the mass media, policy entrepreneurs, businesses, and social groups,[12] all empowered by increasingly diffuse financial and human resources, the Internet, and other tools of instantaneous communication. This ever more complex and fragmented system must now provide answers to the huge policy problems that have arisen as a consequence of the economic and social successes and the tremendous negative externalities of the preceding three-plus decades of reform.

CASE STUDIES

Rather than discuss these changes and their consequences in the abstract, I provide three case studies below to make them tangible. The first case study (on atomic energy legislation) highlights the gridlocked character of the policy process in which bureaucratic interests constantly are at loggerheads, while the second case (on economic policy making) focuses on what the rise of a private sector, powerful corporations, and global economic actors means for policy making. The third case (concerning the Hangzhou Maglev train) underscores the rising importance of popular sentiment in policy making and the growing role of a middle class.

Case 1: China's Atomic Energy Law

China has endeavored to pass an atomic energy law (AEL) since the mid-1980s and, as of early 2013, still had not done so.[13] An AEL would be important because the number of nuclear-radiological facilities has expanded, the value of nuclear and radiological products manufactured for both domestic and foreign markets is growing, and the civilian uses of these materials have multiplied. Since the new millennium, Beijing repeatedly has upped the number of civil nuclear power plants planned and under construction to provide electrical power, jobs, and income to struggling local governments and corporations and to meet carbon intensity reduction targets. This development of the civil nuclear power plant sector raises numerous issues: standards, construction oversight, regulation, disposal of waste, training, site security, emergency response, and adjudication and compensation when mishaps occur. Though the United States has had its problems in these domains, its Nuclear Regulatory Commission (NRC) and the laws in which it is embedded have been the reference norm for the PRC.

In the civilian economy, the medical and agricultural (irradiation) uses of radiological materials have been expanding, and university and corporate research laboratories are utilizing increasing volumes of radiological materials in ever more dispersed locations. One informant told my colleague Bo Kong and me that "'there was [in the reform period] a lot of loss of radiological materials.'"[14] And then there are all the issues that pertain to the nuclear and radiological materials and facilities in the military sector.

In terms of administrative, regulatory, and legal development, an AEL is important if the regulatory bodies and their respective domains are to be clearly defined. Stakeholders include the Ministry of Environmental Protection/National Nuclear Safety Administration, the Ministry of Information Technology/State Administration of Science, Technology and Industry for National Defense, the Ministry of Public Health, the Ministry of Education, and even the Ministry of Public Security,[15] not to mention Chinese citizens. What are the processes by which conflicts among government agencies, localities, enterprises, and citizens are to be reconciled and policy implementation ensured?[16]

To make a long and fascinating story short, in China there has yet to be an AEL passed, despite almost three decades of trying. And it could be a long time until such a law is passed, although this means that the health, safety, national security, and economic costs of problems will grow—perhaps dramatically. What accounts for this political constipation, with five successive draft laws going nowhere from the 1980s well into the second decade of this millennium?

The simple answers are conflicting bureaucratic and economic interests and the complexity of the process by which Chinese policy and law are made. In terms of bureaucratic complexity (as of the end of 2012), safety issues are the principal responsibility of the National Nuclear Safety Administration (NNSA), which is subordinate to a weak Ministry of Environmental Protection (MEP). Among many problems is that a weak MEP does not want to be overshadowed by a potentially powerful subordinate NNSA, so it resists attempts to strengthen it, though in the wake of Japan's 2011 Fukushima plant meltdowns the number of NNSA personnel was boosted. Moreover, the authority for developing and approving the civil energy plan rests with the powerful National Development and Reform Commission (NDRC), and its subordinate National Energy Agency (NEA)—these agencies are prodevelopment, often allying with progrowth power corporations and local officials hungry for revenue and jobs. As one informant put it, "'The local governments support these [nuclear power] plants, but 100 percent of the people oppose them.'"[17] This political landscape pits weak environmental interests against strong development forces. Further, China's state-owned nuclear power companies, often allied with local officials who see nuclear power plants as cash cows and job generators, create a dynamic in which actual construction and preliminary planning often exceed even the ambitious plans of the NDRC.

Beyond this bureaucratic fragmentation and "turf" defending is the complex process by which something becomes law, an often overlooked consideration because of assumptions about the executive-led character of authoritarianism. A prospective law must be placed on the agenda of the State Council's Legislative Affairs Office, which is difficult because of competing legislative priorities. To resolve interagency divisions, the State Council (the cabinet, which in 2012 had twenty-seven ministries and commissions, one special organization directly subordinate, and sixteen regular organizations) must be called in. Then, as is often the case, the State Council in turn tasks interagency leading small groups, a vice-premier, a state councilor, the premier, or sometimes the Politburo Standing Committee to address difficult-to-reconcile issues.[18] Other setbacks can result from periodic administrative reorganizations (there have been seven State Council reorganizations since the 1980s: most recently, at the Twelfth National People's Congress in 2013, the number of ministries and commissions was reduced to twenty-five and other bureaucratic changes were made). These reorganizations change key players through abolition, merger, or divorce, further scrambling the bureaucratic eggs.

Once there is an agreed-upon draft law, it must get on the agenda of the NPC, which meets for about two weeks per annum and has many competing items to consider. Moreover, random events can derail everything. The Fukushima nuclear power plant disaster(s) in Japan in March 2011, for instance, shook up the entire PRC political, technical, and bureaucratic landscape pertaining to civil nuclear energy, further stalling consideration of an AEL.

Consequently, because of the bureaucratic divisions, the complexity of the lawmaking process, and the injection of external events at random intervals, the personal attention of top leaders is often required to break logjams even on relatively minor matters. For example, in the case of deciding whether or not to buy Westinghouse-Toshiba or French (Areva) civil nuclear power plants, the decision was ultimately made by the Standing Committee of the Politburo, which had to rely on expert committee advice. A senior leader of the State Nuclear Power Technology Corporation described the process: "Zhang [Guobao, vice-minister of the NEA of the NDRC] asked for oral and written opinions [from experts], then Zhang sent the report to Wen [Jiabao, the premier], then this went to the Standing Committee of the Politburo, and they endorsed the findings of the expert process—this was their decision."[19]

Case 2: Economic Policy Making

With respect to economic pluralization, outsiders often conceive of Chinese SOEs as responsive to central state interests as if those interests were clear and uniform. The truth is quite to the contrary—as an economic actor, the Chinese state is often an abstraction. Beijing usually exerts little control over (and often has even less information about) the activities and operations of "its" state enterprises overseas. One MOFTEC (Ministry of Foreign Trade and Economic Cooperation, later MOFCOM, or the Ministry of Commerce) official told me in 2002 that for "some Chinese companies, when operating abroad, [investment] flows from one country to another. When a Chinese company is outside of China, its capital flows are beyond our control. They don't report."[20] In a conversation ten years later, the capacity of economic enterprises to resist foreign policy control was spelled out by a knowledgeable official. "You have to be careful in using the word *China*. China is lots of actors." He went on to say: "'In the past, in the Cultural Revolution,' when you used [the word] *China* it was one voice. Now you have different interests. They pursue their interests. Our ambassadors try to coordinate investments [by Chinese entities abroad] but none [no ambassador] is successful. For example, a Sinopec guy told me that the Chinese ambassador told him to do gas exploration in Afghanistan, but he refused to sign the contract."[21]

Corporate power finds its expression domestically as well as abroad vis-à-vis local officials who increasingly depend on foreign, private and/or substantially autonomous "state" enterprises for revenue and employment. As Nicholas Lardy put it: "If profits in tradable goods industries decline, these private firms will invest less; if profits decline further, they will shrink their businesses or even exit from export- and import-competing industries. Local first party secretaries, governors, and mayors may wring their hands over the loss of employment, tax revenues, and other benefits . . . , but by and large they will be powerless to offset the actions of these profit-oriented, private firms."[22]

To keep industries in their localities, local officials and banks (over which they still have considerable sway) cut a variety of deals (involving land, subsidies, and utilities, much like those in investment-hungry American localities) and will throw up internal trade barriers to protect "their" firms from competitors—foreign or domestic. As one Shanxi provincial official succinctly put it to me, "'You have an interest in those who give you revenue.'"[23]

A final layer of complexity comes from the growing private sector. In trying to explain why China's central bureaucracy is unable to ensure faithful implementation of its own export control regulations, a former arms control expert in Beijing explained: "The policy of the government has become clearer and clearer—no proliferation, it hurts China's image. China's instructions to companies are that they should not sacrifice China's interests for their profits. So there are export control regulations; the Ministry of Commerce [MOFCOM] sent people to educate companies, or you will be punished. But China is now not old China, can't control, some small or private enterprises, they don't know or they do things."[24]

There are sharp lines of economic cleavage among bureaucracies, firms, local governments, and citizens, as well as between the public and private sectors. A good example of how these forces collide is exchange rate policy. In the late 1990s and throughout the first decade-plus of the new millennium, China's exchange rate has been a persistent source of friction within China's political system and with major foreign trade partners, especially the United States. In the late 1990s during the Asian financial crisis, the debate in the PRC was over whether to devalue its currency, the RMB, with exporters and export-dependent localities and industries (such as shipbuilding) urging devaluation. By way of contrast, in the post–World Trade Organization entry period, the issue has been whether to revalue the currency, one of many issues kicked up to the Leading Small Group on Finance and Economics and the Politburo Standing Committee.[25]

China's consumers, importers, and the central bank (the People's Bank of China, or PBOC) have an interest in an appreciated RMB, while many business associations (notably in the textile industry), chambers of commerce, exporters (including foreign-invested, export-oriented enterprises in China), textile and cotton-dependent provinces (e.g., Jiangsu, Zhejiang, Guangdong, Hebei, Shandong, Fujian, and others), MOFCOM, firms in the electronics and machinery industries, and others have been committed to minimizing China's currency appreciation.[26] This political gridlock partially accounts for Chinese leaders' inability to move more rapidly to accommodate the appreciation demands of key trade partners.[27] External pressure by the U.S. Congress, the European Union, or even the International Monetary Fund has proven inadequate to overcome this domestic resistance alone. What is needed is a convergence between internal political alignment among key interests and external demands. Only as a result of rising inflation and the need to develop new vehicles of growth in China (given the temporarily sputtering export engine in the post-2008 global financial crisis period) did the PRC again move in the direction of outside pressure.

Case 3: The Shanghai-Hangzhou High-Speed Rail Line and Citizen Action

China's economic, educational, and technological advancement has also fueled societal pluralism. Social groups, property owners who now have assets to protect, and a more informed citizenry aware of the health and environmental consequences of unrestrained growth are increasingly taking action.[28]

One example of this type of social action is the saga of a proposed Shanghai-Hangzhou magnetic levitation (Maglev) train, which was initially approved for construction by Beijing in February 2006. A Maglev is a very high-speed train that uses powerful magnets to lift, guide, and propel a train, thereby greatly reducing friction and raising the potential velocity. Its downsides are enormous electricity consumption and the high per-mile construction costs. Several years earlier, China's first Maglev line had opened, running from Pudong International Airport to Longyang Station in central Shanghai on the east bank of the Huangpu River. The construction of this first line had been extremely expensive, its fare was high, and it blew by houses at 430 kilometers per hour, creating noise and concussions affecting nearby residents. Questions began to arise among residents near the planned Hangzhou line about the effects of long-term exposure to electromagnetic radiation. On January 8, 2008, a public hearing was held on the project. "The noise, vibration and radiation had become major concerns among local residents. They asked the experts to show the environmental assessment and security testing results."[29] This hearing was held two days after a demonstration (benignly called a "collective talking walk") had occurred involving thousands, leading to the closure of part of Shanghai's busy Nanjing Road. Subsequently, after the level of public concern was clear, work on the newly approved line was "suspended."[30]

In March 2010, however, the Ministry of Railroads announced that the second Maglev train line was again, in the words of ShanghaiDaily .com, "back on track."[31] Prior complaints and worries produced some modifications in the initial plan: fifteen miles were added to the line (presumably to skirt sensitive areas), and the speed of the train was to be slowed near densely populated areas. These revisions would make the planned trip longer and the project still more expensive. Then, in October 2010, the slightly slower Shanghai-Hangzhou High-Speed Railroad commenced service, and the rationale for the Maglev project was diminished further—the project was again "suspended."[32] This case reveals how technology that allows people to organize (cell phones, Internet, text message devices, etc.), procedural rules requiring public hearings and the release of information, and a middle class determined to protect its newly acquired property and emerging environmental values can converge to create an empowered social force.

The above cases of the AEL, broad economic policy making, and the Maglev train are all manifestations of the changing character of the Chinese policy-making process and the shifting balance among leaders, society, and interest groups. We now turn to critical and dynamic contexts in which policy making occurs: the information environment and the proliferation of ever-more capable actors.

THE INFORMATION ENVIRONMENT

Making sensible policy requires relevant and accurate information. The policy system to which Deng Xiaoping returned in mid-1977 was an environment almost devoid of reliable and systematic information. Deng and his protégés such as Zhao Ziyang immediately began to rebuild and construct new statistical systems. Subsequently, during Jiang Zemin's era China's leadership increasingly realized the domestic and international implications of the media and information revolutions. In meetings with President Jiang it was not unusual for him to refer to how the information revolution was shaping the conduct of mass politics, policy making, and international relations. In speaking to Henry Kissinger in March 2001, Jiang said: "The world is very different from the one you knew thirty years ago. The information age. [It] would have been very difficult for you [Kissinger] to have come here secretly [nowadays, as you did in 1971]."[33]

Mass Media, Communication, and the Globalization of Information

This realm involves the transmission of powerful visual images, empowering information, and tools that make coordinated action among dispersed citizens possible. In 1978, there were approximately one million television sets in all of China, with very limited programming, in black and white; by 2011, televisions were in 350 million households. The Internet first hit China in the 1990s, and with great force in the new millennium, quickly becoming a new, almost infinite, universe of programming and information to hundreds of millions of mostly urban users. By 2012, China had 513.1 million Internet users,[34] and people could access online and by other electronic means video revealing officials having sex with underage children and adolescents and engaging in all sorts of licentious and corrupt behavior, often at public expense.

This new availability of information has had direct and dramatic effects on politics and policy making. When, for example, U.S.-NATO forces bombed the Chinese embassy in Belgrade in May 1999, killing three Chinese and wounding twenty, President Jiang Zemin was put in a position where he had to credibly react to the visual images of a destroyed embassy and the repatriation of corpses in flag-draped caskets transmitted on the Internet and on cable and satellite television. The deluge of visual images and verbiage pouring in on China's leaders and citizens compressed the time in which Beijing had to make decisions, with the powerful images serving to intensify the response the population was urging its leaders to make—leaders had less time in which to make more highly charged decisions.

With greater access to powerful media and visual images comes the possibility that the propaganda apparatus can strike out on its own (strategically or in error) by disseminating images or information early on in a crisis and thereby shaping the options available to leaders. As one senior PLA officer put it to me in discussing the aftermath of the inadvertent U.S.-NATO bombing of the Chinese embassy in Belgrade in May 1999, "'The propaganda apparatus [in China] went off the tracks, when in doubt go left, so they did not represent the top leadership.' The media could not get responsible people to talk, so only ignorant hacks talked. . . . 'Ding Guangen [the Politburo member in charge of the Propaganda Department] is not a policy maker, but he sat in on policy making meetings after the bombing and saw leaders upset and thought this was their guidance.'"[35]

Today we take a media-saturated environment for granted, but not long ago policy in China was made in a far different setting. A year before Deng's 1977 final return and shortly before Mao Zedong's death, northern China endured one of the worst natural disasters in history—the Tangshan earthquake of July 28, 1976. The epicenter was 150 miles from Beijing, in neighboring Hebei Province. No one knows how many perished, but accepted figures are in the range of 250,000 persons, while initial estimates ran to around 600,000.

In this setting of catastrophe, a group of visiting American congressional staff had the opportunity to witness firsthand just how poor communication within China was and how little even central leaders knew of what had just occurred in their own backyard. If these leaders knew so little concerning what was close by, how much less did they know about the distant reaches of the vast country they nominally ruled? This was a far different reality than that implied by Richard Walker's all-seeing party "eyeball." The American visitors met later the day of the earthquake with Mao Zedong's (leftist) grandniece, Vice-Foreign Minister Wang Hairong.[36] One would have thought that if anyone would be informed it would have been Wang. Yet she was seemingly unaware of the magnitude of what had happened. Beyond a few perfunctory words on the quake at the outset and at the conclusion of the meeting, the conversation went in different directions. Her seeming indifference, I believe, represented her ignorance of the scale of what had happened in a country in which not all counties were yet in reliable, much less instantaneous, communication with the center.

Thirty-two years after the Tangshan earthquake, media and communications development had transformed the situation, not only in terms of what was expected from leaders, but also in terms of empowering social mobilization. In May 2008, a massive earthquake with its epicenter in Wenchuan, Sichuan, struck, killing about seventy thousand persons. Within minutes, broadcast media, Internet communications of all sorts, and cell phones were sending images of the devastation worldwide. This motivated Premier Wen Jiabao to immediately (within ninety minutes of receiving word) fly to the area to bring comfort to quake victims, and provided the PLA an opportunity to be seen as a nurturing and compassionate force rescuing people from the rubble.[37] The heart-wrenching images also inspired volunteers from all over China to descend on the area to help and motivated an unprecedented outpouring of humanitarian support for the stricken area from citizens nationwide. The difference between 1976 and 2008 in both the governmental and the popular response could not have been greater, and much of the contrast is attributable to the information revolution. Information, particularly visual images, makes government indifference much less tolerable to the public and energizes citizens to participate.

Organizational Impediments to the Flow of Information

Thirty-five years ago, China's policy process had an information problem that was apparent in the absence of basic regulatory information that Westerners would consider essential. There were almost no regulatory standards, nor were there any effective national data and sentinel systems that would have supported them. For instance, I went to China with a group of steroid chemists in October 1976, a month after Mao's death, determined to understand how China performed the basic responsibility of regulating the quality and safety of pharmaceuticals; I was particularly interested in this because I had been told by interviewees in Hong Kong in 1972–73 that people in the PRC would pay doctors under the table for Western-manufactured medicines to avoid side effects ("tremors") that often accompanied the use of indigenous pharmaceuticals. It is worth noting in passing that more than three decades later, problems were still rife in the food and drug administration system—the director of China's Food and Drug Administration was executed in July 2007 for taking bribes to approve drugs, most of which were fake, and for which false test data had been submitted, presumably with his complicity.[38]

In my 1976 interviews in China, while I found that every province had its own pharmaceutical standards, there was no uniformity across provinces, and in each province there appeared to be few or no mechanisms to systematically gather data to ensure compliance with whatever local standards existed. According to my notes of that trip presented at a meeting,

> Quality assurance was "assured" by the factory and the local drug control bureau—this means there was no evident nonlocal authority checking things on a random, surprise basis. We got no clear sense of what standards were enforced when inspections occurred. I found out that in terms of food and drug inspections, no products had EVER been removed from the shelves, to my informants' knowledge. Other observations included: scientific research was very stove-piped, with one institute (even in the same city, much less a different locality) having very little idea what the other was doing. There was very little horizontal professional communication, much less collaboration.[39]

Information flow, therefore, is not just about whether the hardware for communication is in place, it also is about whether standards for collecting and interpreting data even exist, whether the pathways exist to convey that information to higher levels in an accurate, useful, and timely form, and whether similar and functionally interdependent units communicate and coordinate with each other. One category of problem is bureaucratic stove-piping, where one organization that possesses information needed by another bureaucracy or level in the system does not provide it. Upper-level leaders remain ignorant, resources are used inefficiently, and the lessons learned by one unit have no benefits for anyone else—everyone is condemned to repeat idiocies. This was China in 1976.

The system has improved greatly over the intervening decades, though the ever greater complexity of the system still confounds attempts to reduce information problems in the policy process. One of the first things Zhao Ziyang did when he became premier in 1980 was to encourage the building of improved statistical and reporting systems (with the help of the World Bank and others) and encourage the establishment of think tanks that could analyze data and make policy-relevant proposals. China's decision making gradually changed from an ideologically driven to a much more data-dependent process. The contrast between the ideological dogma one heard in 1976 and the fact-strewn argumentation of China's leaders today is striking. Both Premier Zhu Rongji and Premier Wen Jiabao (and for that matter Li Peng too) would respond to the assertions of subordinates or foreigners with a barrage of facts.[40]

Nonetheless, there remain systematic biases in the information that subordinates provide superiors throughout the hierarchy. Subordinates often simply lie to superiors and to reporting systems. Moreover, with the development of the market economy and a private sector, the number of units needing to report and to be regulated has multiplied at the same time that these entrepreneurs have many reasons to seek to avoid reporting and regulation altogether—one of the origins of the many tainted-product scandals rocking China itself and the global supply chain since 2000. As one senior Chinese economist put it to a group of visiting U.S. congressmen in 2005: "How fast are we really growing? Statistical reporting is a problem. Local governments, political interference, so some things are overstated. Don't believe that! However, not everyone wants to overreport. Some people want to underreport—the dynamic sectors. Local governments want to underreport in fast periods [of growth] to keep revenues. The private sector and even poor areas underreport to get subsidies."[41]

The Contemporary Information Environment

Into the 1990s, the Chinese people had relatively little information concerning what was going on elsewhere in their own country, elsewhere in the world, and particularly inside Zhongnanhai—the central leadership compound in Beijing. This information-scarce environment had consequences: the capacity of Chinese people to organize to achieve goals was minimal, and the latitude of the elite to make decisions without considering popular reaction was comparatively great.

By the second decade of the new millennium, however, this latitude had decreased considerably; this fact became obvious in the spring of 2012 with the eruption of an elite struggle in connection with how the Eighteenth Party Congress in the fall of 2012 would compose its new Politburo Standing Committee. How this central leadership problem became known to the public and how it was handled demonstrate how different the "information problem" of 2013 is from that of 1976.

The incident involved the first party secretary of Chongqing Municipality, Bo Xilai. The son of a revolutionary elder, Bo had previously been mayor of Dalian (where by most accounts and my observation he did a spectacular job), moving through provincial-level leadership in Liaoning Province to become the minister of commerce and then being posted to the provincial-level city of Chongqing. In Chongqing, Bo was sufficiently removed from the central action that he was motivated to build a local base of political support that he hoped could catapult him to Beijing and the ruling Politburo Standing Committee. Since being posted to Chongqing as first party secretary in 2007, Bo had tried to mobilize popular support by conducting an anticorruption campaign (*da hei*, or "strike black"), building large quantities of public housing, advocating a larger role for state enterprises and clamping down on successful (allegedly corrupt) private entrepreneurs, and promoting a somewhat off-key effort to mobilize nostalgia for the Cultural Revolution's more egalitarian values (*chang hong*, or "sing red"). A more commercialized mass media and instantaneous communications infrastructure had spread news of Bo's efforts nationwide, thereby enlarging his mass support base—he was going populist. By 2011 he was not only a local but a national political force to be reckoned with by a central elite that largely was unwilling to embrace him. Then the complications of a dysfunctional family entered the picture.

Illicit business-related activities, resulting cover-ups, and other involvements led to the murder of a British businessman who had been involved with Bo Xilai, his wife (Gu Kailai), and their son (Bo Guagua)—alleged improper fund transfers abroad apparently were involved. This all unfolded publicly in a media fishbowl and a hothouse of Chinese blog activity. Subsequently, Bo's wife was convicted of murder, with a logical inference being that Bo must have been involved in either the crime or the subsequent cover-up, not to mention other nefarious activities. Bo, as it worked out, had handed his opponents in Beijing the instrument of his own political destruction, resulting in his removal from the Politburo in April 2012 and conviction for corruption and abuse of power in 2013.

In one sense, Bo's opponents in Beijing welcomed this scandal because his political ambitions could be completely discredited by his brutality, corruption, and hypocrisy, as well as the self-evident implication that if he couldn't maintain family propriety, he couldn't very well help rule China. On the other hand, the scandal revealed a network of shocking misdeeds that were systemic in nature, not simply personal foibles; worse yet, all the dirty laundry was getting aired in public view (both domestically and internationally). These kinds of abuses, though the daily lot of many Chinese, had heretofore rarely been on such graphic public display, and the revelations eroded party legitimacy further. Most worrisome to the elite was that for a considerable period during this scandal the regime lost control of the information reaching its citizens.

In the less information-saturated environment of even just a decade earlier, the regime would have used Bo's misdeeds to ease him out behind the scenes (if they did not ignore them altogether), without running the risk of exposing such malfeasance publicly. However, this strategy was not possible, given a commercially oriented media smelling blood, and social media like Weibo (China's "Twitter"), all of which hemorrhaged information probably before the central authorities even knew what was happening. The result was that the regime had to make policy as every lurid detail was emerging publicly, including the unsuccessful effort of Bo's former police chief (Wang Lijun) to seek protection from his then estranged boss, Bo Xilai, at the American consulate in Chengdu—where he ran to spill information, another element of humiliation for Beijing and grist for tabloids the world over. The next day Wang had "safe passage" from the U.S. consulate (thereby presumably avoiding Bo's thugs) into the arms of Beijing's authorities, who soon thereafter charged him with treason, a charge later said to be mitigated by his subsequent cooperation with party authorities.

Professor Zhan Jiang at Beijing Foreign Studies University had no trouble telling the world through the *Financial Times* what he thought this situation meant for China's political system and policy making: "Especially since Wang Lijun [Bo's estranged police chief] fled to the US consulate, there has been a proliferation of political information and opinion spread through Weibo and this is unprecedented in China's history. . . . Weibo represents a political information revolution . . . a huge shift in the relationship between Chinese politics and the media, particularly the Internet."[42]

This inability of leaders to keep their personal and policy behavior behind "the curtain" is quickly changing policy making and mass politics. When Chinese politicians increasingly refer to "public opinion," they are not just figuratively pulling the wool over domestic and foreign eyes. In January of 2010, a Xiamen business leader explained why and how the local populace in his city had just stopped the planned construction of a chemical plant: "Yes, the Xiamen Chemical Plant protests; most people were against the plant plan, and the facility went to Changzhou, next town from here. [The Xiamen protests were] organized by professors and used the Internet. First thing of this sort in China."[43]

The Market Value of Information

One other aspect of the information and policy-making nexus is that information and cultural products (such as movies) have acquired market value that they did not possess before the reform period. An important new area of bureaucratic politics opened up when information and culture products acquired economic value: bureaucracies began to fight among one another and with foreign content providers (such as Bloomberg, Dow Jones, movie producers, and others) for control of the massive revenue streams.

As early as November 1982, for example, it was clear that the then Ministry of Radio and Television was fighting with the Ministry of Culture (not to mention foreign and domestic content providers) over the money to be made. About four years into the reform era, Minister of Radio and Television Wu Lengxi was very clear in explaining the emerging conflicts and the struggles among companies (foreign and domestic) and among domestic ministry-level organizations. The core of the conflict in 1982 was between the Ministry of Radio and Television led by Wu and the Ministry of Culture. One line of division concerned the desire of the television bureaucracy and its viewers to air (often foreign) films on television promptly after release and the desire of the Ministry of Culture (which ran movie theaters) to maximize its box office by not having popular programs or movies shown on television until the theater attendance potential had been exhausted.[44] Similar conflicts between foreigners and Chinese entities, and among Chinese business organizations themselves, over who controls the dissemination of global business news in a market economy are high-stakes games. The propaganda apparatus may be the nominal guardian of values, but film companies and foreign and domestic content providers, as well as state entities, want to make money by producing what people want to watch and read. The values of control and capitalism are often in conflict.

THE CONTEXT OF MORE NUMEROUS AND CAPABLE POLITICAL PLAYERS

When Deng Xiaoping adopted the "open and reform policy," he rapidly committed China to enter the post–World War II Bretton Woods system and the wider global trade regime—as a member of the World Bank and International Monetary Fund (IMF) in 1980, an observer of the General Agreement on Tariffs and Trade (GATT) in 1982, and finally a member of the World Trade Organization (WTO) in December 2001. Chinese leaders had to construct new domestic agencies and create new bureaucratic capacities in order to first negotiate entry into these international agencies and regimes and then manage China's relationship with them. This process instantly embedded new perspectives and interests within a heretofore parochial domestic policy-making system. A similar process occurred when the Ministry of Foreign Affairs created a bureau to deal with arms control issues, which Beijing was being pushed to address by the outside world, especially Washington. This process of building capacity to plug into the global system has had consequences. The number of actors has grown, the complexity of the process has increased, and the balance of interests within the policy process has shifted.

Deng's move toward a market economy at home was also full of meaning for more narrowly defined domestic politics. In a market economy, money becomes a central inducement and no longer a government monopoly. A market economy has hierarchies with status and security that lie beyond officialdom. In newly marketized China, this new reality meant that government had to compete with a burgeoning number of quasi- and nonstate actors for, among other things, talented people and money. As one senior official put it to me, "'The private sector hires good people away from the government. This is a problem in every ministry.'"[45] This gradually alters the state-society balance. This competition for talent is particularly evident in high-tech areas, as one senior official in the government's nuclear regulatory apparatus explained.

> It should be that people who work in XXX [government agency] are highly trained, they should be of high quality, they should be of a high level. But now, work in the government and work in industry, the salaries are quite different. "A serious problem." So before in Beijing we had special policies

on housing, education, so there were more advantages [to working in the government], "but now all gone because of reform. Housing, there is a new policy—no subsidies. So people stop working in XXX [government agency] and work in industry. Those in industry don't move to the government." That is why XXX is in a very difficult position to get qualified people.[46]

Turning to the challenge of bureaucratic coordination directly, there are at least two ways to think about the problem: (1) coordination among agencies in the party-state (the challenge of stove-piping and the uncomfortable interface between functional vertical bureaucracies and horizontal territorial administrations), and (2) the challenge of coordinating government with new sectors of the economy (e.g., a private sector) that have increasing initiative and autonomy.

The first problem—the proliferation of government agencies and the need to reconcile domestic interagency, intersectoral, and interregional disputes—was clear in the protracted (1986–2001) negotiations over China's entry into what was first called the GATT and eventually became the WTO. Every section of an overall agreement that China's trade negotiators reached with the global trading regime required at least grudging acceptance and implementation by a large number of domestic players, all with their particular interests that could have delayed or foiled effective implementation if they so desired.

The first line of combat in the process of reconciling these interests was what now is called the Ministry of Commerce (MOFCOM), a bureaucracy that had a number of organizational antecedents. Even though MOFCOM and its predecessors were not the weakest players in Beijing's bureaucratic firmament, almost every important feature of China's WTO accession package had to be resolved in higher-level interagency meetings presided over, through much of this time, by State Councilor Mme. Wu Yi (later vice-premier and from 1998 in the Leading Party Group of the State Council). When her clout was insufficient, disputes would go to higher arenas, including the premier, the State Council, and sometimes the Politburo Standing Committee. One senior official in the then Ministry of Foreign Trade and Economic Cooperation [MOFTEC] explained how the process worked and what lines of economic, geographic, and bureaucratic division were salient. The internal negotiations involved winning agreement from a variety of alarmed economic sectors: agricultural interests saw threats from commodity producers in the United States, Canada, and Australia; domestic financial services firms feared global multinational financial Goliaths; and automakers feared Western and Japanese imports. To further complicate things, key leaders like Jiang Zemin and Li Lanqing had started their careers in the auto industry. "MOFTEC played a coordinating role among agencies, and if we could not reach agreement, we reported to the Leading Group headed by Wu Yi, and leading ministers. So if we got consensus we [MOFTEC] can negotiate; if not, the Leading Group decides. For example, in 1997, before Jiang Zemin's visit to the United States, WTO had an ITA agreement and China asked to join. Seven ministries were involved. Through the Leading Group we decided to join it."[47]

Turning to the second key problem of coordinating governmental and quasi-governmental entity behavior, and governmental and private sector behavior, Americans tend to think that there is a fairly bright line between private sector and government agency activity. Since 1977 in China, however, there has been a steady expansion in the number of organizations that fall into a gray area in which the control of government hierarchy cannot be taken for granted, and instruments used in the West to regulate private sector behavior—a legal structure, effective regulatory apparatus, or meaningful corporate governance—cannot be counted upon. This means that government officials are often uncertain about what many organizations are actually doing and are therefore unable to bring the activities of wayward entities under control in a timely fashion—even if they want to and corruption hasn't entered the equation. The leaders of these gray-area and private sector entities often exploit the ambiguity of their position to gain personal or organizational benefits.

Two incidents in 2007 and 2011 involving the Ministry of Foreign Affairs and revelations of Chinese military capabilities clearly illustrate this problem of coordination and gray areas. In both cases the Foreign Affairs Ministry was caught unawares by the military's sudden unveiling of new capabilities that concerned the outside world, not least Washington. The explanation I was given by Chinese government analysts was significant in its focus upon the relationship between changes in the economy (corporatization) and government oversight in the national security domain. Some notes of the meeting follow:

> I asked why events like the satellite shoot-down of 2007 and the 2011 unveiling of the J-20 [stealth aircraft] during Secretary of Defense Gates's visit occurred, and this led to a lot of discussion about what I termed "a lack of coordination" (*xietiao bugou*) and what they said was "absolutely no coordination" (*wanquan meiyou xietiao*). They said the 2007 satellite shoot-down was an interesting example of the move from industrial minis-

tries, to corporations, to industries. Each step along this evolutionary chain removed the arms and sensitive technology makers further from the mandatory (*xietiao*) coordination mechanism. Ministries were locked into the mechanism to coordinate actions, corporations were less so, and industries were still less so. XXX went on to say that by the time you were an industry, "it depends how you frame the issues." If the involved industry defines what it is doing as a security or foreign policy issue, it is then obligated to coordinate with that realm of the government; on the other hand, if it is just an industrial product being developed, requirements for coordination are fewer. The point is, as you have gone from a centralized ministry structure to a more corporate, economic framework, government capacity to coordinate in part depends on the self-reporting of industries under loose control.[48]

To put it starkly, industry has an interest in keeping its activities outside the realm of government coordination.

IMPLEMENTATION IS KEY TO THE POLICY PROCESS

Even if the party-state at whatever level formulates a policy and is committed to it, this is just the start of the process of effectively realizing it on the ground—whether across agencies at any given level, down the functional and territorial hierarchies, or among the PRC's increasing number of global entities. Policy formulation is important, but policy implementation is also crucial and usually even more challenging.

Many considerations affect implementation in China, as elsewhere. The following are some central considerations:[49]

1. *The context.* How many and what kinds of actors, with what resources, are entitled to have a voice in implementation, and how large were the initial disagreements over the policy? The more diverse and empowered the stakeholders and the deeper the initial divisions, the bigger the implementation problem.

2. *The content* of policy. Some policies are almost self-implementing, since they align with popular predisposition, while regulatory policies that try to change behavior are inherently more challenging.

3. *The unanticipated consequences* of the policy or unanticipated events in the broader environment.

4. *The time frame* over which policy must be implemented. Policies requiring substantial change that must continually be implemented (such as the one-child policy or anticorruption efforts) are more

difficult to successfully implement than policies that are effectively one-time changes (such as changing a tariff level).

5. *The number and complexity of linkages* with other important policy domains, both at home and abroad. The more implementation of one policy affects, or is affected by, other important policies, the harder it will be to successfully implement a given initiative. For example, the abolition of communes in the early 1980s made it more challenging to implement the one-child policy in rural areas because there was no longer a rural organizational structure to oversee implementation at the grassroots level.

6. *Corruption, both seen and unseen, throughout the system,* starting at the foundational level with the quality of materials put into public works projects. With respect to revenues, one senior economist explained, "Tax evasion is a problem in all sectors."[50]

Moving from the theoretical to the concrete, the three case studies provided earlier in this chapter (the AEL, broad economic and exchange rate policy, and the Shanghai-Hangzhou Maglev train issue) illustrate some of the policy formulation and implementation challenges faced by ever more constrained leaders in China's increasingly complex, globalized, and pluralized system.

The AEL example involves many powerful, yet divergent, stakeholders: the National Development and Reform Commission (NDRC), electric power interests, construction interests, the vast number of civilian and military users of radiological materials, and local governments. It is very difficult to effectively implement already existing atomic energy regulations, let alone adopt a comprehensive AEL. The prodevelopment interests want as little formal constraint as possible, while the regulatory interests (the NNSA and the MEP) are already relatively weak bureaucratic players, further weakened by internal divisions. Also in the mix are Chinese citizens who are anxious about having nuclear power plants in their backyard but who are weaker political actors (unless they take to the streets), though they are increasingly empowered by social networking and communications technologies.

The case of the exchange rate appreciation policy that was adopted in 2005, then suspended (in effect) in 2008, and then restarted in 2011 demonstrates the difficulty of sustaining policy when there are a multitude of interests and when the policy is vulnerable to uncontrollable external and internal events—such as the global financial crisis and, subsequently, spiking domestic inflationary pressures. Only when the world economy seemed to be recovering and China was worried about inflation (2011) was RMB appreciation resumed.

Finally, the Shanghai-Hangzhou Maglev train case demonstrates that even after a policy is adopted (approval to build the transportation line was given in February 2006), local citizens trying to protect their property and quality of life can now organize to delay or stop approved projects. More often these days, local authorities must convene public hearings that make data available to citizens, and members of the public employ networking, mass media, and communication technologies to raise the specter of disorder if their interests are ignored. It is important, of course, to determine the conditions under which popular discontent is effective and the circumstances under which it is not. But if a policy is to be effectively implemented, citizens' opinions must be taken into account.

In the past thirty-five years, China's policy-making system has become increasingly complex and fragmented—dare one say "normal"? This normalcy can be seen along many dimensions. With the rotation of national leaders on a ten-year cycle, for example, leaders tend to be weaker at the beginning and toward the end of their terms, with the greatest capacity to act being in the middle of their tenures. In China, as elsewhere, *important* problems take a back seat to the *urgent* ones, and a genuine crisis is what can focus a policy maker's attention. Finally, in China, if policies are going to be adopted and then effectively implemented, they require sustained attention from top leaders and a bureaucratic "champion."

During the Mao era the principal explanation for policy outcomes had to do with the Chairman, his peculiarities and political strategies, and the tangle of factions in which politics played out—the public was acted upon rather than an active participant. Beginning with Deng Xiaoping's ascension to power and becoming progressively more pronounced thereafter, the explanations for policy outcomes have to do with public opinion, bureaucratic structure, financial limitations, objective conditions, interest groups, and the constraints imposed by global integration. While the basic components are universal, just exactly how these building blocks fit together and interconnect reflects the peculiarities of the PRC. At the same time that we respect Chinese differences, the similarities are becoming more important. That China is becoming a more normal polity, however, does not mean that it will successfully address the enormous domestic and foreign policy challenges confronting it, nor does the country's internal trajectory ensure that the external environment will remain hospitable. Above all, the considerations producing Chinese policies may be understandable, but that is not to say the outside world will always find them congenial.

CHAPTER 4

The World

A power without power will be bullied.

—General Jiang Youshu, November 11, 1982

"If China is too accommodating to foreigners, it creates a
negative reaction in China, and that may slow down reform."
In China we need to consider the political system, the role of
parliament, the kind of decision-making process. We
understand your system has problems that affect your policy
toward us, "but the same is true for China—not because of
bilateral problems but domestic problems."

—High-ranking Chinese economic official, November 1, 1994

"This crisis [the Asian financial crisis] compelled us to
rethink global integration. It is more than trade; it is
investment, then stocks and bonds. So global integration
is going from tangible integration, trade and production,
to intangible integration, including information and
financial system integration. Free capital flows are like
Prometheus's fire—it is warmth but also a source of death.
In the past ten years, network computers have democratized
boundaries."

—Wang Xuebing, president and vice-chairman, Bank of China,
July 2, 1998 (convicted of corruption in 2003)

"China doesn't want to establish a new world order; it wants
to get stronger in the existent world order. All powers have a
stake in the world order."

—Senior Foreign Ministry official, November 23, 2002

"I think the biggest change has been that at the start of reform
leaders had seen the world as the inside [of China] and the
outside [beyond China]. Now, in many respects, they, Hu

Jintao, see there is no distinction—the inside and the outside
are one, interconnected, and mutually influencing."
—Senior foreign policy think tank leader, June 3, 2010

"The twenty-first century is immensely different. Old ways
won't work in the new century."
—State Councilor Dai Bingguo, June 26, 2011

Currently four principal forces shape Chinese views toward, and actions
in, the world: domestic politics and other internal constraints; global
interdependence; realist foreign policy thinking; and technology-driven
action-reaction dynamics. Domestic politics and big-power considerations have been central in shaping Beijing's behavior since 1977, while
the forces of interdependence and the imperatives of technological-
driven change that elicit actions and reactions have been newer developments. Domestic politics is pivotal because leaders must survive the riptides of developments at home if they are to act abroad. Interdependence
alters the home players, their relative political heft, and cost-benefit
calculations in domestic politics. Of course the interplay of domestic
politics and international interdependence does not make China remarkable.

However, the PRC's global behavior is distinctive in its utter pragmatism, or what I call the situational ethics with which these contending
impulses are balanced as Chinese leaders decide how to act internationally. Americans generally describe the making of their foreign policy as a
ceaseless quest to balance America's interests with its values—security,
material, and power needs against more intractable ideas of "right" and
"wrong." Americans often (hopefully) assert that to serve their values is to
pursue their interests. This attraction of "values"—many Chinese would
say "ideology"—has its origins in America the immigrant nation, to which
successive waves of displaced persons and those simply seeking a better
life have come to escape autocrats, material deprivation, discrimination,
and chaos. Given its heterogeneous character, the United States has been
held together by shared ideals and law, not any common place of origin,

ethnicity, or religion. Once in their adopted country, immigrants often have felt obliged to attempt to bring the blessings of liberty, opportunity, and human rights to their brethren left behind in the "old country." There is, therefore, an intrinsically interventionist quality to U.S. foreign policy, with the strength of this impulse varying as the burdens of prior efforts become more or less distant in the collective consciousness. Interventionist and isolationist impulses coexist in the American foreign policy psyche. To the Chinese, however, the interventionist impulse of America is of greater ongoing concern than the isolationist tendency. One senior Chinese intelligence official observed that American interventionist thinking was like having a preference for "surgery" rather than for noninvasive medical procedures.[1]

The intellectual and cultural roots of Chinese foreign policy lie in Confucian and Taoist thought, a long history, China's self-perception in relation to its neighbors, and its unique physical and demographic landscape.[2] China's foreign policy emerges from a matrix in which China is connected to the world, with particular attention given the nation's periphery—everything is interconnected.[3] China's foreign policy view is pragmatic and seeks to maximize benefits in an ever changing yet interconnected global environment. It is not a view grounded in absolute values—it is situational ethics on a global scale. This vantage point is the international politics version of Deng Xiaoping's domestic policy of "crossing the river by feeling for stones" (*mozhe shitou guo he*). This perspective is not a "you are your brother's keeper" vision of international politics. In a 1973 conversation with a U.S. Treasury delegation, Vice-Minister of Foreign Affairs (later foreign minister) Qiao Guanhua recounted that he had spoken with Senate Majority Leader Mike Mansfield about possible U.S. troop withdrawals from Europe (which Mansfield favored and Beijing then opposed, wishing to keep Moscow threatened on two fronts), concluding about the senator: "He is a good person but very idealistic and highly moral." Qiao was not being laudatory.[4]

China's foreign policy is rarely conducted using the vocabulary of moral absolutes and dwells instead on principles such as "mutual benefit," "mutual respect," and "noninterference"—phrases with deep resonance in China given the intervention it has endured in its modern and more distant history. Chinese talk about process much more frequently than they talk about the absolute morality or immorality of outcomes. In stark contrast, Americans often employ the vocabulary of moral absolutes when speaking of outcomes—"universal values." How China acts globally depends on context and its own interests.

In a September 2, 1986, interview of Deng Xiaoping by Mike Wallace of CBS News, Wallace observed, "It seems that Chinese relations with capitalist America are better than Chinese relations with the Soviet Communists." Deng's response is instructive for understanding Beijing's foreign policy framework: "China does not regard social systems as a criterion in its approach to problems. The relations between China and the United States are determined in the context of their specific conditions, and so are the relations between China and the Soviet Union."⁵ For Deng, Beijing's respective relations with Washington and Moscow were about China's interests, not the normative merits of the two superpowers' systems, how they treated their people, or which values they nominally espoused.

In this chapter we examine how the four drivers of Chinese foreign policy have played out in the post-Mao era and what can be expected in the future. Which impulse(s) will predominate in coming decades?

DOMESTIC POLITICS AS A DRIVER OF CHINESE FOREIGN POLICY

Today, PRC analysts and policy makers freely admit that domestic politics clearly shapes China's external policies and behavior. This has not always been the case. Before and early on in the reform era, Chinese leaders, fearing that outside forces would exploit or manipulate internal discord, would never have acknowledged that domestic politics shaped foreign policy. The accepted rhetoric was that 960 million (at that time) Chinese people had one national interest—"The Chinese people stand shoulder to shoulder." PRC interlocutors embedded policy in a grand strategic framework, describing foreign policy not as a domestic political outcome but as a strategic necessity imposed on it by the external world, requiring a reaction guided by ideology. The party tightly held the foreign policy reins.

In a moment of candor in October 1971, Henry Kissinger told Premier Zhou Enlai how domestic opponents in the United States sought to frustrate President Nixon's planned China trip for the following February, saying, "These groups have mounted campaigns against the President's acceptance of your invitation. . . . Even within the bureaucracy some of the established forms [of opposition] continue." Premier Zhou responded, "Also such things like that in China. . . . So we think bureaucracy cannot only be found in the State Department; it can also be found in the Foreign Ministry." To which Kissinger rejoined: "My secret dream is to do to the State Department what the Prime Minister did to his office—reduce it to three [people]."[6]

The fact that domestic populist and bureaucratic politics (as well as underlying economic and social conditions) influence China's foreign policies in many ways is a contention that no credible person in China any longer disputes. Economic circumstances sculpt foreign policy directly by providing the material resources upon which action depends and indirectly by affecting popular opinions concerning national capacities and priorities. Since 1977, China has become economically stronger and more capable, and this is reflected in the nation's growing sense of its own capabilities and subsequent assertiveness.[7] Similarly, China's ongoing social and economic development has empowered new groups inside and outside the bureaucracy and has disadvantaged others, thereby changing the entire framework of domestic interests. As seen in chapter 2, China's national leaders have become weaker in the face of growing societal and bureaucratic pluralization, perhaps the most significant fact of the new political era. Similarly, Chinese Foreign Ministry and central trade bureaucracies are less able to manage the nation's multitude of external connections, and territorial administrations and nonstate economic entities have been relatively empowered. Just as China's "supreme leaders" have loomed progressively less large as the reform era has unfolded, so too have China's central foreign policy leaders become less dominant.

Within Chinese society, rural perspectives have declined and urban, more internationalist (and nationalist) views have risen in salience. In one striking set of statistics, one sees the multifaceted effects of urbanization. In 2012, when a sample of urban and rural Chinese was asked whether they "like American ideas about democracy," 60 percent of the urbanites said they did while only 43 percent of rural dwellers gave the same response.[8] Urbanization, the rise of a middle class, and coastal development have empowered economic interests and underscored the importance of interdependence. The Chinese populace has also come to see the PRC as more empowered in the global power hierarchy and hence has become more demanding of leaders who often are viewed as excessively deferential to foreign demands—"public opinion" has become a fashionable explanation for policies. As Premier Li Peng said when explaining why he would not capitulate to American demands to improve human rights in exchange for continuation of normal trading relations with Washington in 1993: "But I don't think I can report what you told me to the Chinese people via television, because they would say that the Chinese premier is making China's policy based on the American president, and they would overthrow me."[9]

Bureaucratic struggles, turf battles, and normal organizational change and evolution, along with the personalities of various office-holders, also affect China's foreign policy. Today's PRC governmental organization chart differs substantially from its 1977 analogue, with the current structure embedding functional and geographic interests that were unrepresented, underrepresented, or simply nonexistent at the time of Mao's death. For example, in 1980 China's Foreign Ministry had no equivalent of the Arms Control and Disarmament Agency, and, unsurprisingly, these types of interests were not effectively represented in the bureaucracy; today these concerns are built into the structure of the ministry.[10] Similarly, at the onset of the reform era the Foreign Ministry had no unit responsible for protecting citizens overseas, a function that became essential once China had businesspersons, contract workers, students, and tourists living and traveling around the world in great numbers. Conversely, many of the economic ministries of the planned economy that existed at the onset of reform have simply been abolished or relocated on the organizational map, with many becoming more autonomous economic, semi-market-oriented actors at home and abroad. Many of these corporations and industrial sectors are substantially controlled or influenced by politically well-connected extended families born of the party and the revolution.[11] Former premier Li Peng and his family, for instance, are nearly synonymous with electric power. Chinese corporations abroad create problems by fighting among each other in foreign markets—"China and its banks are growing out of the posture of China Inc."[12]

In terms of territorial administrations, at the end of the 1970s, once a few special economic zones were created, other territorial administrations began to push for their own access to the outside world under favorable terms and free of Foreign Ministry constraints or the limitations imposed by central trade and economic bureaucracies. A continual feature of the reform era has been the attempt of the Foreign Ministry system in Beijing to maintain its control over external relations, and the countervailing attempt by other bureaucracies, localities, and other economic, educational, and cultural entities to break free of the traditional monopoly.

Similarly, as the relative influence of the central diplomatic and military establishments has waxed and waned (see chapter 6), the tone of Chinese foreign policy has varied accordingly, with military perspectives gaining strength as the PLA's budget has grown briskly since 1990 and its retired officers have become more vocal. And merging territorial administration and national security issues, at the onset of reform, Hainan Island was an undeveloped tropical island that was part of Guangdong Province, not terribly important in either provincial or national politics. However, in April 1988 it gained provincial status, and since it has developed considerably, having important military facilities and seeing its interest as expanding its administrative span of control to as many South China Sea land features and fishing grounds as possible.

Also germane to the connection between domestic and foreign policy is elite succession. Succession has changed the dominant individuals shaping policy, as occurred with Mao's death and Deng Xiaoping's ascendancy at the start of reform. Similarly, the shift from Jiang Zemin to Hu Jintao in 2002 was more critical than often realized, since a leader with a high commitment to the United States-China relationship was succeeded by one with less connection to Washington. In short, in China as elsewhere, domestic politics is the soil in which the plant of foreign policy grows. The domestic ebb and flow of money, people, bureaucracies, and the reigning ideas of any given era all affect foreign policy.

Personality, Position, and Power Shape Foreign Policy

Jiang Zemin's abrupt and unanticipated rise to power in mid-1989 in the wake of the Tiananmen debacle illustrates the many domestic forces shaping foreign policy in China today. For his debut on the national stage, Jiang was in a weak position—China was isolated internationally; the older, nominally retired elite was divided but still powerful and lurked ominously off center stage; and the younger members of the elite were weak, divided, and traumatized by the Tiananmen violence. Jiang was chosen precisely because he was weak, initially, and therefore unthreatening. It took Jiang time to get his hands on the levers of foreign and domestic policy power, as he had to gradually consolidate his position. In foreign policy, he was constrained by Premier Li Peng, who held the chairmanship of the critical coordinating body—the Leading Small Group on Foreign Affairs—until about 1998, leaving Jiang with imperfect control over external policy prior to that.[13]

In this setting, Jiang Zemin wanted to respond strongly to the United States' May 1995 announcement that Washington would grant a visa to Taiwan president Lee Teng-hui to visit the United States the following month. This was because the preceding January he had made what he thought was a conciliatory policy statement on Taiwan ("Jiang's Eight Points," or *Jiang Ba Dian*).[14] Lee's announced trip was a perceived slap in Jiang's face, with Jiang's calls for more cross-Strait cooperation effectively rebuffed by Taipei's show of assertiveness. Compounding that sting, the Chinese leadership had thought it had an understanding with the Clinton administration that a visa would not be issued to Lee. In the end, Lee's trip to Cornell University set off protracted Chinese reactions, including the temporary withdrawal of Beijing's ambassador to Washington, Li Daoyu, in mid-June, and missile firings (with dummy warheads) off the northern and southern shores of Taiwan in July 1995 and again in March 1996, just prior to the island's presidential elections.

What requires explanation is that President Jiang wanted to respond immediately to the Lee situation in June 1995 but that the reaction was delayed by domestic considerations. President Lee Teng-hui delivered his speech at Cornell on June 9, but the first salvo of missile firings did not start until July 21, followed by a second salvo about eight months later. Why the delay? A senior PRC foreign policy analyst explained:

> In 1995, you remember that after Lee Teng-hui was given a visa there was an announcement by the Foreign Ministry that the day he [President Lee] took off for [from] Taiwan something big would happen. But on the day Lee took off, the Foreign Ministry spokesman in effect backed off, the reason being that no decision had been made. At that point, Jiang actually had his own desire, to respond in a strong fashion, but he did not yet have the power of unilateral leader to decide rapidly. Jiang Zemin simply did not have the political capital to decide alone; he had to build a consensus and this took time. So while some in the military did want to take a hard line— one suggested firing missiles the day Lee took off for the United States to force Lee to turn his plane around and return to Taiwan!—Jiang wanted a strong response too, though perhaps not that strong. The Foreign Ministry spokesman had to back down because the center was unable to decide what to do for some period of time, and Jiang had to build a consensus without the power to make a more unilateral decision at that time. Further, Jiang at that time would not have wanted to decide unilaterally because had he "decided wrong" he would have given a weapon to opponents. . . . He wanted a collective decision so as to avoid subsequent blame, if it was to be assigned.[15]

The need to build consensus also is seen in Beijing's other crisis behavior with Washington. At critical foreign policy moments Jiang Zemin was unwilling to receive a call from President Clinton until he knew he was on solid ground with his colleagues. One PLA officer explained, "'Until there is leadership agreement, no one dares to pick up the phone and risk leadership.'"[16]

The role of personality, individual interest, conflicting bureaucratic responsibilities, and domestic politics is also clear in Beijing's policy toward Hong Kong in the wake of June 4, 1989, and in the run-up to the reversion of the British colony to mainland sovereignty on July 1, 1997. From 1983 until early 1990, China's ranking representative in British Hong Kong was the director of the Xinhua News Agency, Xu Jiatun. Xinhua News Agency constituted a shadowy, parallel administration to the British colonial government. Xu Jiatun was well liked locally, he was seen as relatively open and as someone who was mindful of Hong Kong people's concerns and interests and tried to convey them to Beijing in an effort to smooth the path to reversion. However, Vice-Foreign Minister Zhou Nan and Director Lu Ping of the Hong Kong and Macau Affairs Office back in Beijing were not particularly appreciative of Xu's approach in Hong Kong.

The violence of June 4, 1989, in Beijing, and the unrest elsewhere in China greatly unsettled the already nervous Hong Kong people, raising for them the question of what reversion to mainland sovereignty in mid-1997 would mean for their freedom and their bank accounts. Many in Britain and America were likewise concerned—not least the U.S. Congress. In this context Director Xu consented to meet with Professor A. Doak Barnett and me in September 1989 while the colony was still reeling from the globally televised violence in Beijing. In that meeting, Xu did not abandon or directly criticize Beijing's line (indeed he defended "the necessity" of the crackdown), but he nonetheless argued that part of the key to stability in Hong Kong was reform's continuation in China—that what Beijing did internally would have great bearing on attitudes in Hong Kong and that most Hong Kong people were not anti-China. Xu said: "Three factors in Hong Kong are key: stability in China; open door and reform; and cooperation with the United Kingdom."[17] In short, Xu was arguing that the problem was not in Hong Kong but in Beijing—not exactly in line with Lu Ping and Zhou Nan, who told the journalist David Gergen more than a year later, "Prosperity and stability in Hong Kong largely depend on close cooperation between China and Britain during the latter half and that is where we are now."[18]

Such contradictory comments give a hint of the behind-the-scenes infighting over the issue of how to deal with the people of Hong Kong that was taking place in the wake of the June 4, 1989, violence. Xu wanted to adopt a relatively open, interactive style and get out among Hong Kong's people. He was telling Beijing that it needed to reassure people in Hong Kong and around the world by continuing reform and opening, and he was warning his bosses back in the capital that the status quo of local relations was not good. Back in Beijing, as Xu recounted in later writings, Vice-Minister Zhou Nan and Director Lu Ping were advocating a less open approach vis-à-vis Hong Kong while reassuring their superiors in Beijing that all was going fine down south—happy talk.[19] Other leaders in Hong Kong were clear in their views of Lu Ping and the office he ran. In 1992, Governor Chris Patten commented, "'Lu Ping is just an operator.' . . . They don't know much about Hong Kong—they are conservative."[20]

To make matters worse for Xu, he was closely associated with now fallen former general secretary Zhao Ziyang, who had parted ways with Deng Xiaoping over how to handle the June 4 turbulence, among other things.[21] Within two months of our meeting with Xu in late 1989, Zhou Nan had set up a committee to investigate Xu, and in January 1990 Zhou himself was appointed director of the Hong Kong Branch of Xinhua News Agency, replacing Xu. Apparently sensing that he might be arrested, in early May 1990 Xu fled to America.

Unsurprisingly, in the wake of Zhou Nan's assumption of the Xinhua directorship in Hong Kong, negotiations with the British became more contentious. Zhou Nan's inclinations were more muscular, he was more responsive to Beijing's tougher attitudes, and his defeat of Xu reinforced directions that help account for the acrimony of the next period of Sino-British relations and friction with the local population in Hong Kong. Zhou Nan, one British governor of Hong Kong told me, loved jumping out in front of the British governor if they were in proximity to one another—staying a few steps ahead of the colonialists, as any good nationalist would.[22]

Public Opinion

In this digitally interconnected world, public opinion in China, as elsewhere, can become mobilized and metamorphose into assertive nationalism before the political elite has time for any thoughtful reaction. A good example of such mobilization can be found in the May 7, 1999, NATO-led (U.S.) accidental bombing of the Chinese embassy in Belgrade that killed three and wounded twenty Chinese and was followed by the emotion-laden homecoming of the dead and wounded.

Large and violent demonstrations against the U.S. embassy in Beijing and other U.S. counselor facilities in the PRC followed the bombing, along with U.S. explanations of what happened and why—"a grave mistake and tragedy that occurred as a result of a series of failures in U.S. intelligence and targeting procedures." The demonstrations continued, and Washington's explanations were considered inadequate, insincere, and incredible by most Chinese—giving rise to four core PRC demands: "apology," "conclusions," "punishment," and "compensation."[23] The entire episode dragged on for months, leaving the scar of deep distrust in both countries from which the relationship had not fully recovered more than a decade later. Why did this episode last so long? What accounts for its dynamics?

At the time China's leaders needed a compelling explanation for how the bombing had happened so that their people could feel that the regime stood for their national interests, dignity, and justice. The explanation offered by the United States, however, simply was not credible to the average Chinese person,[24] and therefore the CCP leadership could not accept what its own people would categorically reject. Shortly after the bombing, a Chinese vice-minister expressed the general frustration and anger, saying that PRC citizens believed Americans were more concerned with Bill Clinton's peccadilloes with Monica Lewinsky than with the death of Chinese at U.S. hands.[25] U.S. undersecretary of state Thomas Pickering personally delivered Washington's official explanation one month after the incident. A Chinese interlocutor explained how the U.S. explanation was viewed: "Actually, the Pickering report [given to the Chinese some days before] hasn't offended any U.S. department, but it offended the Chinese because they think it is too far from the truth. The [Pickering] report mentions three maps. . . . Pickering mentioned a dozen such mistakes, a probability of one in a million. It is hard to accept such an explanation."[26]

From the vantage point of 2013, I have yet to find a Chinese person who believes the tragic incident was accidental. The point here, however, is not to discuss how the misadventure happened, how the crisis was managed, or what lessons in crisis management might be drawn— this largely has been done in an excellent edited volume by Michael Swaine and Zhang Tuosheng.[27] Our current purpose is to understand how domestic constraints shaped Chinese leadership behavior in the bombing's aftermath.

Once public opinion is aroused, this provides an opening for various Chinese bureaucracies to promote their interests and to express shared outrage. The military and propaganda apparatuses were quick to see such an opportunity with the bombing incident, and of course the most ungenerous interpretation of U.S. motives was fully consistent with their organizational cultures. The military saw an opportunity to advance its budgetary and other organizational interests. As to the propaganda apparatus, it is one of the least progressive gears of the Chinese bureaucratic machine, and it saw its chance to whip up nationalism, which it did with substantial television time devoted to the incident. As one senior military person put it to me shortly after the event, "'The world's two worst propaganda machines, China's and CNN, play off each other.'"[28]

In this context, Jiang Zemin and the Chinese civilian leadership sought to understand what had happened; manage domestic bureaucratic politics; manage student outrage (by selectively letting student demonstrators into the embassy quarter but keeping the numbers manageable); and minimize damage to China's long-range interests by maintaining minimum communication with the United States. Initially, there was lack of Chinese leadership consensus about what course to take, accounting for lack of responsiveness to President Clinton's efforts to speak directly to President Jiang in the tragedy's immediate aftermath. Even domestically Jiang seemed to be keeping a low profile; one popular joke about his seeming absence was: "Chinese police stations received missing-person reports on Jiang [Zemin] and Zhu [Rongji]."[29]

Sometimes public opinion in China has become an independent force that Chinese leaders can, at best, benignly manage. At other times, the center may believe it advantageous to arouse popular indignation—always running the risk that, once aroused, popular passion could veer in antigovernment directions. Within the government, different bureaucracies use public opinion to legitimate their own policy proclivities and interests, making it hard to reach consensus—sometimes "the center" is not of one mind. The strategy Beijing adopted to deal with this NATO bombing crisis was to minimally communicate with the Americans while making demands for satisfaction, to permit controlled demonstrations, and to let time heal the situation. It wasn't simple or pretty, but U.S.-China relations lived to see another day.

Economic Forces

Premier Zhu Rongji's visit to the United States in early April 1999 offers a good example of domestic economic constraints on foreign policy. There was hope in China's upper leadership that this U.S. trip might close a deal with Washington on Beijing's entry into the WTO, after well over a decade of negotiations. One think tank analyst delineates how Chinese domestic politics had gotten in the way of this deal for so long:

> Three periods on WTO [accession negotiations]. If not for Tiananmen, we would have been in. In 1992/1993, China could have joined WTO but the [Chinese] auto industry implored [that China not join]. This time, 1997/1998, also [the] internal factor played a big role—for example, the SOEs and the workers. Demonstrations and hunger strikes. Students are manageable, but workers are even more difficult to manage. "Everyone knows that if China opens up most SOEs are finished." Zhu Rongji said, "Three people are doing one job; one is doing, one is watching, and one is making trouble." Zhu went to inspect SOEs in Manchuria in 1998 and said this (a couple of months ago).[30]

In the lead-up to Zhu's 1999 mission to the United States, President Jiang Zemin and Zhu worked together to override vociferous popular and elite opposition and put together what they viewed as a workable offer to Washington concerning WTO entry terms. There had been three meetings of the Standing Committee of the Politburo and full Politburo to decide whether Zhu should even go to the United States and related issues.[31] Once Premier Zhu arrived in Washington, however, it became clear that, fearing adverse labor union and congressional reaction, President Bill Clinton was unable to promptly accept the offered terms. The United States was constrained by domestic politics as well! To make matters worse for Zhu and Jiang, the Clinton administration went on to make Beijing's offered concessions public.

Premier Zhu returned to Beijing amid a hail of criticism from PRC interest groups arguing that he had offered Washington far too much. This was an outcome Zhu had been greatly concerned about prior to his U.S. trip, telling members of Congress visiting Beijing: "I can tell you they [my domestic critics] won't accuse Mrs. Barshefsky [the U.S. trade representative] of trading principles. Chinese people will accuse Zhu Rongji [me] of trading principles."[32]

To make matters worse, this was not a time any Chinese leader would have wanted to appear excessively pliable in the face of Western demands widely perceived in China to be unreasonable. Jiang Zemin and Zhu Rongji were well down the track of what would become a layoff of more than twenty-five million state-owned enterprise (and other) workers,[33] a consequence of restructuring the Chinese economy to make it more competitive ahead of WTO accession and the ensuing global competition it would bring. There were legions of unhappy, unemployed workers and fearful managers throughout the PRC. There were also upcoming meetings of the NPC, and top party officials feared that voting at the NPC might publicly reflect the dissatisfaction.[34] Consequently, Jiang and Zhu had to let things cool down for several months (as did Bill Clinton in Washington), with the two sides finally reaching agreement in November 1999. China entered the WTO at the end of 2001.

Thus far we have presented economic considerations as a constraining influence on Chinese external behavior—but the quest by domestic groups for economic opportunity can also influence the face China presents to the world. A core feature of Deng's reforms was to provide economic incentives to increasing numbers of actors, even those who were somewhat removed from direct state control. Since the state's capacity to regulate these actors has not kept up with the global reach of their activities, one finds Chinese entities (whether corporations, individual or collective entrepreneurs, or local governments) promoting their parochial interests on a global basis, sometimes at the nation's expense. Answering questions such as what constitutes "China" as an international actor and "who speaks for China" are becoming complicated by economic decentralization in the absence of a rule of law and well-developed regulatory institutions.

The above examples illustrate the multiple ways domestic considerations affect foreign policy in China—bureaucratic politics, mobilized citizens, economic constraints or economic opportunities, and the need for relevant international partners to simultaneously be in a permissive domestic environment. Domestic considerations, however, are not the only factors shaping foreign policy: interdependence, while not entirely distinct from domestic politics, is a growing force, inasmuch as it reshapes the domestic playing field, its actors, and their incentives.

INTERDEPENDENCE AND FOREIGN POLICY

Globalization and interdependence have altered the way China's leaders and its citizens view the world. The PRC's stake in a stable global economy became obvious to many of its citizens as the global financial crisis of 2008 unfolded, with one very senior Chinese bank official explaining to American visitors: "The real thing that is hurting us is the Western recession. Trade is 79 percent of our GDP—38 percent is exports, and of this, 18 percent is exports to the U.S. and 20 percent to Europe. In 2007, there was 11 percent growth (2.7 percent of this was from net exports). Now export growth has got us [down] to 9 percent."[35]

Globalization and interdependence have altered domestic politics by creating linkages that make China more reliant on the world for food, energy, and export markets. And this reliance and interconnectedness are not just an urban phenomenon; farmers are exporting significantly, so they too have interests beyond China's borders. As the mayor of Zhangzhou City (Fujian) said to visiting American foundation leaders in 1993, "We export a lot of mushrooms to the United States. . . . We export thirty thousand tons of mushrooms to the United States. Now we export asparagus, clothes, and shoes to the U.S. market. We have two cities that want to have relations [with us]—Cedar Rapids [Iowa] and Salinas [California]."[36] For much of China's citizenry in 2013, international markets are a fact of life, with around ninety million employed in export manufacturing and total employment in export production (including agriculture and services) at one hundred million—about one in eight working Chinese.[37] Officials at both the local and central government levels rely significantly on revenues from customs duties, on taxes derivative of foreign participation in the Chinese economy, and on revenues from China's domestically owned export-oriented enterprises. Local leaders are quick to acknowledge this powerful interdependence— Shanghai's mayor Xu Kuangdi noted that in 1998 one-third of Shanghai's GDP came from foreign-invested enterprises.[38] Beijing may be about high politics, said one think tanker, but Shanghai is "'most concerned'" about "'executive jets.'"[39] Globalization creates new constituencies even before taking into account the corrupt links abroad that enrich officials with gatekeeping functions throughout the system.

Interdependence is not just about money and employment; it also is about acquisition of technology and know-how from abroad that will enhance national capability to continue to move up the value-added chain—a key to China's future. Interdependence does not make international conflict impossible, and indeed it can create conditions that make conflict even more destructive should it occur, but it does provide incentives to keep conflict with major partners manageable.

There is the thinnest of lines between interdependence and dependence. At the onset of the reform era Chinese leaders wanted to avoid dependence rather than to achieve whatever the gains of interdependence and comparative advantage might be. "Self-reliance," the mantra of the 1960s and much of the 1970s, was the shibboleth that Deng shattered with his "open policy." The real fears of dependence centered on the economic and military realms. In the security domain, Mao Zedong (as well as Deng in the early reform period) was scarred from interactions with Moscow in the 1950s and 1960s, convinced that the USSR had sought to make China a security vassal. Vice-Foreign Minister Qiao Guanhua explained this to visitors in 1973: "Khrushchev also held strategic products—the atom bomb—therefore thinking he could strangle China. In 1957 they said they would cooperate with us, producing a bomb, but in 1959 they tore up the contract. But he [Khrushchev] spoke directly to the Chinese people saying, 'You are so poor you don't even have trousers to wear and you think you can produce a bomb.' He said this in 1960, and the day after his downfall in 1964 we exploded the bomb."[40]

In the economic realm, from the 1950s until the early 1970s Washington and its allies placed an embargo on the PRC. After this period of enforced self-reliance, there remained in the early years of reform (and to some extent even today) a fear of dependence and a belief that it was foolhardy to depend on others. In 1973 Michael Blumenthal asked Vice-Foreign Minister Qiao, "To what extent does self-reliance influence trade?" Qiao's instructive reply was "The main things [will be produced] ourselves—grain, you [America] produce a lot of grain, but if China stops producing for one year could you supply us?"[41] Of course, the fact that the United States used food as a weapon only reinforced PRC determination not to become nutritionally dependent at that time. A measure of how attitudes have changed is clear in PRC Ministry of Agriculture statistics and an explanation from the PRC's Development Research Center in 2012: "Along with the rising trade volumes, there has also been a growing trade deficit in the agricultural sector. In 2011, the agricultural trade deficit rose 47.4 percent to $34 billion, whereas in 2004, China was still an agricultural net exporter. . . . China is already the world's largest importer of soybean and cotton and has become the largest agricultural export market for the U.S. since 2010."[42]

One of the clearest expressions of this Chinese strand of thinking on interdependence was provided by a person knowledgeable about how Jiang Zemin was briefed prior to his 1997 trip to America. The Chinese president was searching for a positive way to intellectually frame his U.S. trip, and he decided to make the argument that economic, security, and political interdependence provided the compelling rationale for cooperative U.S.-China relations. The conversation Jiang had with his advisers is recounted below:

> In 1997 in preparing for his trip to the United States . . . Jiang Zemin asked
> . . . formally what ought to be his strategic view for his trip to the United
> States. . . . [The person responded that] his trip's strategic viewpoint should
> be built around the notion of common interests. Jiang asked what they
> were. . . . The five common interests were (1) the avoidance of conflict;
> (2) neither side can do without the other in the economic realm; (3) both
> sides need a stabilized Asia in both the security realm and the economic sta-
> bilization realm [the person had in mind the Asian financial crisis at this
> point]; (4) transnational issues, but of course at this time antiterrorism was
> not so serious, rather drugs, human smuggling, and environmental protec-
> tion; and (5) our leaders' personal interests in both countries. With respect
> to this latter point, what . . . [this person said] means is, "If a leader deals
> with it [the bilateral relationship] well, they will be great leaders."[43]

This same respondent said that despite the many subsequent issues
that negatively affected bilateral US-PRC relations since that briefing to
Jiang in 1997 and his trip to the United States (the 1999 NATO/US
bombing of the Chinese embassy in Belgrade, 1999 moves by Taiwan
president Lee Teng-hui toward what was perceived in Beijing as separation, the 2000 election on Taiwan of independence-minded Chen Shui-
bian as president, and the 2001 US-PRC military aircraft collision near
Hainan Island), interdependence was still a reality: "'We have experienced so many shocks, but these points [the five mentioned in the quotation above] still are there after all. . . . They are becoming more
important than five years ago.'"[44]

Turning to the era of Hu Jintao, one of his very senior foreign policy
advisers argued that economic interdependence is stronger glue for
bilateral relations than a common strategic enemy such as "the bear to
the North" during the 1970s and early 1980s or counterterrorism in the
post-9/11 era. He continued:

> Take all this, it would give us a solid foundation for U.S.-China relations.
> The volume of trade between our two countries is very big. So "I believe the
> very development of China provides opportunity for the United States and
> development of the United States provides China opportunities. Our rela-
> tionship should not be based on external factors. So our relations today are
> much stronger than in the 1970s and 1980s. Because back in the 1970s/1980s
> we had very little to give you [the United States]—poor/backward. But in the
> past twenty years, its [China's] road has implications, but in a phrase, the
> road we are taking is integration into the world, not separation, and this is
> win-win for our two countries."[45]

Notably, at the opening of the new millennium, China became a
major exporter of capital—gaining an ever growing stake in the stabil-

ity of the entire international economic system, not to mention in the prosperity of the United States (with over half of the PRC's foreign exchange reserves denominated in U.S. dollars). This was signaled to me in a 2002 meeting with then minister of finance Xiang Huaicheng, as recounted in my notes: "'You know, China is now the number one foreign purchaser of U.S. Treasury notes. . . . We have a current holding of U.S. Treasury notes of $80.9 billion [outstanding]. Further, this is not all the U.S. financial instruments China holds.' He noted that they also have corporate bonds and the bonds of localities and municipalities in the United States. The current outstanding total of all these financial instruments is $150 billion. 'So, you can see we have a great deal in common.'"[46]

With such a proportion of its assets denominated in dollars, China has a strong interest in not having the U.S. dollar continually depreciating. As one of China's chief economists explained to members of the U.S. Congress, "Your biggest problem is the fiscal deficit—your dollar will go down and down. If your dollar drops, it costs people [China] who hold reserves in dollars."[47]

Fast-forward about a decade to 2011: with the United States alarmed by its weakening international credit rating, and its fiscal and credit health in serious jeopardy (with China the single biggest foreign holder of U.S. Treasury and agency debt), Vice President Joseph Biden felt compelled to reassure a Chinese audience he was addressing about the security of China's massive U.S. dollar-denominated asset holdings: "You're safe. Please understand that no-one cares more about this than we do, since Americans own 87 percent of all our financial assets."[48] Similarly, on her first trip to Asia as secretary of state in February 2009, shortly after the fall 2008 collapse of Lehman Brothers, Hillary Clinton said to a Beijing audience, "By continuing to support American Treasury instruments the Chinese are recognizing our interconnection. We are truly going to rise or fall together."[49]

Finally, in addition to the obvious economic interdependence, there is certainly political interdependence, as Jiang Zemin's advisers pointed out to him in his briefing for his 1997 trip to the United States: "'If a leader deals with it [the bilateral relationship,] well, they will be great leaders.'"[50] If political leaders in two highly interdependent states cannot deal effectively with one another and their common problems, they both run the risk of being defined as ineffective by their own constituents. During the Cold War, the litmus test for any U.S. presidential candidate was "Can he deal effectively with Moscow?" At this point in world affairs, a similar test must be administered to the custodians of the U.S.-China relationship in Beijing and Washington, respectively: "Can he or she effectively deal with Beijing/Washington?"

Despite the emphasis here on the binding qualities of interdependence, it is not an unalloyed contributor to cooperation. China's going global has increased its points of contact and interests around the world. With contact comes friction. With interests come desires to protect them. Thus increased interdependence is an impulse that tends to promote more cooperative behavior, but it also generates friction.

THE REALIST IMPULSE
Power and Interest

Considerations of power and interest are never far from the thinking of Chinese foreign policy practitioners and citizens alike. Weak states have less say than strong ones, or, as General Jiang Youshu put it at the beginning of this chapter, "A power without power will be bullied." In talking about why the Taiwan issue is so hard to resolve, President Jiang Zemin put it in very straightforward terms: "Why is a solution so elusive? I was thinking and wondered if I should share my frank thoughts with you before this meeting. I think of an analogy. Taiwan has a population of 20 million, and us, 1.2 billion. Though Taiwan sees itself as rich, but the mainland is bigger. Like a skinny and a fat person. I weigh over eighty kilos. Well, if we have a fight, it won't be a problem for me to win, but if a big guy stands by him and says, 'Don't fight,' I will think for a while."[51]

With respect to interest, General Zhang Wannian put it succinctly: "I suggest that both sides [the United States and China] proceed from the big picture—not seek small interests at the expense of larger interests."[52]

Balance and stability are core interests in the realms of Chinese domestic governance and foreign policy, and for good reason—when balance and stability are lost in a society of such demographic and geographic scale, or in such a fractured region as Asia, it becomes exceedingly difficult to restore equilibrium. The cascading ramifications of instability in such circumstances can be huge and unpredictable. The cultivation of balance and stability in both domestic and foreign policy is a major aspect of leading China and has been for thousands of years. Maintaining macrostability requires Beijing to keep adjusting its specific microrelationships. In April 1991, Foreign Minister Qian Qichen told journalist David Gergen, as the USSR was rapidly declining and the United States was approaching its unipolar moment, "No one in the world wants to see one center [the United States]. Nor do I believe it is possible."[53] In the Chinese worldview, there is an expectation of fluidity and constantly shifting alignments. Shortly after the Soviet Union collapsed, Foreign Minister Qian Qichen predicted that its demise would create conditions for more conflict between Washington and its Cold War–era allies in Europe and Japan: "With the old enemy gone, conflict with [your] allies will increase."[54]

Power is central to maintaining stability and balance, not to mention achieving dominance or hegemony. The acquisition of power is the absolute precondition for survival, a lesson learned repeatedly throughout Chinese history. Invasion by the Mongols resulted in the establishment of the Yuan dynasty (1279–1368); invasion by the Manchus resulted in the founding of the Qing dynasty (1644–1911); Japan's invasion and occupation of China in the 1930s and 1940s led to unspeakable consequences. This history—along with the record of encroachment by the West in the nineteenth and twentieth centuries—was a harsh teacher. Many late nineteenth-century and early twentieth-century Chinese scholars and modernizers simply defined China's national task as becoming "rich and powerful" (fu qiang guojia). In twenty-first-century China an analytic industry of considerable size is devoted to measuring the nation's growing power in relationship to its chief comparators, the United States, Japan, India, Europe, and Russia.[55] Chinese leaders and citizens alike see China as moving up the global power hierarchy and are very interested in accurately measuring that progression. However, while most Chinese citizens feel pride and empowerment in their progress toward modernization, they also know that their country has a long way to go and that the progress to date is fragile—a realization that has hit with renewed force after the initial exuberance in the wake of American difficulties and China's continued but slower rate of growth following the global financial crisis. In 2009, 41 percent of Chinese saw their country as the world's leading economic power—by 2012, this had declined to 29 percent.[56]

Mao Zedong had power and balance at the forefront of his foreign policy thinking: in 1949 allying with the Soviet Union to offset a dynamic and threatening America, then strategically reversing himself in the early 1970s to effectively ally with a Vietnam-exhausted United States in the face of a more assertive Soviet Union. As Zhou Enlai put it to Michael Blumenthal in 1973:

We should take lessons from history. The British Empire ruled the world for more than 300 years. During World War II, Churchill told Roosevelt he would not dissolve the British Empire, but actually he did. That is the way of the world. . . . After World War II, the United States was quite overweening. As President Nixon pointed out in July, 1971, in Kansas City, to correspondents: Whenever there is trouble America just sends in troops and/or money. But America has taken care of too many world affairs. He spoke the truth. The prestige of the United States is at an undreamed of low. The United States contributed to the anti-Fascist war; that is an eternal and cannot be wiped out. The same is true of the contribution of the USSR during World War II. The people of the world are grateful to the two countries. But since the United States has overextended itself, it is impossible for it to return to its isolationist position.[57]

In 1982, Mao's successors, Deng Xiaoping and Hu Yaobang, once again modified the PRC's alignment in the Sino-Soviet–United States triangle, this time to a more equidistant position. They saw a Soviet Union of waning strength as an offset to Reagan's more assertive America— Beijing's "independent foreign policy" was born. It is remarkable how rapidly China moved to this more equidistant policy, which was quite clear in Zhao Ziyang's words to a group of American governors in 1983: "Very straightforward, but not too pleasant for you to hear. The threat to China's security comes from the United States."[58] Later, in the era of President Xi Jinping, one of Xi's first moves to respond to the U.S. "pivot" to Asia announced in late 2011 was to improve relations with Moscow, which was also estranged from Washington. Xi's first trip abroad after becoming senior leader in late 2012 included Russia. The message? China has geostrategic options.

The proclivity toward balance and stability is evident not only on the grand strategic chessboard but also at China's periphery.

Southeast Asia

The degree to which equilibrium, balance, and stability dominate Chinese thinking never was clearer to me than in Beijing's decision to support the bloody Khmer Rouge regime in Cambodia from 1975 to 1979—a policy commitment that spanned the Mao Zedong/Deng Xiaoping divide. These two very different leaders came to essentially the same policy: support Pol Pot and his regime in order to keep Phnom Penh from falling under Hanoi's sway and to keep Vietnam pinned down and distracted. While Americans visiting Chinese leaders at that time sought to encourage Deng Xiaoping to withdraw support from Pol

Pot's genocidal regime, China's long-standing policy to limit Hanoi's domination of its neighbors could not be changed through reference to humanitarian concerns. If supporting Pol Pot was the price of containing Hanoi's ambitions, this was a price Beijing was willing to pay. In a June 22, 1979, conversation between Chen Muhua, vice-premier and minister of economic relations with foreign countries, and Joseph Califano, visiting U.S. cabinet secretary, Chen basically said: "If the Cambodian people have to pay for China's interests, so be it." In a conversation with Deng Xiaoping at about the same time, Deng made it clear that what bothered him was not the massacre of the Cambodian people by their own government but the fact that Vietnam's invasion of Cambodia had created a regional (indeed global) refugee crisis.

> The reason for the creation of the refugees is mainly the attack by Vietnam on Cambodia. But before that, and of course I am not going to comment on the policies of the Pol Pot group when it was in power, and to be frank we didn't agree with some of those policies. To be frank, some of the policies weren't popular. But at the time there were no refugees. . . . The cause of the exodus and a big number of refugees has to a certain extent been the result of the policies followed by Pol Pot. But the direct reason is the aggression of the Vietnamese troops against Cambodia, so the genuine settlement requires wholehearted assistance to give moral, material, and political help to the Cambodians, to force Vietnam to withdraw, and only after that will the problem be settled.[59]

Of course, giving "wholehearted assistance" to the Cambodians meant helping Pol Pot, despite his appalling human rights record. Also of great concern to Beijing was what it saw as Moscow's growing influence in Hanoi. As Vice-Premier and Foreign Minister Huang Hua put it to an American group in 1980, "So anyone trying to harm Democratic Kampuchean forces [Pol Pot] is only helping the Soviet Union."[60]

The tendency of Beijing to try to limit Hanoi by building support among regional neighbors was again clear in 2012. In July of that year Beijing induced Cambodia at a foreign ministers' meeting of the Association of Southeast Asian Nations (ASEAN) to frustrate through parliamentary maneuver other ASEAN members from adopting a concluding joint communiqué. The proposed communiqué would have addressed South China Sea disputes that the PRC wanted left unmentioned.

Central and South Asia

In Central Asia, there is an ongoing effort to balance Russian, Indian, and, since 9/11, American influence in the region. China's relations with Pakistan to offset India's power on the subcontinent demonstrate the balancing game in its clearest form. Also instructive are China's relations with Kazakhstan and China's leading role in the Shanghai Cooperation Organization (SCO). While America seems devoted to changing the world, China, as a rule, strives for balance, albeit a dynamic and ever-changing balance with few or no permanent friends *or* enemies.

North Korea

Turning to Beijing's attitudes toward and interactions with the North Korean (DPRK) regime, the PRC applies pressure to its wayward neighbor only when the DPRK's international behavior affects the PRC's international interests and Beijing is reasonably certain such pressure will not create instability that could spill into China. As one of China's senior intelligence officials explained: "'The first Chinese interest is a non-nuclear Korea. When the foreign minister of the ROK was in Beijing, he [NPC head Wu Bangguo] said he had three nightmares: (1) a nuclear DPRK; (2) war; and (3) DPRK collapse. So our national interest is to avoid all three. Kim's personality or ideology has nothing to do with us!'"[61]

China sees its main challenges with respect to the DPRK as maintaining complex balances and stability between North and South Korea, not promoting the welfare of Pyongyang's subjects (despite famines and human rights abuses); maintaining balance among the major powers entrenched on or near the peninsula (Japan, Russia, China, and the United States); and maintaining balance and stability along its own border with North Korea, where its northeastern provinces have important economic and border security interests. Yanbian Autonomous Zhou in Jilin Province, for example, has 70 percent of its trade with the DPRK,[62] not to mention a large population of ethnic Koreans with relatives across the border in the floundering North. Stability in the DPRK matters to the PRC, as the then vice-chairman of the Central Military Commission Zhang Wannian put it to former defense secretary James Schlesinger, "Any measures that contribute to stability are welcome."[63] Moving forward in time, Beijing joined with other U.N. Security Council members to sanction Pyongyang for a nuclear test in early 2013 (Pyongyang's third), but it supported only limited sanctions and even those only when it was reasonably sure that the added pressure would not destabilize the North Korean regime.

The Taiwan Strait

Though it is appropriate to emphasize the role of both foreign and domestic balance and stability in Chinese thinking, PRC leaders want to produce change from time to time. With respect to the Taiwan Strait, for example, Beijing remains committed to maintaining balance in the short and medium runs while tipping the balance in China's favor over the longer term. The problem from Beijing's strategic point of view is how to deter dangerous, secessionist moves on the island in the short and medium runs while simultaneously weakening U.S. resolve to intervene on Taipei's behalf. With a longer time horizon in mind, Beijing pushes for a fundamental change in the Taiwan-mainland relationship, counting on a steady shift in the balance of cross-Strait economic, cultural, and military power to work its magic. In 2002, one well-placed senior Chinese scholar put it to me this way:

> They [Chinese leaders] are all realists, they believe in military power, and all [of them] will think it [Chinese military power] is inadequate. In ten years [it is] unlikely to have the force to do it, take Taiwan over; after ten years [the situation] is murky. This [ten years] is the best time for Taiwan to go independent. In ten years we'll have enough strength to deter the United States in the Strait—[in] ten years we'll have [a stronger] air force, cruise missiles, a bigger strategic force, more warheads, including short-range missiles. If we devote 25 percent of our public military budget to these four items [above], U.S. intervention is not an option. Even if we attack without provocation, [it would be] tough for the United States to intervene. But we are not working on it at this pace. Once we have the capability, we should not have a first strike. Taiwan will become more careful as they know the U.S. might not be able to help. This [right now] is a dangerous time—[we are] getting the capability but [we] don't [yet] have it. Taiwan may move first.[64]

Evolving Realist Views

There has been some evolution of realist views and attitudes in China, with the gradual appearance of serious discussion among intellectuals about the degree to which "universal values" (*not* Western values) should guide China's definition of its interests and foreign policy.[65] These discussions, however, have not yet achieved a critical number of adherents among the PRC's decision makers. If an area of proposed big-power intervention is distant from China's immediate periphery, and the United Nations and/or a regional organization is calling for outside intervention (as was the case in 2011 with respect to Libya), under limited conditions Beijing may accede to a more interventionist, "universal values" approach, preferably not requiring any tangible PRC commitment of resources beyond diplomatic acquiescence. On the other hand, because the Libyan operation of NATO expanded from the responsibility to protect civilians into a regime change operation, when an analogous situation arose in Syria the following year Beijing adamantly opposed going down the interventionist road (as did Moscow).

Chinese who hold a strong realist, big-power orientation and articulate it with great passion also recognize the constraining impact of the domestic agenda. "'As long as China [faces] domestic challenges, [it] won't fight, and as it gets stronger, the U.S. [will become] more reluctant to fight.'"[66]

This brings us to a fundamental problem in the thinking of Chinese realists—they underestimate the resilience of the American system. Many focus on the technological power of the West, particularly the United States, rather than the power in its ideological, political, or cultural institutions, though in a fascinating poll of Chinese citizens' views in 2012 the Pew Global Attitudes Project found that 52 percent of surveyed Chinese "like" American ideas about democracy.[67] Nonetheless, the still apparent tendency to downplay the centrality of social/value systems is reminiscent of an older strand of late nineteenth- and early twentieth-century thinking that postulated "Chinese thinking for essence and Western thinking for use" (ti yong). In mid-1979, in a remarkable moment of introspection with China's party vice-chairman Li Xiannian as the "Democracy Wall movement" was being torn down, Li made an observation that apparently had been nagging at him—"It is very strange that in Western countries science and technology are very developed but religion is so important."[68] Reformers and some realists influenced by interdependence in the new millennium are coming to see that national power has its origins in a complex fabric of political and social institutions, patterns of thought, and values. Innovation springs from societies organized to foster it. The problem is that to be at the forefront of innovation and technology central to national power, leaders must embrace a fluid and dynamic (open) society that ultimately threatens their grip on concentrated power.

ACTION-REACTION DYNAMICS

Beyond domestic politics, interdependence, big-power politics, and realist foreign policy thinking as drivers of China's international behavior, another factor is gaining prominence in China's interaction with the

United States and its neighbors—an action-reaction dynamic driven by technological change. One nation's military-related technological advance, or even the possibility of advance, can constitute an actual or perceived threat to another state, which in turn develops what it views as offsetting, defensively inspired capabilities, thereby eliciting additional technological countermeasures by the first party. This process can create an endless upward spiral of capabilities that produces more cost and less security for everyone. An example of this dynamic involves China's 2007 successful test of an antisatellite (ASAT) weapon (which created substantial and dangerous space debris that disabled a Russian satellite in January 2013), the early 2008 U.S. use of an antisatellite weapon to destroy an aging satellite (in what many suspect was a reaction to the PRC test), and a rejoinder by the director of China's Institute of Space Law, Li Juqian: "Judging by the current development of U.S. ASAT weapons, missiles, high-energy laser weapons, particle beam weapons, microwave weapons and micro-satellites are all effective ways to destroy a satellite. They might also be the methods that China adopts."[69]

In the Chinese language the concept of *maodun* (矛盾 "contradiction") very aptly captures this process in the two ideographs that make up the word—"sword" (矛 *mao*) and "shield" (盾 *dun*). The sword and the shield each have their distinct primary purpose: usually the sword is offensive and the shield defensive (though each can be used in contrary ways when necessary: a sword can block an offensive thrust and a shield can be used to smash an adversary). The user of either the sword or the shield may have defensive motivations, but the opponent *fears* the other's offensive potential. Military development is thus a continual race between the sword and the shield, with eternal ambiguity as to how each may be used—feeding the distrust and innovation of the rival. As one Chinese general put it to visiting Americans in mid-2011, "'For China [there is] no other way but to follow the tide of military development.'"[70]

This dynamic is well under way in the U.S.-China relationship. Beijing understands this dynamic and its perils but, like security establishments elsewhere, is disinclined to assume the risks of not responding to the technological gains (or even possible gains) of other states. There is a long list of examples where this technological competition can be seen unfolding, including

- Mobile platforms to ensure the survivability of China's strategic nuclear retaliatory force

- Submarine warfare—China is developing and deploying quieter submarines
- Anti–ballistic missile defenses and penetration aids—the development of dummy warheads and multiple warheads on missiles
- Stealth technology
- Antisatellite capabilities
- Innovative missile capability to degrade U.S. aircraft carrier advantages
- China's move into space
- Cyber-warfare and intelligence capabilities

In each realm, America has existing and developing capabilities that China has sought to address or neutralize, so a dynamic of technological competition has set in between Beijing and Washington—which is sometimes reflected in the behavior of some of China's neighbors as well. Professor Sun Zhe of Tsinghua University put the Chinese perception in terms that mirror how many Americans see their situation: "We need to be able to defend ourselves, and our main threat, I'm afraid, comes from the United States."[71]

The thinking in China to which this action-reaction dynamic gives rise is illustrated by one of the PRC's foremost strategic analysts. In this quote he was responding to a question about how Beijing thinks about ensuring the security of its nuclear retaliatory force as Washington develops and deploys anti–ballistic missile (ABM) capabilities and transfers some of this capacity to U.S. friends and allies in Asia and elsewhere.

> What number of warheads does China need? It depends on how much [U.S. missile] defense we have [to deal with]. The U.S. earmarked four hundred to five hundred strategic weapons for China without missile defense. So it depends on what we [China] assume the survival rate [of Chinese missiles will be]. Then [we have to consider] what it takes to deter [the United States]. All these assumptions are superficial. . . . If the U.S. builds a space-based program, then we go for submarines. However, the U.S. may not build the antimissile system because the president changes, technical problems, and it will take a long time to deploy the system in any case. But we will go more mobile, MIRV [multi-independently targetable reentry vehicles], more survivable platforms, greater numbers, countermeasures, and penetration aids and decoys. So they [U.S. military planners after dialogue with China] can watch us and not feel surprised. We are not sitting idle. We are smarter [than to just get in a shouting match with Washington]; we don't want a rhetorical war. We don't need to stop the U.S. from enhancing its security, we only need to offset the bad parts for us.[72]

The United States has employed much the same logic in determining its program of strategic development. In June 2012, China launched its Shenzhou 9 manned space capsule with a three-person team aboard (carrying China's first woman into space) to link up with an orbiting module, Tiangong 1. The mission succeeded in docking twice, once robotically and once manually, thereafter returning safely to Earth. The year before, Beijing had unveiled plans to accomplish a manned lunar landing by 2020, and "its space agency has publicly suggested establishing a 'base on the moon as we did in the South Pole and the North Pole.'" One U.S. reaction has been to call for action to prevent a lunar land grab by Beijing, pointing to such a potential development as a "game-changer for international security."[73]

This dynamic of endless reaction and counteraction can be controlled only through greater mutual transparency; dialogue on intentions and capabilities between militaries and their national command authorities; mutual restraints agreed upon in negotiations; and cooperation. The United States and China are not close to seriously following this path, though there was a strategic component to Sino-American discussions in the first Obama administration as an add-on to the Strategic and Economic Dialogue; this process was continued as the second Obama administration began. It is ironic that Washington cooperated more with Moscow on space initiatives at the height of the Cold War than is possible with China under current U.S. law and political constraints.

So how has the Chinese worldview changed and how has it remained the same as the reform era has unfolded?

In terms of change, China has become a much more complex and pluralized actor, speaking with many, sometimes contradictory, voices. Though one should avoid exaggeration, China has also moved from being a relatively weak, inward-focused, and continent-bound nation to being a major international player with coercive, economic, and ideational power exerted not only regionally but globally. China's people and its leaders now feel empowered to be full and equal participants in regional and world affairs. Beijing is increasingly comfortable with the institutions of the global economic order—wanting to boost its influence within them—and *un*comfortable with the U.S.-led security order, founded as it is on bilateral and multilateral alliances of which China is not a part. The United Nations–led security institutions are much more congenial to Beijing.

What has remained relatively unchanged is the Chinese foreign policy tradition of realist thinking, situational ethics, and a deeply embedded sensitivity to being "bullied." Thus productively managing U.S.-China relations is possible, but it will not be simple; it will be made more complicated by a Chinese leadership that pays increasing attention to deeply embedded nationalism and public opinion.

The four contending forces shaping Chinese foreign policy discussed above lie in uneasy juxtaposition. Domestic politics can be a force pushing for either cooperation or conflict, depending on the context. Often, however, domestic politics in one country feeds caution and anxiety among outsiders, and when domestic politics feeds nationalism the ensuing sense of national empowerment can be problematic. Interdependence is a growing reality, and as China's economy and society continue to become more interconnected with the world, domestic politics is itself changed. While interdependence should moderate international conflict, it does not inoculate against it. In the aggregate, interdependence boosts the costs of conflict and therefore reduces its likelihood.

To wade into more pessimistic waters, nation-states feel compelled to constantly assess the power, intentions, and capabilities of other key actors; all these assessments are subject to misjudgment. Concern with the distribution of power among states and its uses breeds wariness that is exacerbated when there is a new, dynamic, and very large entrant into the front ranks. For example, in 2011, Vice-Minister of Foreign Affairs Mme. Fu Ying made clear a widely shared perception in her country that power among nations "is [in] a process of diffusion. It used to be within the Western world, but now it is also diffusing to a wider world."[74] In turn, all these assessments are made more subject to error by technological developments that relentlessly jeopardize the capacity of each state to protect itself.

In short, there are reasons for both hope and concern about the character of China's future global interactions. Interdependence and an imperative to focus on domestic needs will create incentives for cooperation for a long time. On the other hand, nationalism and the action-reaction cycle generally will not be constructive. How these contending forces are managed by the leadership of the United States and China will go a considerable distance in defining the character of the twenty-first century. There is a struggle for the soul of Chinese foreign policy between the realities of interdependence and the impulses of assertive nationalism.

PART TWO

China, an Up-Close View

CHAPTER 5

Nightmares

It is true that Deng [Xiaoping] brought great reforms, but since 1980 resentment of the people has been boiling up. No channels to express this, and therefore outsiders [meaning foreigners] believe China has no problems. But if you look at recent history, every two years incidents have occurred which show the resentment. In 1985 young intellectuals understood they must work to bring down the government, and the older generation of intellectuals has lost hope for the party. Realize that the only hope is that new forces released by economic reform will be the future hope of China, not the party.

—Liu Binyan, dissident Chinese journalist, speaking in New York
   City, May 31, 1989

There are in today's China eighteen regions where the people are yet to rise above the lowest standard of subsistence. Of these regions, which are historically revolutionary bases, China's back country, underdeveloped regions, or those inhabited by ethnic minority peoples, two are to be found in east China, five in central China, and eleven in the western part of the country.

—Former first party secretary of Fujian Province, Xiang Nan, July
   20, 1993

I only have one final wish before I go see God the Lord—that I will see clear scenery.

—Premier Zhu Rongji, Zhongnanhai, Beijing, April 5, 2002

"The expectations of the Chinese people are rising much faster than the capabilities of the nation. This is a big problem we have to pay attention to."

—Director general of a Beijing ministry, 2005

With this chapter we move from Part 1's focus on the principal continuities and changes in the PRC's governing, policy making, and world
outlook over the last four-plus decades to Part 2's concern with more
topical and human aspects of the system. This part is centered on what
keeps Chinese leaders awake at night, civil-military relations, and how
the Chinese negotiate. This chapter examines the many persistent anxieties of Chinese leaders.

Each post-Mao Chinese leader has experienced a particular slice of a
massive and complex society and history and, therefore, has had distinctive formative experiences. For Deng Xiaoping, the Long March,
the Anti-Japanese War (World War II), the civil war, the founding of
the PRC, and Mao's missteps of the Great Leap Forward and Cultural
Revolution were all very personal.[1] Jiang Zemin and his predecessor
General Secretary Zhao Ziyang both entered this national saga during
the "War against Japanese Aggression," as World War II is termed in
China. Zhao recounted his background by saying, "I was not in the Red
Army. I did not participate in the Long March. I joined the army and
took the gun in order to oppose the Japanese aggression."[2] For Hu Jintao and Xi Jinping, it was the Cultural Revolution and early reform era
that shaped them, albeit in differing ways: Xi Jinping had revolutionary
ancestry and thus possessed a kind of red noblesse oblige, while Hu
Jintao was a "shopkeeper's son."[3] Such categorization was common at
the time, suggesting a claimed purity attached to the offspring of revolutionaries but not to one whose father was a mere merchant. Personally, and vicariously through their family, friends, and associates, China's reform-era leaders have all survived different riptides of the first
sixty-plus years of PRC history. No matter how they came up in the
system, however, as C.H. Tung reminded us in chapter 2, they are all
"cautious."

Prior to reaching the pinnacle, China's post-Mao leaders all held jobs
in provinces and municipalities (administrative units frequently bigger
than European nations in land area and/or population) in which they
were responsible for everything—housing, food, education, public
health, disorder, the malfeasance of subordinates, and central policy
goals of all descriptions. For example, Xi Jinping's experiences in local
government in Hebei, Fujian, and Zhejiang provinces, and in Shanghai
Municipality before his step to the upper reaches of the national elite,
were critical elements of his formative experience.[4] None of these leaders ever forget that the costs of political failure in China remain high,
though not as lethal as in the Mao Zedong era.

Because the currents of Chinese politics are so strong, and the problems confronting leaders so large and complex, their default position is not to stay awake at night worrying about the United States or, for that matter, the outside world beyond Taiwan and the near periphery. The outside world rises to the top of the agenda only when unruly external actors or circumstances threaten to connect with unstable and truculent internal forces, thereby upsetting the fragile domestic balance. What has struck me in reviewing more than forty years of interviews and meetings with Chinese leaders is the consistency of their broad concerns, even if the specifics change: the peasantry, the enormous population, and the problem of feeding the people; the preservation of elite cohesiveness and mass stability; the achievement of passable policy implementation within the context of geological layers of territorial and functional administrations; economic growth, employment, and inflation; and the need to prevent "outside forces" from linking up with internal malcontents. These concerns are shared by forward-looking thinkers as well as by recalcitrant hard-liners. Leaders at all levels differ, not in their worries, but in the solutions they can envision to address them and in their governing styles.

Mass media and telecommunications are becoming ever more central, in that they instantaneously provide fodder for discontent and the means to organize and focus it—new means of communication and social networking technologies multiply the ramifications of missteps, be they domestic or international. Chinese leaders now worry about whether they appear at the scene of a domestic tragedy quickly enough, whereas Mao could stay in the vermillion walls of Zhongnanhai as tens of millions starved.[5] Public opinion has become more important, new communications amplify it, and, paradoxically, a China that is increasingly open finds its leaders trying to control proliferating channels of communication.

Chinese leaders look at the world from the perspective of how it affects China, rather than how China affects the world, though this narrow aperture is gradually enlarging as China's capacities and interests extend ever farther from its shores. Chinese leaders' nightmares concern huge social groups while Americans focus on individuals, as we heard in chapter 2 when Premier Wen Jiabao told a visiting member of the U.S. Congress that he didn't have time to think about individuals because he had to worry about a mass of 1.3 billion.[6]

DOMESTIC BAD DREAMS

The Peasantry, Population, and Food

In the initial stages of reform, China's national and local leaders feared there would be a "blind influx" of peasants into cities as preexisting social and economic controls eroded, communes disintegrated, and opportunities expanded in urban areas. The initial strategy, therefore, was to find nonagricultural jobs in the countryside for displaced agricultural labor, as Sichuan's governor Yang Xizong explained in 1983: "Once agriculture is mechanized, we must find appropriate jobs for the peasants in the countryside. We can't absorb them in the cities."[7] Nonetheless, as big-export industries and globalization kicked in, and the need for factory and construction labor grew rapidly in China's big cities, especially along the coast, the rural-to-urban migration turned from a trickle into a torrent.

At the end of 2011, for the first time in China's history, the rural population fell below half of the total population—to 48.7 percent. China today has passed the tipping point of becoming an urban nation. Consequently, PRC leaders will become progressively more preoccupied with urban problems, including the difficult challenges of governing a growing middle class. Despite the population shift, however, rural issues remain very important for leaders at all levels.

The Chinese population remaining in dismal circumstances in the countryside remains large—the average rural resident's per capita income was a little over $US1,100 (6,977 RMB) in 2011, with wide variation among localities.[8] This rural mass has a long history of instability and tragedy, something that Mao's successors have not forgotten—his was a peasant-led revolution, after all. This historically induced (though gradually fading) focus on rural areas is exacerbated in contemporary China by the current massive conversion of agricultural land to other uses. An individual who was present at a conversation between President Obama (on his first trip to China) and Premier Wen Jiabao reports that the premier expressed his concern about the rural problems he faced, saying—"How would you like to have eight hundred million farmers when you only need two hundred million? I have six hundred million [surplus] farmers"[9]—nearly three hundred million more people than in the U.S. population.

Although China's rural households have experienced growing average incomes over the reform era, they have numerous grievances, many of which stem from the means by which local governments finance the centrally imposed mandates for which inadequate national resources are provided. Local finances are substantially dependent on land transfer taxes, taxes on resource extraction, and taxes on industrial enterprises—with the "real estate industry" accounting for between 40 and 60 percent of local government revenues.[10] In addition, a large number of provincial and lower-level bureaucrats depend on real estate–related revenue streams to pay their salaries. The strategy many local governments have employed is to force peasants off the land and into modern apartment blocks in nearby towns, thereby creating high-density living complexes, freeing up land that can be sold (or used as collateral) by government to finance operations and projects (and fuel corruption).[11] The dispossessed are usually paid far less for their land use rights than any reasonable free market appraisal would suggest. Much of the rural populace feels cheated, torn from the land, and deprived of the security that land traditionally has provided. In Chinese, *laojia* is a concept that means an ancestral home, where one's relatives are buried and where one always has a place to return. Millions of peasants' native homes are being ripped from their possession.

In addition to being a source of discontent in the villages, this process affects the rural migrants who have moved into cities, because they are often uncertain how long they may remain there. The appropriation of land back in their villages severs the lifeline that land in their home villages has traditionally represented. So, for example, when there is an economic downturn affecting construction and export industries in the cities that employ huge numbers of rural migrants, as in 2008–9, and waves of migrant workers return to their official residence where they no longer have land use rights, there have been some significant disturbances.[12] The entire process inflames those peasants who move into high-density apartments or have otherwise become dispossessed from the land on which they have relied, in addition to making urban migrants less secure and fueling corruption among local officials. The central government has great difficulty controlling these situations happening all over China. And there is a lack of will locally to control these land grabs, given the need to finance unfunded central mandates.

These developments, combined with the environmental consequences of new, often polluting enterprises in rural areas, are two of the three largest causes of "mass incidents" in the countryside. "Mass incidents" is a large catch-all category comprising everything from small-scale demonstrations involving a handful of peasants to large-scale and protracted local violence. Chen Xiwen, director of the Central Rural Work

Leadership Group Office, reportedly explained that there are three principal sources of written peasant remonstrance to local governments nationwide: half concern land expropriations, nearly a third are due to village committee embezzlement, and the remainder relate to local environmental pollution.[13] In combination with the urban problems enumerated below, the reasons why the 2010 national budget's actual year-end expenditures for "public security" rose 14.6 percent over the preceding year (and the comparable figure for "national defense" rose "only" 7.3 percent) are quite clear.[14]

Turning to the issues of population and food, in leadership statements from over four decades it is striking how central the issue of *gross population size* has been to Beijing. In recent years, this concern has been compounded by justifiable alarm at some structural features of China's population. During the reform period there has been an evolution from worrying about having the ability to feed people toward a concern about becoming dangerously dependent on the world food system (even though the country is benefitting greatly from its nutritional interdependence). Ironically, obesity is a concern in cities.

Reform-era Chinese leaders' consistent concern about the absolute size of the PRC's population is notable. In the early days of reform, the almost universal perspective was that a large population made it very difficult to *raise per capita income*—Deng's principal indicator of success, as explained in chapter 1. Prior to Deng's return to the stage in mid-1977, however, this was not the reigning population paradigm, and, indeed, it was in this realm that Deng's return to power marked a huge and immediate turnaround. In the year prior to Deng's return, Wang Hairong, Mao Zedong's grandniece and then vice-foreign minister, gave Mao's line on population when an American visitor asked, "How will China and other countries of the world cope with the problems of four to five billion people in this century?"

> *Wang:* Increase in population is good.
>
> *American visitor:* Can be good if there is enough food and resources. . . . I don't worry about China, but about countries like India and Pakistan. How are the other countries going to help them come up without the minimal means of existence?
>
> *Wang:* Each country must take care of its own living standards. It isn't a matter in which a certain amount of aid provided by other countries can resolve. As far as China is concerned, population has increased continually since Liberation. Some people say China has almost eight hundred million people, and this number is double the pre-Liberation [number].

But the standard of living of the eight hundred million is [now] better than that of the [previous] four hundred million.[15]

In contrast, led by Deng, from the late 1970s on, China's leaders saw their country as having a window of opportunity for dramatic economic progress, a window that might remain open for only a limited time. Deng worried that if the party didn't quickly produce significant gains in per capita income the regime would lose what (little) legitimacy remained. For Deng, every new mouth to feed slowed per capita gains. So for the next two decades very little attention was given to the long-term results of the harsh one-child policy, one of which was to help produce an inverted age pyramid that would create a rapidly aging population—a huge elderly cohort with a relatively small group of younger individuals to support them. It is this consistent concern with per capita income in the short run that goes a considerable way in explaining the more than three-decade-long adherence to the (evolving) one-child policy. Central Committee Secretary Hu Qili put it concisely in 1985: "Population growth is closely linked with per capita income. We must take care and work hard to speed up economic development."[16]

As exemplified by Vice-Premier Li Xiannian's 1979 commitment to prevent starvation, food was very much on the minds of those who were or had been military officers because for the most part they (e.g., Li Xiannian) as well as their troops came from agricultural areas. Issues of the PLA's *Bulletin of Activities* (*Gongzuo Tongxun*) during the crushing famine of the Great Leap Forward's aftermath record the privations of both army troops and their families who were essentially stranded on islands of starvation across the sea of rural China.[17] I was struck by General and Vice-Premier Geng Biao's 1978 conversation with an American delegation—it was almost as if he were responding directly to the leftist claptrap of Vice-Minister Wang Hairong cited above: "It is futile to deck oneself out as a beauty if you are ugly and people won't believe you. In the past the Gang of Four described our backwardness as progressive and advanced. No, our country, but our people must learn from their past and from their experiences. Then our people become rich, our country will become strong. To take food grains, for example. The average food grain consumption is three hundred [kilos?] per year [per capita]. Not enough. So, among the Four Modernizations, one is on agriculture."[18]

Moving on to the year 2000, Geng Biao's secretary (*mishu*), Xi Jinping, who became China's most senior leader in fall 2012, recalled the nutritional privation he had encountered in the late 1960s and 1970s in rural Shaanxi, where he had spent seven years:

> I grew up in the seven years I was in Shaanxi. I learned two important things. First, I had the opportunity to understand what real life looks like, what is right and wrong, and who ordinary people are. These were experiences for life. Right as I had arrived at the village, many beggars would often appear. As soon as they turned up, the dogs would be set on them. At the time we students had the opinion that all beggars were "bad elements" and tramps. We did not know the saying *"In January there is still enough food, in February you will starve, and March and April you are half alive, half dead."* For six months all families would live only on bark and herbs. Women and children were sent out to beg, so that the food could go to those who were working in the fields with the spring ploughing. You had to live in a village to understand it. When you think of the difference there was at that time between what the central government in Beijing knew and what actually happened in the countryside, you must shake your head.[19]

In the second decade of the new millennium, Chinese leaders often express concern about the structure of the population, in no small part due to China's rapid urbanization, demographic transition, and the cumulative consequences of the one-child policy. As one senior American diplomat put it succinctly in 2012, "The math just doesn't work." The one-child policy produced an age structure with one child, two parents, and four grandparents.[20] A young married couple will need to plan to potentially support four parents. There now is a continually rising retiree-to-worker ratio, just as more internal mobility allows children to move far from their place of birth, and therefore their parents.

These population developments will be a drag on economic productivity and raise social safety net costs. Keeping labor productivity growing in the face of a rising retiree-to-worker ratio requires substituting capital for labor, expanding education, improving labor quality, and increasing R&D. With the tide of elderly rising, the costs of building even a modest social safety net will increase dramatically. Any one of these tasks on its own is a challenge—taken together they cause insomnia among Chinese leaders. And this is before the skewed gender ratio in which about 119 males are born for every 100 females is taken into consideration. This gender imbalance has arisen from the confluence of the one-child policy, a cultural preference for males, and the widespread availability of ultrasound sex determination technology. This confluence has created a reality in which tens of millions of young males (mostly rural) are without the prospect of finding a mate.[21] There is pressure to change the one-child policy, and, as described earlier, in

2013 steps were taken to put the policy under more professional medical scrutiny.

Workers and Urban-Industrial Issues

In the era of reform, several developments constitute the tinder of worker discontent in industrial enterprises, with flare-ups periodically erupting as "mass incidents." In 1979, then vice-chairman Li Xiannian put his finger on one of the causes of worker unrest very succinctly: "How to solve unemployment. To tell the truth, it is a problem."[22] Twenty-six years later, a senior Chinese economist told visiting members of Congress, "'The whole world is talking about jobs going to China, but we are talking about where to get another two hundred to three hundred million jobs.'"[23]

Thus far, periodic, localized "mass incidents" have not coalesced across geographic areas, nor have workers been permitted to organize in a way that makes them an effective unified force. Were either of these phenomena to develop, it would be a game changer for the entire Chinese political system. China's leaders have used the All-China Federation of Trade Unions (ACFTU) to try to preempt discontent and, if unrest breaks out, to keep it contained. Nonetheless, there is some indication that the ACFTU itself is beginning to act as a somewhat more effective advocate of worker interests (particularly with respect to multinational firms), as seen in the Labor Contract Law of 2008 and in light of the Walmart experience in the PRC.[24] With respect to Walmart, for instance, in 2006 the generally antiunion company agreed to have the ACFTU present in all its outlets and two years later capitulated to PRC union demands for worker pay increases. It is hard to imagine that ACFTU can support worker demands in foreign-owned enterprises and not soon be subject to its members' demands that the union also represent the interest of workers in domestic facilities.

The sources of the workers' discontent, expressed in job actions, worker suicides, and other violence, include

- Layoffs of workers stemming from restructuring, winding down, or consolidating small, medium, and some large state enterprises (as occurred on a vast scale in the latter part of the 1990s and into the new millennium), and layoffs stemming from volatility in the global economy and trade-related export peaks and valleys (as occurred in the wake of the global financial crisis in 2008–9)

- Poor environmental and other working conditions in factories—
notable examples include multinational firms such as Taiwan's
Foxconn (in part, an Apple subcontractor that in 2012 employed
about 1.2 million workers in China and was accused of using
forced student employees on assembly lines, among other
things)[25]
- Straightforward issues of pay and overtime
- Conflicts of interest between "permanent" or "regular" workers
(with legal residence) in the cities and "migrant" or "contract"
laborers working in factories without permanent legal urban
status: the former group generally has better terms of employment and quality of life, while the latter group lives in legal
limbo, enduring less favorable terms of employment and inferior
access to educational, health, and other services for themselves
and their families

In April 2002, some members of the U.S. Congress met with Zhu
Rongji as he was entering the last year of his premiership, a time at
which the government had been laying off, retraining, or otherwise
dealing with tens of millions of displaced urban industrial workers. One
senior congressman asked the premier: "[I have been] reading about
protests regarding economic dislocation. Most recently, worker actions
and police actions, [protesters] have been indicted, put in jail. 'What do
you think is the proper response?'" Premier Zhu's answer revealed that
his daily routine included receiving a list of urban, worker-related disturbances:

> In the last few years of reform, China has been deepening reform of the state
> enterprises. Without these efforts it would have been impossible for China to
> have such great economic success. In the restructuring, it is inevitable that
> some plants are closed, that workers are laid off. Even the famous oil field of
> Daqing has declining production, so our only choice is to reduce the work-
> force—there is no other choice. I think if we simply show no regard for
> workers or use violence against workers we betray our ideas—we are the
> Communist Party. Therefore, we are trying to establish social security and to
> meet their needs. However, because we are poor, it is impossible to have
> benefits like the Western or Nordic countries, so active workers have more
> benefits than laid-off workers. This current period is one of transition from
> the plan to the market. Where before we emphasized egalitarianism, but
> now they [the workers] feel disoriented, and that is why they take to the
> streets. It is inevitable. Every day such things happen, and each day I have a
> report telling me where workers have taken to the streets. From January 1 to
> March 28 [2002], from my bulletins, altogether there have been 265 cases of

protests with more than 50 workers. But 99 percent, not 100 percent, of workers who participated in making trouble have basic [unmet?] needs. The problem is that they [laid-off workers] think that they have made great contributions in the past and they think [ask], Why should they have less than current workers now? I think that these laid-off workers with poor education, even labor heroes, I think that their skills are not appropriate to the new economy, even with retraining. It is inevitable that large numbers will be laid off, provided with social security, but it is impossible to avoid troublemaking. But development of the market economy will lead them to have "rebalanced thought." In all these cases, all these people, we have not used violence and jailing, we generally use persuasion.[26]

If one looks at the overall picture—tens of millions dislocated from economically unviable SOEs in the late 1990s and early 2000s, ongoing tens of millions of rural migrants entering the urban labor force in various capacities and facing discrimination in both the workplace and the cities themselves, and the added number of people seeking employment because of the natural population increase—it is not surprising that there are numerous localized labor actions. The surprise is that there has not yet been more instability and that what instability there has been has been relatively effectively contained. Chinese leaders, however, can never assume that this will remain the case.

Looking to the future, as China's demographic pyramid becomes increasingly inverted, the worker-to-retiree ratio will become progressively more burdensome. Additionally, urban wages will rise as the quantity of available labor declines and the skills required of workers increase. This, in turn, will generate new challenges, including cost pressures on exports and domestically consumed items. Chinese and foreign industries are already responding to the demographic shift by pushing ever farther into the PRC interior or even outside China to find cheaper production sites. Further, increasing productivity will need to compensate for rising labor costs if the PRC is to remain competitive.

Environmental, industrial, and urban issues increasingly converge on disputes concerning plant location, particularly polluting facilities, often in the petrochemical industry. In October 2012, demonstrations against a Sinopec petrochemical plant's expansion in Ningbo, Zhejiang, became a particularly alarming example for central authorities. The protests began with suburban farmers and then spread to the city's urban middle-class and student population, turning violent and engaging riot forces with thousands of citizens, with demonstrators calling for resignation of the city fathers. After substantial violence the government backed down on the project, leading the Beijing environmental activist Ma Jun to say: "We've seen the same pattern over and over again. . . . Ignoring public concerns leads to confrontation. We can't resolve all our environmental issues through street action. The cost is just too high."[27]

Environmental concerns also impinge on the sustainability of industrial and urban growth. Since the 1950s, for example, China's leaders at all levels have been concerned with the sustainability of growth in the cities, industry, and agriculture of the North China Plain—Where is the water needed to nourish such growth going to come from? As early as 1982, my field notes from interviews at the Yangzi River Valley Planning Authority in Wuhan record that there was consideration of this dilemma: "The idea of diverting water from south to north was proposed even before Liberation, but no research was done. After Liberation, this idea was proposed by Mao, among others, in 1952. The idea of moving water north out of the Yangzi was part of the 1958 general basin plan, although no specific route was picked."[28]

These early plans, finally being implemented in the new millennium, were a response to the fact that cities on the North China Plain were fighting for water—urban areas were clashing with upstream rural areas, and provinces were already at each others' throats for water. In the past fifty years, all these problems have only become worse, with the water table across the entire northern plain dropping about one meter per annum. Effectively coping with this problem requires more efficient water use and demand management rather than a focus on engineering projects to supply more water from distant locales. Increasingly throughout China, but particularly in the arid north and west, China's leaders will find themselves dealing with ever more contentious water problems that could explode into significant instability.

Economic Growth and Volatility

The CCP holds power and obtains legitimacy on the basis of performance. *Performance* is defined principally as improved and more secure material conditions, though quality-of-life considerations are gradually assuming more salience, particularly in cities. Yet choking (literally) on urban air in China is becoming an explosive issue. It has thus far been hard to balance ecological, public health, and economic growth considerations when China's leaders are hard-wired to prioritize economic growth. The first five "Main Goals" specified in the Twelfth Five-Year Plan (2011–15) are: "We will achieve steady and rapid economic development. GDP will increase at an average annual rate of 7%. Forty-five million new urban jobs will be created. The urban registered unemployment rate will not exceed 5%. The overall price level will remain basically stable."[29] Economic growth and stability are the central preoccupations of Chinese leaders.

Local leaders and those responsible for economic units are evaluated for promotion and reward principally on the basis of the economic performance of their localities or units. The holy trinity for Chinese national leadership on the topic of the economy is: achieve high growth, avoid great volatility (both in prices and in employment), and avoid losing control over domestic economic policy and performance because of linkages to the global economy. Of all the economic topics mentioned over the last forty-plus years of interviews, inflation was by far the most frequently raised and the most anxiety-laden. My notes of a 1994 meeting with China's chief science official, Song Jian, illustrate this anxiety: "Inflation of 13 percent is not good, too hot, so now we need to cool it off. We need to reduce the construction scale. If these [hot, inflationary forces] are not controlled, 'it is very dangerous' [hen weixian] and social problems are a lot. There could be student riots. Bankers should tell us how [to avoid inflation]!"[30]

The regime's preoccupation with inflation dates back to the second half of the 1940s, when a dramatic upward price spiral corroded support for the Kuomintang (KMT) during the civil war. In the 1980s, growth rates and price volatility were substantial. In 1985 Politburo member and Central Committee secretary Hu Qili told visitors, "[I] hope within three years the growth rate gradually will slow down. . . . July to September, [the growth rate was] 21 percent; September it was 14.7 percent. . . . Circulation of currency is under control and prices are stable."[31] Early in 1989, inflation topped out in the 20-plus percent range according to China's State Statistical Bureau—a development that motivated urbanites to hit the streets in the Tiananmen-related disturbances of May and June, as NPC head Wan Li explained to majority leader of the U.S. House of Representatives Thomas Foley on the eve of the crackdown.[32]

Post-1989 performance in achieving price stability (as measured by the annual change in the Consumer Price Index) has improved somewhat over time, but it remains a real concern, with the regime relying on a hard-to-implement mix of administrative and macroeconomic tools.[33] Since 1995, inflation has remained below 10 percent and volatility has gone down dramatically, but whenever prices rise (as they did for periods in 2004, 2007, and 2010) leaders worry enough to take prompt measures.

Economic growth and price stability are seen as preconditions for political stability, which is an overriding goal for Chinese leaders. The policy challenge is that high rates of growth create upward price pressures ("overheating"), environmental impacts, and social dislocations that are actually incompatible with political stability. Reconciling all of these not entirely consistent objectives of political stability, modest price increases, high-speed growth, and low unemployment certainly keeps China's leaders awake at night. As then vice-premier Zhu Rongji reflected on one episode of dealing with inflation, "In 1993, I couldn't sleep when the economy was overheated."[34]

In the period from the late 1990s on, episodes of high price volatility (particularly the move from high inflation rates to deflation over a short period) have been connected to instabilities in the international economic environment. In 1997–98 the Asian financial crisis caused prices to deflate rapidly in China, as did the 2008–9 global financial crisis. In such cases, China's leaders move rapidly to stimulate growth and insulate the domestic system as much as possible from the vagaries of the international economy. Insulating Chinese domestic economic performance from the international system's condition, however, is becoming progressively more difficult given China's growing linkages to global trade and finance. Moreover, understandable attempts to insulate China from international volatility can be viewed abroad as naked protectionism.

In March 2007, on the eve of the global financial crisis, Premier Wen Jiabao presciently sensed the turmoil ahead, talked about the sources of economic instability in China and its links to the international system, and explained how PRC leaders could never take economic stability for granted. "China's economy has maintained fast yet steady growth in recent years. *However, this gives no cause for complacency, neither in the past, nor now, nor in the future.* My mind is focused on the pressing challenges. 'A country that appears peaceful and stable may encounter unexpected crises.' There are structural problems in China's economy which cause unsteady, unbalanced, uncoordinated and unsustainable development. Unsteady development means overheated investment as well as excessive credit supply and liquidity and surplus in foreign trade and international payments" (emphasis added).[35]

Income inequality (as measured by the Gini coefficient, discussed earlier) is a second-order concern, most apparent when fears concerning social polarization and instability are growing. Reducing poverty has been a central goal of China's leaders since the beginning of the reform period, but the bedrock belief is that a rising tide lifts all boats. So at any given moment addressing rural poverty and income inequality has its champions, but it is not generally a first-tier priority.

Disasters—Natural and Manmade

China's enormous population inhabits a dangerous continent. Chinese history, from ancient times, is often recounted by reference to the mileposts of natural and sometimes manmade calamities. Some of the markers of the communist era are the Yangzi River Flood of 1954, the Great Leap Forward policy-induced famine of the late 1950s and early 1960s, the Tangshan earthquake (1976), simultaneous inundations in three parts of China in 1998, and the Wenchuan earthquake (2008). These calamities are calibrated in hundreds of thousands or even millions of dead, injured, and displaced persons, and they leave imprints on leaders and citizens for decades—sometimes centuries—after their occurrence. A 1992 conversation with President Jiang Zemin made this fact of life clear, even when it was stated in President Jiang's stream-of-consciousness manner.

> Last year we had heavy floods, and it reminds me of the serious floods in 1931 in Yangzhou, my native city—flood, walked around in bath towels. Last year during the floods I went to the Huai River. My heart was sad to see water at the banks. Then I saw young people playing there. I wondered why they didn't take the flood seriously—because of bumper harvest, we had huge grain reserves. Then I remember last winter, cold and no clothes, so we provided them to flood victims. Three months later I went back to flood areas and saw construction everywhere. The fact that we have nine hundred million farmers and have stability in the countryside and this contributes to overall stability.[36]

Each day as they get out of bed, Chinese leaders have in the backs of their minds the knowledge that natural forces or incompetent (and perhaps malevolent) subordinates in the system may create a catastrophic circumstance with which they must deal and which may also strike a blow at regime legitimacy. The degree to which leaders handle crises well can bolster regime legitimacy; the degree to which the regime is responsible for crises or mishandles them (as in the case of the man-made policy calamity of the Great Leap Forward or the collapse of shoddy infrastructure during the 2008 earthquake in Sichuan) can just as easily erode regime legitimacy.

Vice-Premier Zhu Rongji, speaking with former U.S. ambassador to China Leonard Woodcock, verbalized this "you never know" attitude that seems to be a part of the DNA of a Chinese leader, saying, "I sometimes wake up on the agriculture problem. In 1993–94, China suffered drought and flood, food reserves dropped by half. Last year we had a good harvest, summer harvest, so no need to import grain at all. But we still want to import at good prices. We want better grain stocks—*you never know*" (emphasis added).[37]

Under a media microscope, the way world leaders respond to floods, earthquakes, and all manner of natural and manmade tragedies can affect their capacity to effectively govern, as U.S. president George W. Bush found with Hurricane Katrina in 2005 and Russian president Vladimir Putin found when he failed to end his vacation to personally take charge of the disaster surrounding the sinking of the Kursk, a nuclear-powered submarine that went down in 2000, losing 118 seamen. China's premier Wen Jiabao made widely acknowledged efforts throughout his two terms to expeditiously and personally respond in such circumstances, as did President Hu Jintao—seeming to learn from the mishaps of other world leaders. Indeed, in August 2009, Taiwan's president Ma Ying-jeou was caught unprepared by Typhoon Morakot, which dropped 109.3 inches of water on the island in a matter of days, killing more than six hundred people.[38] As a result of what was widely perceived to be inadequate government disaster planning and response, President Ma's approval rating dropped to what was then an all-time low of 16 percent.[39] This represented a decline of 25 percentage points since June of that same year.[40]

Given the rush to build infrastructure in China, both to spur economic development and to provide stimulus to keep domestic demand and employment up in the face of slowdown, China has built breathtaking numbers of roads, bridges, buildings, dams, high-speed railroads, power plants, and other structures since the 1980s. Some of this, often poorly built *doufu* (bean curd) construction, decays rapidly and requires serious maintenance almost as soon as it is completed. Consequently, major project failures provide a constant stream of tragedies that China's leaders must address. Infrastructure failures almost immediately veer into discussions of how the projects were overseen, how licensing occurred, who got paid to look the other way as concrete was adulterated or reinforcing bar not used, and how high up the leadership chain corruption goes. In August 2012, for example, a brand-new ramp on a river bridge in Harbin collapsed, killing three, with one Internet commentator immediately saying: "Corrupt officials who do not die just continue to cause disaster after disaster."[41] The 2008 Wenchuan earthquake morphed from a natural disaster into a political disaster when large groups of grieving parents demonstrated against officials they held accountable for the substandard construction of the collapsed schools in which their children had died.

Earthquakes are a good example of the degree to which dealing with calamities is a prominent part of a Chinese leader's job description at every level. In the 1900–2012 period, China had four of the world's top twelve earthquakes ranked by the number of deaths (two in the top five). The Tangshan quake of 1976 killed at least 242,769 persons, while the Huaiyan quake of 1920 killed 200,000. The Wenchuan earthquake of 2008 killed 87,587. By way of comparison, Europe had one earthquake in the top twelve (Messina in 1908, killing 72,000) and the United States has had none; the 1906 San Francisco earthquake killed three thousand—a toll that ranks number 63 on the U.S. Geological Survey global earthquake list of events with one thousand or more fatalities since 1900.[42] From 1900 to 2012, China had eleven quakes that inflicted three thousand or more deaths, with most eclipsing three thousand fatalities. This reflects the relatively seismically active area in which China is located, poor building standards, inadequate code compliance, substandard construction materials, and density of population. In short, China's leaders must deal with this relatively high level of danger in addition to the corruption that frequently becomes part of the explanation for why calamities are so devastating.

Now we turn to the flood danger, an age-old fear because of the way people have historically settled near water sources, particularly in China's rice-dependent culture. In the summer flooding of 1998, concurrent with the Asian financial crisis, President Jiang Zemin had to face nearly simultaneous inundations in south central China, southern China near Vietnam, and the north near Russia, with the last flood area being the most devastating. The heaviest downpour was in June and July in Qinzhou, Guangxi, reaching a biblical 68.28 inches (six and one-half feet) of rain during the storm's duration. The U.S. National Oceanographic and Atmospheric Administration reports that 3,656 people were killed in these inundations, with an overall impact on upwards of 240 million people—demolishing or damaging seventeen million homes, leaving fourteen million people homeless, and causing an estimated $20 billion in damage.[43]

In the wake of these disasters, there is often a component of official action or policy found wanting by the Chinese public or international observers, not to mention Chinese leaders themselves. Before the development and spread of broadcast television, cable TV, the Internet, cellular communication devices, and social media, the regime could limit the knowledge and visual impact of such events. For example, in the 1975 collapse of the very large, poorly constructed Banqiao and Shimantan dams in Henan Province, a reported 85,600 persons died and the disaster affected millions—flooding twenty-nine counties and municipalities following a typhoon, the worst dam collapse in world history. Ask Chinese who were around at that time, and generally they will not remember the details because the government was able to hide the extent of the damage. The media and communications machines were still highly controlled, commercialization of the media was nonexistent, and the personal communications revolution had not yet started.[44]

In other cases, there were significant delays in reporting (particularly manmade) disasters, such as the November 13, 2005, Songhua River benzene spill that started in Jilin Province and rapidly affected the drinking water of major downstream cities. The pollution plume was well on its way to Russia before the problem was publicly acknowledged by local and company officials (and the State Environmental Protection Agency, or SEPA). As a United Nations Environment Programme Field Mission report delicately put it, PRC "authorities at different levels" did "take timely and appropriate mitigation measures," but "unfortunately, this effective effort of SEPA had not been communicated with the public sufficiently. Had this communication been adequately provided, the level of uncertainty and fear by [the] public would have been lower."[45] In plain English, I believe this UN report translates to something like this: local officials were slow in reporting the initial large incident to superiors, and more dilatory still in communicating pertinent facts to the Chinese public and to the Russians downstream. International authorities were not informed of the spill until November 26, thirteen days after the petrochemical plant explosion set off the incident. "Both the President and the Prime Minister [of China] extended their apologies to the Russian Government."[46]

A final example of the range of calamities that await all Chinese leaders comes from the biological realm. In late 2002 a coronavirus (severe acute respiratory syndrome [SARS]) hit China hard. This disease had its probable origins in the wet markets of South China and initially was extremely alarming because the mode of transmission was not well understood and its mortality rate was high. Beyond creating global alarm, the viral outbreak also brought worldwide criticism down on

PRC leaders for delaying acknowledgment that there was even a threat and for not being forthcoming with accurate and timely information. The accumulated result of the initial unknowns concerning the disease and the lack of information in (and from) the PRC set off panic in Chinese cities and villages to the point that alarmed citizens in many places threw up road barricades to prevent "outsiders" from coming into their areas. Most importantly, the disease took a substantial human toll— 8,098 stricken and at least 774 deaths worldwide, with the most fatalities occurring in the PRC (348), Taiwan (84), Hong Kong (298), Singapore (32), and Canada (38).[47]

This episode provided a discordant note on which Jiang Zemin left office. In addition, the minister of public health, Zhang Wenkang (who was personally close to Jiang), and the mayor of Beijing, Meng Xuenong, were sacked by incoming general secretary and president Hu Jintao, thereby boosting Hu's initial public standing. Beyond the lessons concerning disease management in a globalized world, there are other lessons for Chinese leaders: a leader's legacy is insecure until he or she is fully out of office (and perhaps not even then), and a central leader can turn calamity, if properly handled, into political support.

EXTERNAL FEARS

Taiwan

Though considered an "internal affair" by Beijing, Taiwan has been beyond Beijing's control since the PRC's founding and hence is appropriately treated in this section. From the earliest interview among those used for this volume (a July 17, 1971, meeting in which Premier Zhou Enlai was conversing with a group of visiting American scholars), the island has been identified as *the* dominant issue in U.S.-China relations: "Taiwan is a province of China and it is an inalienable part of China's territory," the premier instructed his young visitors in 1971. Indeed, the island underlay much of the Sino-American Cold War–era conflict, dating from when President Truman inserted the U.S. Seventh Fleet between Taiwan and the mainland in June 1950.

From 1950 into the 1990s, Beijing consoled itself about the division of the motherland with the belief that people on either side of the Strait saw themselves as Chinese and as part of an entity conceived of as "China," albeit at that moment divided. The rise of the Democratic Progressive Party (DPP) on the island in the mid-1980s, the 1988 death

of Chiang Kai-shek's son, President Chiang Ching-kuo, and the evolving presidency of Taiwan-born Lee Teng-hui thereafter in the late 1980s
and 1990s gradually called into question prior assumptions about a
shared cross-Strait Chinese national identity. The period of a shared
national identity was less perilous for Beijing (even with an American
security commitment to the island) than the period when Taiwan's self-
concept drifted ever farther from that of the mainland, as was the case
from the 1990s into the new millennium. Beijing became increasingly
vulnerable to the mercurial politics of a resentful and autonomy-minded
population on the island that PRC leaders had not had to consider during the KMT's martial law period that ended in 1987.

Compounding the problem for Beijing was the unfavorable conjunction between the Tiananmen violence of June 4, 1989, and the development of democracy on Taiwan—an attractive development from a Western perspective. Consequently, Taiwan became more worrisome to the
PRC in the 1990s and into the new millennium. The situation was perilous for Beijing because any formal move by the island that was construed on the mainland as an irretrievable step toward independence
would present PRC leaders with the choice of using force in the Strait to
assert Beijing's claims or forfeiting the regime's legitimacy in the eyes of
its own people. Bluntly, Taipei had the capacity to precipitate cross-
Strait conflict and drag Washington into it by virtue of the ambiguous
U.S. security link to the island in the form of the 1979 Taiwan Relations
Act (TRA).

In May 2000, DPP candidate Chen Shui-bian was inaugurated as
Taiwan's first non-KMT president in the first peaceful transition of
power between political parties in the island's history. Given Chen's
own personal record of favoring independence, and the DPP's charter in
which the concept was embedded, the Taiwan issue moved from the
category of a long-standing worry for Beijing to that of an acute problem. By the end of his two terms (2000–2008), President Chen felt free
to tell a visiting U.S. group that China was, in effect, a paper tiger that
would be forced to accept the realities Taipei would create. The subtext
of Chen's thinking was that Washington was too deferential to the
mainland and that, in the final analysis, America would not let a democracy go down the drain:

> "In the past, the PRC opposed Taiwan during the election of a president, etc.
> Whenever Taiwan tries to consolidate democracy; it was displeased when
> martial law ended; displeased with elections; similarly displeased when we
> recognize referendum rights and human rights—many in the world have

these; China opposes it. Similarly, in the KMT administration [till 2000] many democratic activists called for more freedom—the KMT said it could not do it, China will invade, to scare them away from democracy. Democratization is the world trend and our twenty-three million people's objective— we don't back down in the face of threats. So after the past two decades ended martial law, bonds on the media, overhauled the Legislative Yuan, elected mayors, held presidential elections, and in less than three years a referendum law, and we held a referendum. Last year we caused the National Unification Council to cease to exist and by so doing abolished the One China Policy." And now people on Taiwan can decide issues through referenda. "So, in the last few decades we insisted on principles and we will not stop because of oppression. The 'One Country, Two Systems' principle is a way to convert Taiwan and make it a local government. People cannot accept this, or being a part of the PRC, or China. So China can oppose, but the twenty-three million Taiwan people will not be affected or stop pursuing their ideals or objectives. I may not see this dream in office but I may live to see it."[48]

From the 1996 inauguration of Lee Teng-hui as president after the first island-wide popular election, Beijing progressively felt that no matter which tools it employed to try to dampen this independence tendency, it elicited increasingly pronounced reactions from Taiwan and its people. In 1995–96, Beijing ill-advisedly launched missile shots off the island's shores in the hope of driving votes away from Lee, only to have that effort boomerang. In 2000, Premier Zhu Rongji warned Taiwan voters against electing Chen Shui-bian—Chen won in a cliff-hanger that Beijing may have helped push the challenger's way. After Chen's election, Chinese President Jiang Zemin entertained the idea of a "time line" for reunification, but this too proved unable to rein in the island. After he succeeded Jiang Zemin as president, China's new supreme leader, Hu Jintao, struggled with how to minimize the risks posed by Chen, eventually settling on a two-pronged approach: (1) passing an "Anti-Secession Law" in 2005 as a deterrent (accompanied by an ongoing buildup of missiles that could be targeted on the island and proceeding with naval and military modernization), and (2) changing the policy emphasis from "reunification" to "no independence" and cross-Strait "peaceful development." This move put a number of Beijing's eggs in the basket of interdependence, which, in turn, pulled the two sides of the Strait together on the economic front, while not perceptibly changing Taiwan's identity in a more "Chinese" direction.

In the Taiwan election of 2008, Beijing hoped that the DPP candidate, Frank Hsieh, would lose to his KMT adversary, Ma Ying-jeou, with whom Beijing felt more comfortable. Having learned its lesson about the boomerang effect of interventions, Beijing remained largely silent throughout the election, figuring that anything it did would backfire. Ma won, and, as a senior Beijing analyst put it, President Hu Jintao "'can have high-quality sleep.'"[49]

Even so, on the mainland increasing pluralization of society and the rise of "public opinion" (nationalism) are growing forces in policy. Combined with Taiwan's own developing democracy and the attendant uncertainties, and an antiunification sentiment that has grown across the political spectrum on the island, this means that there is the ever present possibility of a fast-emerging crisis that might be only minimally under mainland (or Washington's) control. One senior Beijing analyst put the PRC perspective thus: "'Taiwan has too many collective irrationalities. Though our leaders have more and more interest groups and while leaders pay attention to Taiwan, the public may not. If mainland people lose patience, then people [on the mainland] will abandon this sophisticated approach and go for a simple solution. Our society is very diversified and we underestimate political change on the Taiwan side, we underestimate the instability of establishing democracy. [Mature] democracy may be stable, but not getting there.'"[50]

The point of this case study of Taiwan is simple: Beijing's leaders may be authoritarian, they may have an enormous span of control, and they may have growing resources at their command, but on this issue they are at the mercy of events and passionate publics on both sides of the Strait. It is not clear that Beijing's "good sleep" with respect to Taiwan will last.

The Perils of Being "Bullied"

As China historically (and even today) sees itself as having been bullied, it proves prickly to deal with, even as it becomes stronger—creating the fear among its neighbors that it will itself become the bully.

Every nation has its national narratives structuring popular and leadership thinking about foreign policy, providing frameworks by which citizens assess the fitness of their leaders, and setting standards that contending domestic leadership groups use in their own internecine struggles. These narratives help establish the "boundaries of the permissible" that fence in leadership decisions and create a blinking red light on specific issues in the minds of leaders that they ignore at their peril. Understanding the PRC's national narrative is essential if one is to understand how China sees itself in relationship to both its neighbors and distant powers.

A key component of China's national narrative is that "China should never again be bullied as it was in the nineteenth and twentieth centuries." From casual conversation to formal exchanges, this narrative repeatedly appears. In passing, Vice-Chairman Li Xiannian told visiting U.S. mayors in 1979, "We were bullied by the imperialists."[51] Nearly two decades later, President Jiang Zemin gave voice to this thought, even bringing Victor Hugo into the discussion.

> Looking at China's modern history, I see suffering and bullying. I'm not so old, but from my childhood I experienced the northern warlords, the civil war, eight years of the Anti-Japanese War, the struggle between the Communists and the KMT, and then liberation. If you go to the ruined site of the Yangmingyuan [part of the Summer Palace complex destroyed in 1860 by Lord Elgin] you can have lots of reflection. This reminds me of Victor Hugo's words about Yangmingyuan. A Frenchman who took part in burning it down wrote to Hugo about it. Hugo replied: "You have destroyed a cultural pearl in the Orient. It is like two thieves: one who started the fire, and the other who stole the jewels." I admire Hugo's work, such as *Les Miserables* and *Notre Dame*.[52]

A core aspect of any Chinese leadership's legitimacy is to protect national sovereignty and dignity and never again permit China to be bullied. This shared national orientation makes China challenging to deal with because which issues are perceived to be "bullying" are, to a considerable extent, in the eye of the beholder. Is Tokyo's detention of a Chinese boat captain who is inebriated and rams into a Japanese vessel in disputed waters "bullying"? Are U.S. warships in the Yellow Sea trying to deter North Korea "bullying" China?

China's central leaders must constantly be on guard against their reactions to a particular external development morphing into a referendum on their own fitness to rule. They are in constant danger of having conciliatory behavior toward foreigners refracted through the domestic lens of "allowing China to be bullied." We see this in the South China Sea, where a sloppy, eleven-dashed line drawn by Chiang Kai-shek's ROC government in the late 1940s was bequeathed to the successor regime of the PRC, a line that Beijing modified to nine dashes after Liberation. In turn, Beijing's leaders fear that if they show flexibility with foreigners on this line that they cannot adequately explain or define, it will be construed at home as weakness—Is the CCP a less fierce guardian of China's sovereignty than Chiang Kai-shek was? If China shows weakness regarding its maritime claims in Southeast Asia, what conclusions will Japan and the Koreas reach about Beijing's steadfastness on maritime disputes with them? There is a vicious cycle of sorts, with anxious PRC leaders reiterating "China's indisputable historical rights" and thereby not only alarming smaller neighbors but also further diminishing their own domestic room for future maneuver, even if they wished to avail themselves of this space.

In no instance was the implication of the "China is bullied narrative" for PRC leaders on clearer display than when the United States/NATO inadvertently bombed the Chinese embassy in Belgrade in May 1999, as mentioned in chapter 4. As one progressive and cosmopolitan vice-minister put it:

> Therefore, to resume and improve relations the U.S. must launch an investigation, punish [the perpetrators], and compensate the victims, otherwise Chinese people won't accept it. "Chinese people have a long memory, five thousand years of history, the Opium War, and Chinese bullied, and they have a deep feeling of being humiliated and they should never again be bullied." Some Western media thought the protests were fanned up by the government; they don't know, but the Chinese government played a restraining role, cooled [it] down, otherwise the protests would have lasted longer.[53]

Looking to the future, as China's interests expand globally, its citizens and material assets are increasingly vulnerable to political turmoil in other countries or failed states, terrorism, piracy, and natural or manmade catastrophes. China's citizens expect their leaders to protect them from both ordinary dangers and bullying abroad, just as the citizens of any other major power expect of their governments. PRC naval activity in the Gulf of Aden to protect PRC ships from piracy (increasingly in cooperation with international naval forces) and Beijing's extraction of about 35,860 citizens from Libya as the regime of Muammar Gaddafi came tumbling down in 2011 are indicative of what the Chinese people increasingly expect of their leaders.[54] That same year, when thirteen Chinese sailors were murdered by a Burmese drug lord, the Chinese public was outraged, and Beijing considered using a drone strike to kill the kingpin and his confederates.[55] Indeed, in various anti-Chinese incidents in Indonesia dating back to the 1960s, there have been periodic (albeit unrealistic) calls by PRC citizens (and Overseas Chinese) on Beijing to protect or assist Chinese brethren in the Indonesian archipelago from persecution. In almost all of these earlier cases Beijing was incapable of doing much to assist and generally had to stand by as disasters unfolded. Today's Chinese leaders will have decreasing ability to stand idly by, and they are acquiring logistical and strike capabilities that increasingly will give them options. In a conversation with a Chinese general during the period of the U.S. invasion of Iraq, the officer expressed frustration that PRC citizens caught up in the maelstrom had to be extracted using other countries' air transport.

In a 2005 conversation with members of the U.S. Congress in Zhongnanhai's Purple Pavilion, Premier Wen Jiabao summarized the challenges interrupting his sleep, evoking Martin Luther King's "I Have a Dream" speech. He responded to a congressperson who stated, "I am aware of inequalities in education and health care, especially in rural areas," with the following:

> You have raised the question I am most interested in and also something I think about even in my dreams. China is very big and also very unequal. There is uneven development—inequalities among cities and between east and west. GNP per capita is one-twentieth that of the U.S., so it is still an uphill journey. There are 250 million people in urban areas, 24 million of whom are looking for jobs and only 12 million can be successful. Twenty-thousand million [?] urban dwellers are entitled to subsidies. We have successfully lifted 250 million from poverty, but still 30 million are in absolute poverty. . . . We have to work fifty years to reach the level of a moderately developed country. To catch up with the modern countries we have to work for generations, tens of generations. This leaves us with no choice but to follow the peaceful road to development. . . . To make sure this country of 1.3 billion is stable, prosperous, and growing is our greatest contribution to the world. . . . We have a dream, and our government is making efforts to realize these dreams, that from last year to next year, three years, we will relieve farmers from agricultural taxes, and there is a special $90 billion fund for this. Also, there are other policies. By about 2007, nine years compulsory education in poor areas [will be realized], in 592 poverty-stricken counties, students get exempted tuition, books, and subsidies for dorm expenses. We also have a plan for the road network to link townships to county towns by 2010—asphalt roads. Last year we provided [jobs to] 8.9 million unemployed [people], and this year there will be 10 million. Gradually we are addressing health care in the cities—expensive, hard to see a doctor. I have a dream.[56]

It is revealing when, in the twenty-first century, China's premier still has an unfulfilled aspiration for asphalt roads that might one day reach all villages in the country.

It is notable that shortly after his installation as China's new leader, Xi Jinping, on December 29, 2012, gave his own "dream" speech, saying that by the one-hundredth anniversary of the CCP (2021) China would be a "well-off" (*xiaokang*) society and that by the one-hundredth anniversary of the PRC (e.g., 2049) China would be a strong, modernized, and democratic, and socialist nation. "This is the greatest dream of the Chinese nation in modern history."[57]

The domestic agenda is China's leaders' overwhelmingly dominant concern, except in the halls of the foreign affairs bureaucracy. It is true that increasing numbers of domestic agencies and localities have involvement with, interests in, and concerns about the outside world, but these are largely refracted through the lens of domestic needs, hopes, and fears. The concerns of Chinese control agencies such as public security, state security, and the propaganda system outweigh concerns of the Foreign Ministry the vast majority of the time. The reflex in the Chinese system is to ask what global developments imply for China rather than to contemplate how China can change the world. This may be shifting, but only slowly, and only noticeably where interdependence has created compelling external interests that relate to domestic concerns. Foreigners become relevant to Chinese leaders when they facilitate the PRC's dealing with its massive internal challenges; engage in actions threatening the delicate domestic balances that PRC leaders seek to manage; or are popularly perceived to be "bullying" China.

In sum, in the near and midterm futures, the Western world is likely to face a China preoccupied by its own enormous domestic agenda—a country that rises to the challenge of providing "global public goods" only when doing so also meets compelling internal needs. Efforts to influence China's internal situation by applying external pressure, or pressure from China's periphery, run the ever-present risk of igniting the "I won't be bullied" knee-jerk reaction that unifies even unpopular Chinese leaders with "the masses." As a senior Chinese foreign affairs official put it, "'Every time China gets into trouble with its neighbors, the U.S. is always on the other side.'"[58]

Another powerful theme of this chapter is the extent to which China, despite its new modern visage, remains hostage to the forces of nature and unfortunate geographic circumstances. Cities, as well as agricultural regions, are vulnerable to massive floods, dramatic seismic events, and other catastrophic occurrences, many of which are worsened by human error or corruption, and all of which are compounded by China's huge population. China remains a society in which natural and manmade calamities can measurably affect national prospects. Being a Chinese leader is no simple task.

CHAPTER 6

Soldiers and Civilians

In the councils of government, we must guard against the acquisition of unwarranted influence, whether sought or unsought, by the military-industrial complex. The potential for the disastrous rise of misplaced power exists and will persist.

—President Dwight David Eisenhower, "Farewell Address to the Nation," January 17, 1961

The Chinese military is quite different from the U.S. military that takes orders from the civilians. Power comes out of the barrel of a gun, [it does] not just take orders like the U.S. military. To the military it is a shame of fifty years' duration that Taiwan is not solved. Whereas, if MFN [most favored nation tariff treatment] is the issue, the military is much less involved. MOFTEC [The Ministry of Foreign Trade and Economic Cooperation] was not much in favor of military exercises [in the Taiwan Strait] because it would spoil the international environment, hurt relations with others—the military doesn't care so much. The Foreign Ministry is different from the military.

—Shanghai think tank analyst, June 20, 1998

"Deng Xiaoping could say mostly blunt things to military generals and the newer leaders cannot. Deng never minced words and they [the generals] listened. With Jiang, it is different; he needs to be much more suave and persuasive— directly admonishing them would be avoided. This doesn't mean that the military is out of control."

—Senior Chinese diplomat, August 15, 2002

China has now stood at a new historical point and its future destiny has never been more closely connected with those of the international community.

—Preface to *China's National Defense in 2010* (white paper)

At this point in history, China faces two critical tasks: to adapt its political institutions to the reality of a pluralized society and bureaucracy, and to control the military and associated industry as President Dwight Eisenhower (in different circumstances) urged his fellow Americans to do with respect to their military-industrial complex in 1961. This chapter considers this second task. China's military, the People's Liberation Army (PLA), can still be brought to heel by civilian leaders when they are unified and serious, but the military has considerable room to maneuver with limited oversight. When civilian party leaders are divided, the existing problem of civilian control over the military complex is compounded.

From 1929 until well into the post-1949 era, the ethos of the PLA, and its antecedent Red Army, was that it was a party army—that the party controlled the gun, even though Mao Zedong played an outsized role from the earliest years. During Mao's post-1949 reign, the PLA progressively became guardian of the Chairman as the embodiment of the party and its ideology, particularly in the 1960s through mid-1970s. In Mao's later years, the PLA effectively had become his personal army. A few weeks before the Chairman's 1976 death, a division-level officer described the army's relationship to Mao by saying, "The PLA is personally led and commanded by Mao Zedong and the Chinese Communist Party."[1] There are many examples of Mao's control over the PLA, including the sacking of Defense Minister Peng Dehuai in 1959 (for criticizing Mao's Great Leap Forward) and the September 1971 fiery airplane death of the subsequent defense minister and onetime successor to the Chairman, Lin Biao.

Reasserting the traditional understanding of PLA subservience to the party as an organization, rather than an armed force loyal to a single individual, had to await Mao's death. While preferable to the cult of personality and blind loyalty to a single leader, this PLA-party relationship is not fidelity to a constitution or long-held principles enforced under a rule of law. A simmering argument in today's China is the degree to which the PLA ought to be an instrument of the state (a "national army"), not the instrument of a single political party.

To provide some comparative perspective, when in 2000 the Democratic Progressive Party (DPP) on Taiwan took power from the Kuomintang (Nationalist Party, or KMT), with which the Republic of China (ROC) military long had been identified, the new civilian administration of President Chen Shui-bian was concerned that the military would not be loyal to their new government. President Chen's chief civilian foreign policy adviser, Chiou Yi-jen, put it this way at the time:

> Civil control of the military is a more serious problem for us—we have no experience. He's [President Chen] trying to stabilize the military, "but [we] don't know if it is having a result. [We] don't change any top military intelligence leaders. If this works we don't know. We don't know if they will do what we say. The chief of the joint command said, 'Show loyalty to the new [DPP] regime.' The joint commander said, 'Fight independence.' I worry about this tendency." . . . We are worried about the reliability of the military and want to establish good relations [with our military].[2]

In short, in circumstances where the military is an arm of a political party, as on China's mainland today, when there is turmoil within that party, or there is a change of ruling party, the political alignment of the military cannot be assumed.

In this chapter we examine issues constituting the crux of the PRC civil-party-military relationship in the reform era, as they are crucial to both China's domestic political evolution and its relationship with Asia and the world. Among those issues are: How does the PLA relate to civilian political leadership? How much latitude does the PLA have to act in areas that have consequences for the broader society, the civilian leadership, and China's foreign relations? What is the PLA claim on budgetary resources, how is this claim articulated, and where do corruption and associated business activity fit in the picture? Finally, what is the relationship between the PLA and other parts of the decision-making system?

REFORM-ERA TRENDS IN THE MILITARY

A PLA major general succinctly summarized the major strategic mileposts along the reform era's pathway of military modernization in a 2005 meeting:

> There has been a string of important decisions along the road of Chinese military modernization: "The important decisions on PLA modernization are: 1985, reduce military troops by one million troops; 1985, there was a strategic task change to strengthen the navy; 1989, we began to increase the money for the military by a big margin; 1993, the strategic task was defined as to win a war under high-tech conditions; 1995, the strategic military and S&T task was realizing the transition from quantitative forces to qualitative forces and technology intensive; 1997, there was another five hundred thousand troop reduction announced; 1998, there was a reorganization of the State Commission on Science and Technology and the establishment of the

fourth department, the General Armaments Department; 2000, there was reform of the logistical system and joint logistics support; 2002, we decided to push the RMA [revolution in military affairs] with Chinese characteristics building informationalized war; 2003, we announced another troop reduction of two hundred thousand to reach a size of 2.3 million in the PLA; 2004, we further adjusted the strategic guideline to preserving the maritime interests of China and Taiwan. These are key tasks."[3]

In the years between Mao's 1976 death and 2013, the PLA's development and role in society proceeded along several avenues. The first was that, despite the June 1989 entanglement of the armed forces in domestic politics and struggle, as it professionalized the military generally retreated from mass politics. Nonetheless, the PLA remains the ultimate regime backstop, and as military affairs become more technically complex and civilian leaders are often without experience in this domain, the civilians rely increasingly on expert advice from those in uniform. As one well-connected senior Chinese scholar put it in 2005, "'As the military is becoming more professionalized and the political leaders more civilianized, the civilians need their advice and professional input more deeply, in a narrow range of issues, related to Taiwan and military force issues. So it is not that the military will take over, but their expertise is indispensable in a specific set of issues.'"[4]

In the early days of the PRC almost all the political elite had significant military experience, many having been senior officers during the revolution and the Anti-Japanese War. But since the elevation of Jiang Zemin to party leadership in 1989, and the death of Deng in 1997, very few members of the Standing Committee of the Politburo or the party's commanding heights have had military experience—China's current ruler Xi Jinping being a modest exception, having served as General Geng Biao's secretary (*mishu*) in the Central Military Commission (CMC) for a brief time. As David Shambaugh explained, "The 'interlocking directorate' has been completely broken by generational succession. . . . The party-army elite is clearly becoming bifurcated."[5]

A second avenue of PLA development has been the relative diminution of the land army as a service component, and the relative rise of the navy and missile forces, and to a lesser extent the air force. As one PLA general put it to me, "'Ground forces in the past were big brother but now are the younger brother.'"[6] Since 1982–83, the PLA land army's personnel count has been reduced by approximately 31 percent, the navy has held constant, and the missile forces have achieved an 11 percent increase. The navy, missile forces, and air force have also procured the greater number of modern systems.[7] These budgetary and procurement patterns reflect the fact that Deng Xiaoping shifted the emphasis from a "people's war" of attrition fought on Chinese territory by low-tech land forces to a progressively higher-tech war, fought beyond China's boundaries by combined services. This shift is more easily conceptualized than achieved, but in the intervening years the PLA's gains have been significant.

This reorientation of the Chinese military has had a number of implications, including an upgrade of the education and skills of personnel recruited, a larger defense budget to pay for more complex systems and more highly trained personnel who now can sell their skills in a higher-paying civilian economy, and a parallel increase in the sophistication of China's defense and defense-related industry (most notably missiles, shipbuilding, IT-related industrial capability, and some improvement in the aviation industry).[8] While one should not exaggerate, these new capabilities (including new generations of quieter submarines, new aircraft, an aircraft carrier, new types of ballistic and cruise missiles, and a stealth aircraft under development) enable the PLA to contemplate more expansive goals, in turn boosting the anxiety of China's neighbors and more distant powers. All this also raises issues of command and control. As China moves into the maritime, air, and space domains previously monopolized by the United States, the opportunities for frictions and accidents multiply.

As the PLA has become more technologically sophisticated, the services with the greatest power projection capacity are slowly increasing their relative strength in military-related decision making—these high-tech services within the PLA will gain importance in the Chinese economy as well. Air force representation on the party's Central Committee went up 200 percent in the 1990–2007 period, and navy representation increased by 133 percent, while the representation of the land army declined.[9] To be sure, the ground forces remain an important force in intramilitary politics.

All this change finds reflection in the changing face, character, and outlook of the military people one has met in China over time. In 1976, at Mao's death, the PLA's face was the land army, and those one encountered looked rumpled, often spoke poor Chinese, and were rough-hewn in every sense. They had no vision that extended beyond the locales in which they had served, they were not big on conversation, and what they said was formulaic ideological rhetoric. In the new millennium, one meets officers who have had experience abroad; many speak foreign languages, and they have aspirations that parallel their uniformed counterparts in all modern militaries. It was quite in character when one senior Chinese general expressed the desire to land on an American aircraft carrier! "I want to land. No helicopter, fixed wing."[10]

Turning to military-related industry, the process of converting former government armaments ministries into more autonomous economic actors (there are now ten corporations under the State Administration of Science, Technology, and Industry for National Defense and the State-Owned Assets Supervision and Administration Commission) has contributed to improved innovation and profitability. These corporations have more freedom of action for commercial activities, which can create coordination and policy implementation problems in foreign and national security policy.[11] In short, China is building a military-industrial sector, still of modest proportions, characterized by selective deep pockets of excellence and more moderate capability elsewhere. This industry will become increasingly important in the polity, the society, the economy, and foreign and national security policy making. In his report at the Eighteenth Party Congress in November 2012, Hu Jintao essentially wrote a potential blank check for allocations to the military, saying: "Building strong national defense and powerful armed forces that are commensurate with China's international standing and meet the needs of its security and development interests is a strategic task of China's modernization drive."[12]

As the PLA acquires increasing power projection capabilities, there is a resonance with popular nationalism—a convergence of popular pride and the military's desire to increase its capabilities and resources. This convergence was evident when China launched its first aircraft carrier in 2011, and when its space program launched the Tiangong space station module in September the same year (and as of mid-2013 had successfully placed twelve people in space). The space program is a hard-power asset and has a soft-power, attractive potential as well, with Yang Liwei, the PRC's first man in space, traveling to the United States in 2004. It is no stretch of the imagination to say Colonel Yang is gregarious, even charismatic, with both foreigners and his countrymen; his mass popularity made it predictable that he would be the lowest-ranking officer elevated to the Seventeenth Central Committee in 2007.[13]

The overall architecture of the policy-making system must also be considered. Under the current and traditional structure, the military has a direct channel to the chairman of the CMC (who generally, though not always, is the general secretary of the party) and through him to the

Standing Committee of the Politburo. This creates a structural problem in decision making because other intelligence and foreign policy institutions report up through separate state and party channels. There generally is insufficient horizontal coordination between these channels and the military, almost guaranteeing there will be instances (sometimes important) where the left hand (the diplomats) do not know what the right hand (the military) is doing. There is anemic horizontal communication between bureaucracies that are separate in structure but interrelated in function. Further, coming out of the Eighteenth Party Congress of fall 2012, the foreign policy apparatus had no seats on the Politburo, while the uniformed military had two. Concisely, the military is under civilian control, but it could be under better coordination within the security-foreign policy system. It is this fact, for example, that accounts for Xi Jinping, shortly after taking office as general secretary and chairman of the CMC, establishing an interdepartmental task force (which he personally oversaw) to deal with a growing crisis with Tokyo over the Diaoyu/Senkaku Islands—a volatile situation in which dozens of Chinese agencies, localities, and other actors needed to be coordinated, not least the diplomats and military.[14]

Other important developments in civil-military relations concern the activism of retired military officers and corruption within the military—including the purchase of ranks, often related to one's retirement security.[15] The concept of retirement was nearly nonexistent under Mao, when the three principal exit paths from a position were political disgrace, dementia, or death. But the professionalization of the military, education requirements, and age limits have created a body of high-ranking retired officers.[16] These officers, once retired, do not sink into obscurity; instead they are often beckoned by the market economy. Growing numbers of institutions (education, think tanks, etc.) are anxious to hear their views, and more diverse and receptive media have provided these retirees avenues for the expression of their views and sources of considerable income on the PRC speaking and opinion-editorial circuits. Unsurprisingly, the most balanced and moderate voices are not the ones the market and media reward, although it is unclear what these new voices actually represent. As one PLA colonel put it: "'PLA officers are not supposed to have personal views, but China is in the process of transformation, so people's understanding of the situation is different. Some in the PLA want to show their personal view, that they have freedom of speech, some go on TV to become personal stars. I hope you can forgive some wrong views.'"[17]

The military has a zone of technical competence and information that may or may not be easily accessible to the PLA's supposed civilian masters—to what degree do civilian leaders defer to military expertise? The PLA can endlessly hypothesize future threats requiring more response, which in turn require greater budgetary allocations. Standing for pride and muscle means that the military can more readily become aligned with popular nationalism than the civilian leaders and diplomats who have broader, more nuanced responsibilities. China's military is increasingly operating in the wider world, a world that used to be nearly the sole preserve of China's Foreign Ministry. Now Beijing's Foreign Ministry competes with the military for attention and policy support of the party center.

Many of these changes are underpinned by a rapidly increasing Chinese military budget. Though what is recounted in the quote below is the opinion of only one well-placed senior Chinese scholar, it forecast well the trajectory China has followed since these views were articulated in 2004 and describes—accurately, I believe—the broad direction in which PLA and security thinking in China is headed.

> "Today China spends US$30 billion [official budget] on its military. By 2020, it will be four times higher, and at least for the last decade-plus China's military budget has increased at the rate of GNP increase, about 12 percent per annum. By 2020 our military budget would be $180 billion at this rate of growth—almost 50 percent the U.S. military budget of last year. I don't know where the U.S. budget will go. But with Chen Shui-bian there is no hope that we will be restrained. And if you put this in PPP terms, our military budget would be close to $700 billion. We now spend about $2 billion per year on Russian equipment, so we can buy a lot more. And these figures don't include off-budget procurement."[18]

These dimensions of development have fundamental implications for civil-military relations, not to mention China's relations with its neighbors and more distant big powers.

THE PARTY/CIVIL-MILITARY RELATIONSHIP

Strongman leadership within the party has progressively weakened since Mao's death. The functional responsibilities of various senior central political leaders have become more explicitly delineated and separated. Schisms among members of the most senior political elite periodically become publicly visible. China's post-Deng civilian leaders (with the modest exception of Xi Jinping) have had slim to no military experience. These developments raise a key question—if the party center splits, "who" is the party? If this occurs, it raises the possibility that the military (or various parts of it) may align with that fragment most congenial to its interests, thereby creating "factionalism."

This brings us to the problem of "two centers," meaning that it may be unclear at times where (or who) the authoritative party center is. This became a challenge in late 2002, when Jiang Zemin (who was no longer on the Standing Committee of the Politburo) retained the chairmanship of the CMC (where critical security decisions are made), while his successor, Hu Jintao, headed the Politburo Standing Committee and nearly all of the other foreign policy–related leading small groups. As one senior Chinese scholar explained,

> *Scholar:* "First, there is a difference between foreign policy and security policy, not to mention domestic policy. Hu [Jintao] is in charge of foreign policy, and Jiang [Zemin] much more so in security policy. Hu is in charge of domestic policy."
>
> *Lampton:* But Hu Jintao is in charge of most of the Leading Small Groups, so it looks like he is in charge, and he is chairman of the Politburo Standing Committee, which Jiang is not even on.
>
> *Scholar:* Yes, but remember that Jiang is chair of CMC, and the way the military works is often decisions are made by the CMC; there Jiang is number one and Hu number two.[19]

This circumstance of divided power between Jiang and Hu lasted two years. During this period, one interviewee said to me, "'We are in a most vulnerable period in PRC history to be indecisive, to make decisions on national security.'"[20] Another strategic analyst said, "The ultimate survival [of the party] depends on the military. The military did demand Jiang stay on—not good—interference. 'The military is more involved in the international crisis management system.'"[21]

In a November 2002 meeting with outgoing general secretary Jiang Zemin shortly after the conclusion of the Sixteenth Party Congress, he pointed out to his American visitors that there had been a split in the party center in 1989 (Deng Xiaoping had remained chair of the CMC after leaving the Politburo Standing Committee in 1987, and he personally motivated particularly reliable military units to repress the protesters in Tiananmen Square when the Politburo Standing Committee on which he no longer sat was unable to act in the face of its own division). Jiang told our group: "What also is important is that the leadership has been stable for thirteen years; in 1989 we had 'two headquarters.'"[22]

Jiang Zemin went on to explain why he was retaining the chairmanship of the CMC: "According to my character and morality, I would not keep it [the CMC chairmanship,] *but all the people in the military wanted me to keep it*" (emphasis added). I construe Jiang to have been saying that the military was not yet confident about Hu Jintao's leadership. In keeping his CMC chairmanship, Jiang set the stage for the "two headquarters" problem, which he said he had avoided for the preceding thirteen years. And of course, explaining that he was keeping his CMC chairmanship post because that is what the military wanted is not what reasonably can be counted as civilian control. It is significant that at the end of that meeting, as we were moving toward the exit, he said to us, "'I will not interfere in the work of the new guys.'"[23]

Jumping ahead to the run-up to the Eighteenth Party Congress in the fall of 2012, there was considerable internal debate, and external speculation, as to whether Hu Jintao would relinquish his chairmanship of the CMC "on time" or choose to retain that position for some period beyond the Party Congress. As one senior person in the military put it to me prior to the Eighteenth Party Congress, "I don't know if Hu Jintao will leave 'completely.'"[24] Had he retained the CMC chairmanship, this would have created yet another potential "two headquarters" problem with his successor Xi Jinping. In this sense, one can count Hu's seemingly complete departure from positions of power in the 2012–13 transition as a modest step in the direction of both institutionalization and more unified civilian/party control of the military. That the debate went on so long and was subject to such internal horse trading, however, is an indication of how far institutionalization still has to go and just how fragile norms are.

Beyond this issue in 2012 was also the open fight preceding the Eighteenth Party Congress to select the next Politburo Standing Committee. The fight involved the attempt by Chongqing party secretary Bo Xilai to strong-arm his way onto the Standing Committee by mobilizing popular support, the resistance of the bulk of the party center to this attempt, and Bo's March 2012 dismissals from his post in Chongqing and from the Politburo a month later. Bo's removal was followed by a nationwide effort to ensure that military units having personal and historic connections with Bo or his family remained loyal to the party center, not to Bo Xilai, whose father had earlier led the Fourteenth Group Army. The center also seemed concerned about possible Bo loyalists in the Second Artillery (the strategic and conventional missile forces) and the Chengdu Military Region,[25] consequently making efforts to ensure that the military remained unified and under central control. It is not inconsequential that Yin Fanglong, head of the political department of the Second Artillery, came out in *People's Daily* at the time saying, "We should boycott all wrong ideas and refute those key issues like 'The military should not be led by the party.' When encountering a situation when it is hard to choose between emotion and principle, we should choose to put personal relationships subordinate to the development of the party's cause."[26]

In short, as the CCP becomes more pluralized and as intraparty groups vie for power, the meaning of military loyalty to the party at key junctures may be unclear. In the case of Bo Xilai, the PLA seems to have responded to the center's call for displays of loyalty in a disciplined fashion.[27] Nonetheless, the fact that the party center's opening move against the effects of Bo included making sure the PLA was under unified party control reveals the underlying problem and embedded anxieties. This is one of the dangers of military subordination to a political party rather than to a constitution, the law, or the state. Even though in the 1982 State Constitution an effort was made to increase state and civilian control of the military by the creation of a State Central Military Commission, this effort has had no discernible effect.

One also can discern the character of the civilian-military relationship in the information the military provides, or fails to provide, the civilian leadership. While evidence in this area is ambiguous, several interviews with senior Chinese military and foreign affairs officials lead me to question whether civilian leaders can count on the military to provide accurate and timely information at key junctures; these concerns extend beyond ordinary military uncertainties, the fog of war.

A probable example of the misinformation problem occurred in April 2001 with the collision of a U.S. reconnaissance aircraft (EP-3) and a Chinese fighter off Hainan Province, over international waters but within the Chinese Exclusive Economic Zone. The Chinese pilot, Wang Wei, died and the disabled American plane made a forced landing on the Hainan airfield from which the now dead Chinese pilot had taken off. In a meeting with a senior Chinese military officer during the extended crisis that followed the accident I was, in effect, told that the Chinese pilot indeed had run into the U.S. aircraft ("'It is difficult'" to control young pilots, was the way it was put)[28] and that the local Hainan military authorities had initially explained the accident to their superiors in the chain of command as caused by the American aircraft. One senior member of the foreign affairs system said, "You know, last year, [with respect to the EP-3 incident, we] 'didn't handle it so well from my point of view. The Foreign Ministry didn't know the situation, it got information from the Ministry of National Defense, so [the Foreign Ministry] can't say anything. So at the very beginning [we made] mistakes.' . . . The problem became big. [Vice President] Hu Jintao was in charge and communicated with Jiang every day. . . . Hu [was] in a difficult situation and Qian [Qichen] in a difficult situation. 'They were in charge but didn't know the real situation.'"[29]

Soon after the collision was announced publicly (presumably on the basis of incomplete or misleading information provided by his own military), President Jiang Zemin demanded that the United States cease its surveillance of the Chinese coast and demanded an apology, setting the stage for an eleven-day period in which twenty-four U.S. military personnel remained unable to leave Hainan.[30] Later, the issues of U.S. compensation and the conditions for the return of the U.S. aircraft also arose. The immediate crisis involving detained U.S. personnel was resolved when the U.S. Department of State and China's Ministry of Foreign Affairs took the lead in negotiations, not the respective militaries. As the PLA officer put it to me, it was a mistake for China "to make a national incident out of it."[31] In the end, the PLA did what it was told by the civilian leadership, but that doesn't hide the fact that the initial reports were at best inaccurate and at worst intentionally misleading, leading Beijing to take a more intransigent position than the incident could, in the end, sustain.

Another category of information problem is that local commanders and various military services may exaggerate the threats they face in order to get policy attention and resources, while the job of higher-level military staff and executive leaders is to adjust these distorted figures and assessments. This situation gives rise to debates within the security establishment as to how much threat China may actually face. With respect to U.S. air reconnaissance along China's coast, for instance, I was told in 2012 by a senior military officer: "Many [PLA] operational military commanders give examples of close-in reconnaissance [by the United States] in our South China Sea. [Local operation] commanders give a number of slide briefings, figures, they show what feels like a front line." I then asked whether China's leaders thought the number of U.S. reconnaissance sorties was rising or falling as of early in 2012 and was told: "'[It is] obvious that in sensitive areas they [the PLA] see an increase.' Facts provided [to upper-level decision makers] by the general staff sometimes are lower than the figures from these regional commanders. 'The result of this debate will have far-reaching impact and the debate extends all over our research community.'"[32] Concisely, different entities within the Chinese armed forces and other components of the security and foreign policy establishments provide information to superiors that best serves their interests.

In this discussion the focus has been on tensions between civilian and military authorities, but this is only part of what is evolving into a more complex story. Portions of the economy increasingly find their interests aligned with the military. One striking example is seen in the alignment of interests between the China National Offshore Oil Corporation (CNOOC) and the PLA Navy. As one individual in the intelligence and foreign policy realm explained, "As for the military, oil companies, CNOOC, are a natural ally. The navy wants to be more active. CNOOC, 'oil, wants to be a partner with the navy, to be more assertive in dealing with small countries.'"[33] In its broadest sense, civil-military relations constitute a much bigger universe than simply the chain of command.

THE BUDGETARY WARS

In the opening days of reform until 1989, the military was a low (and sometimes declining) budgetary priority. Top echelons of the armed forces grudgingly accepted the low status because they understood the need for basic economic development and a modernized economic foundation if a strong military was ever to be created. As Admiral Liu Hua-qing, China's most senior uniformed military officer, put it to Robert McNamara in 1994, "'Therefore, we [the PLA] have had great patience because we believe in the common interest, and when China modernizes we'll have more resources.'"[34] The PLA *share* of GDP reached its nadir in 1994–95, as documented in chapter 1.[35] The period of a relatively calm external environment made the low economic priority of the PLA feasible. To make the slim budgetary diet more palatable, in the latter half of the 1980s and in much of the 1990s the military was permitted to retain revenues it made in subsidiary industries and enterprises (everything from hotels to missile sales)—a volume of cash that was of a large, albeit uncertain, magnitude. By the mid-1990s, two things began to happen that would affect the military budget: China's civilian leaders became anxious about the problems created by large off-the-books PLA revenues, and China's military became progressively less satisfied with its low budgetary priority.

From 1995 to1998, China's civilian leaders sought to shut off most irregular sources of income to the military and to compensate for the

PLA's losses through increases in the regular military budget. They took this action because irregular sources of revenue flowing into military units at various levels had a number of pernicious effects, including fostering corruption, generating diplomatic problems, diverting soldiers from training to business, and weakening civilian control because the civilians (and perhaps even the upper levels of the military itself) could not be sure what resources were flowing to subordinate units through various channels.[36] From the perspective of PRC leaders (both civilian and senior PLA), if you don't control the money, you don't control the organization.

With respect to dissatisfaction of the military, by the early 1990s the PLA was becoming less and less patient with its budgetary straitjacket. The first stage of increasing the defense budget occurred in the wake of the June 1989 Tiananmen violence; increased budgets became a reward for loyalty to the party in its moment of need. Shortly thereafter, PLA budgetary demands went up further as the United States powerfully demonstrated its new military technology in the First Gulf War of 1991—Saddam Hussein's army, not unlike the PLA, was pulverized by newly unveiled smart weaponry and incredible U.S. logistical feats.

The PLA argument for resources was further strengthened by increasingly loud calls by Taiwan's president Lee Teng-hui for more international space and by the progressively louder voice of proindependence forces on the island. President George Herbert Walker Bush's 1992 approval to sell 160 F-16s to Taiwan further strengthened PLA demands. Then, with Deng Xiaoping's 1992 Southern Tour, economic growth took off, so soon there was more money—from 1987 through 1991, the GDP growth rate averaged 8 percent; from 1992 through 1996, it averaged 12.44 percent.[37] The PLA wanted more money, the economy was able to provide it, and the technological and educational base of Chinese society was qualitatively improving, so better human and technical resources were becoming available. Moreover, the PLA had to compete for talent with the civilian economy, which drove personnel costs up. As one general put it to me a decade later (after there had been pay increases): "The young are reluctant to join the armed forces. A general gets one-half the pay of his daughter two years into the workforce. 'So the increase of the military budget to some extent is new hardware, but most is salaries and welfare for soldiers.'"[38]

By 1994 (even before the 1995–96 missile crisis in the Taiwan Strait, in which the PLA deescalated in the face of U.S. counterpressure), the PLA was becoming more public in its calls for resources. Sometimes the calls were gently put, sometimes they were strident—either way, they were unmistakable. One very senior PLA general, in addressing former U.S. defense secretary Robert McNamara and a group of senior retired U.S. military officers, gave the soft sell, letting the numbers speak for themselves:

> This year the defense budget reached 52 billion RMB, which is only US$6 billion. We can give you three figures, appropriate for a country pursuing "active defense." From 1980 to 1993, our defense [expenditures were] up 1.16 times, while in the same period prices went up 1.3 times—so, in real terms, it declined and we reduced [our forces] by one million persons. If we take out inflation, from 1980 to 1993, the U.S. defense budget was up 25 percent in real terms. Our defense budget from 1980 to 1993, the percentage in GNP declined—in 1980 it was 4.33 [percent of GNP]; 1993, 1[?] percent. . . . So China's strategy of defense is manifested in this budget.[39]

In a 1994 group meeting I attended with Admiral Liu Huaqing, China's highest uniformed military officer at the time and patron saint of the navy, Liu also voiced the soft, patient approach:

> In China, the contribution of defense is always subordinate to the development of the economy—defense is not a top priority. Although [there have been] increases [in budget] lately, still limited, and that is why we are so slow to modernize and we cannot borrow to finance it. So our defense expenditures are kept to a minimum. We are aware that our weapons of all services are far behind the present equipment of the United States. We are aware of these differences and we hope to modernize, but the problem is that we have no resources and if we compete with economic needs, we'll be in competition with the economy and that is not in China's interest. . . . The weapons and equipment of the U.S., Russia, Japan, and even South Korea are much more advanced than ours—the latter two because of U.S. technology. We are aware of this, but we put economy as the first priority. But we believe a large war won't break out and if small wars [occur], not too tough for us to handle. But if we don't have economic growth now, we won't modernize later. One point two billion people need housing, shelter, and so if we have a strong military, but they are poor, "What is the use?"[40]

On the other hand, a subordinate, but nonetheless a very senior general himself, was less restrained and left less to the imagination in describing the need for more PLA funding:

> We are concerned with military expenditures. Take 1993, our military expenditures, according to state allocations, were 40 billion RMB; however, the exchange rate was 1:6. That means $US 6 billion. The year 1994, military expenditure is 52 billion RMB, but the exchange rate changed to 1:8.7, or this is $US 5.97 billion. One-third [of military expenditures] are spent on maintenance of daily life [*renmin shenghuo*], salaries, and other expenses;

maintenance and this is one-third; and equipment, including R&D and procurement, [is the remainder]. Compare this to the United States in 1993—[defense expenditures] were $US 279 billion; Japan was $30 billion. Incomparable to the United States. Japan was $37 billion,[41] and China much smaller than Japan's. China has an "active defense" policy. To protect sovereignty we need to have a limited degree of military expenditure. Also, we have inflation, and [real] military expenditures are dropping. We give priority to economic development. Apart from reducing staff by one million persons, we are trying to reduce expenditure. There is a $1 billion deficit for our military staff, and we are subsidizing ourselves. For example, from 1980 to 1993, the rate of increase of inflation for civil products was 1.3 percent, and [the rate was] much higher for military goods. In substance, it [military expenditure] has been reduced.[42]

Then one of the American visitors angered this same PLA interlocutor by saying that outside assessments of the PLA's budget were much higher than officially acknowledged. The PLA general responded, hotly:

> Our policy is defensive. China's expenditures are small. Minimum expenditures; with inflation, difficult to maintain our armed forces. There are many complaints in the armed forces, so we are asking for a quota in the national budget, but this is not very practicable. Deng once said that it is impossible to raise military expenditures. We should place priority on other economic sectors. XX [American delegation member mentioned by name] said that the Chinese military budget is $US 30 billion. In 1993 the total national income was 514.82 billion RMB. "Is it conceivable that we have spent that much? The truth is, XX [American delegation member mentioned by name], we are poor!" This would hamper our development—that is groundless. Is it that useful?[43]

This tension over budget priority was between the military and the party's supreme decision makers, as well as the NPC. According to a senior Chinese general speaking in frustration, expressions of opposition to increased military spending were rife in the NPC in the 1990s:

> At each National People's Congress session the military complains that the budget is too small, but each time the NPC delegates vote for cuts. And in the 1980s, when Deng was elected chair of the Military Affairs Commission [MAC or CMC], and "when Deng met with the MAC he said that the military would have to be patient." [He said], "Now you have selected me, I want to cut one million [troops], and I can tell you that you will not have the increases you want, you will have to be patient. I can tell you that the army still has to be patient. The reason that we restrain our budget is that we are now building Chinese socialism, and according to the theory we can't have an arms race that would drain away our resources. This is a rational approach because to seek truth from facts, it is because we have to keep up with inflation and readjustment and market factors, so we have to maintain

a minimal level for the PLA. So when there is price readjustment, inflation, we have to increase the budget. But for us, our first concern is salaries and rations for the men, and second is maintenance and repair of weapons, and procurement is our third priority."[44]

Moving into the new millennium, China's military was still not reconciled to what it viewed as its persistently insufficient budgetary priority, given that it saw itself confronted with many threats: modernizing neighbors, a globally more interventionist United States, an increasingly independence-minded Taiwan, a need to protect the PRC's growing global interests, and a revolution in military affairs (RMA). As China's defense minister put it to a U.S. group headed by Henry Kissinger in 2001:

> We need to maintain arms, give good salaries. The U.S. spends $354 billion—Japan spends $40 billion. The ROK spends $9.8 billion. Taiwan spends $9.9 billion, and last year increased to $12.6 billion. But China is only at $14 billion. To introduce new weapons and to develop an effective deterrent are our objectives. Facts speak louder than words. Some media are trying to stir up trouble by reporting [unintelligible]. Facts. [China is a country of] 9.6 [million?] square kilometers. One point three billion population, an eighteen-thousand-kilometer-long coastline, borders fifteen countries [unintelligible]. Yet our budget not only does not compare with that of the United States, but even with that of our smaller neighbors. We want to cut down the military. But a 17.7 percent increase in our military [budget] has given rise to charges of China threat, yet . . .
>
> The USA was the first to introduce the RMA. I remember being in the United States in 1996 and visiting Bill Perry, the National Defense University, and a Texas base. First time I heard about the RMA. So efforts are being made to bring China's military into the twenty-first century. We know we need to change, along with the rest of the world. Jiang Zemin said so. Therefore, we are beginning. We lag far behind. Trying to modernize weapons and systems. Strengthen the military through science and technology.[45]

In a quotation above, a general said that the PLA was asking for a budgetary "quota." I subsequently was told by another PLA general that, at about the same time as Jiang Zemin was worried about the implications of the PLA having off-the-books revenues from its enterprises, a broad deal was worked out: namely, the PLA would get a fixed share of the GDP through the budgetary mechanism. If PLA allocations through the budget grew at the rate of the overall economic expansion, then when the GDP was rising rapidly, as in the 1990s, the PLA would get rapidly increasing amounts of money through the budget without changing its overall priority in the economy. In exchange, the PLA agreed to divest itself of most of its enterprises generating funds outside the budget. As a senior officer put it to me in 2011, "The Ministry of National Defense had a sort of fixed slice of the GDP, 1.2 to 1.4 percent of GDP for the last twenty years. It [the PLA] had asked for 3 percent, but that had been turned down. This is what 'defense in balance with the overall economy' operationally means."[46]

As one would expect in the bargaining system described in chapter 3, the PLA asked for a percentage that was twice as much as it got. In exchange for the PLA receiving growing funds through the budgetary mechanism, civilian leaders were to get more transparent and controllable money flows into the military. As of 2013, however, despite the agreement, individuals and organizations in the PLA have been creative in devising channels for off-the-books revenues—land sales, sales of promotions in rank, and other sundry means. And the PLA remains unhappy with its allocations given what it views as its geographically expanding responsibilities, the need to acquire and master ever more expensive technologies, and an increasingly complex threat environment.

Part of that threat environment is U.S. military cooperation with and weapons sales to Taiwan, which the PLA uses in its arguments for more money. As one general put it in 2010, "'As a soldier, I support U.S. sales [to Taiwan], and then we [the PLA] can ask the [Chinese] government to give us a bigger budget.'"[47] Then, in the fall of 2011, in connection with his trip to Australia and Indonesia, President Obama announced a "pivot" (later renamed "rebalancing") to Asia, telling the world that U.S. military, economic, and diplomatic attention would be methodically shifted to Asia as the United States presumably drew down resources devoted to the Middle East and Central Asia. An initial installment in this effort was the announced rotation of a small contingent of American marines through Darwin, Australia, and Secretary of State Hillary Clinton standing on the deck of the U.S. destroyer *Fitzgerald* in Manila Bay proclaiming: "We will stand and fight with you."[48] With this stance by Washington, the PLA is able to argue that the threat environment has further increased. As one Chinese analyst put it in early 2013, "With tension in this area, 'the PLA will have another golden age.'"[49]

The budgetary deal outlined above in which the PLA got a fixed percentage of a briskly growing GDP (albeit not the percentage it desired) has many implications, two of which are central. First, because China's GDP has rapidly increased, defense expenditure has grown at a double-digit rate for all but one year since 1990.[50] This rapid increase has, in turn, energized the fears of neighbors and distant powers. Beijing has tried to compensate for this budgetary growth and resulting concern by increasing transparency, military-to-military exchanges, and other reassuring moves, but the reality of China's growing power and some hamhanded diplomatic and military actions (in 2009 and thereafter) have contributed to anxieties in the region. Looking at China's PLA budget growth from another angle, however, it is positive inasmuch as off-the-books monies that previously went to the PLA but were of unknown magnitude by outsiders are being substituted for regular budget flows that at least have a chance of being seen. Further, the PLA has less incentive to make money by doing things that are disruptive to China's foreign relations.

Second, this budgetary deal with the PLA suggests that if GDP growth slowed for a sustained period (as it already has begun to do as China shifts to a growth model that presumably will be less dependent on exports and investment-intensive growth), particularly if such deceleration were concurrent with the military feeling more threatened by U.S. "rebalancing" in the region or other large security concerns, the PLA would be distressed that its revenues were constrained just as external challenge was mounting. This presumably would increase PLA pressure on civilian leaders for more resources, for a new deal.

The military now is making the argument that it is not simply an instrument of hard power but an instrument of soft power as well. One example is the PLA navy's 2007 launch of the "Peace Ark," a hospital ship that undertakes humanitarian missions around the world. The military will never believe it is being given adequate financial and human resources to accomplish its tasks, which are limitless, in a sense. The problem is not simply budgetary allocations but the fact that the PLA must increasingly compete with an ever more dynamic domestic economy for technically capable human resources.

THE MILITARY IN CIVILIAN MINDS

For civilian leaders, although the military missions enumerated above are central to ensuring security, maintaining domestic order, and mobilizing mass support on nationalistic grounds, as one very senior former U.S. intelligence official put it in 2011, "Military modernization is not on Hu Jintao's top ten 'to do' list when he wakes up."[51] Rather, when the members of the Standing Committee of the Politburo—a body on which no uniformed officer sits as of 2013—arise each morning, their agenda is usually close to home: managing an internal rural-urban migration of gargantuan proportions; generating jobs by the tens of millions; quelling tens of thousands of mass public disturbances;[52] cleaning up the garbage and piping away and (sometimes) treating the sewage of 20 percent of the world's people; and so on and so forth. I remember a meeting with President Jiang Zemin after he became president, and asking him what he most remembered about a trip he had made to the United States. He said, without skipping a beat, "When in 1981, I went to Chicago and people asked what I wanted to visit, I said I'd like to know about garbage. Chicago has these difficult problems, but does a good job in garbage relative to Shanghai."[53]

In a remarkable 1996 group meeting with Vice-Premier Zhu Rongji, he explained which issues worried him most, including inflation, agriculture, and growth. Then the vice-premier went on to say: "Regarding defense burdens, China may not be the lowest, but one of the lowest in the world in the budget. China doesn't need a huge arsenal; we have 1.2 billion people; no nation is crazy enough to fight a ground war [here]. 'What we need is a deterrent force. Don't need to spend much in the military budget, but we need to maintain our deterrent force for defense.' Nothing here that I lose sleep over."[54] Of course, much has changed in terms of China's global role, interests, and the environment in which it finds itself in 2013. Nonetheless, Zhu's domestic politics vantage point is shared by the bulk of Chinese officials, most of the time.

Against the background of this agenda for civilian leaders that is overwhelmingly domestic, the military is viewed, in the words of a former senior U.S. intelligence official cited above, as "just another pressure group."[55] If one imagines China's uppermost leaders to be at the top of a huge, inverted policy funnel, as described in chapter 3, with only the most significant, thorny, and generally domestic policy disputes landing on their desks, it is easy to see how they would tend to see the PLA as just another noisy claimant on scarce resources. Add to this situation the fact that no paramount Chinese leader since Deng Xiaoping, except Xi Jinping, has had any active military experience. This missing life experience connecting China's civilian leaders and the military could play out in a number of possible ways, from a complete lack of ability to communicate on important issues to the possibility that civilian leaders with no prior connection to the military might be even more solicitous toward military demands. On balance, however, it appears that China's civilian party leaders are not mere pawns in the hands of officers they fear to cross. Most of the problems in civil-military relations have their origins elsewhere.

One of the ways the civil-military relationship can play out is cyclical. Some "supreme" leaders, at the start of their terms, use external conflicts to shore up their positions with both the military and the populace, exerting more control over the PLA and external relations once they have consolidated power. As one knowledgeable senior person explained, it is like Deng Xiaoping coming back and then in 1979 pursuing a strike against Vietnam. "Do something to control the army, and indeed Jiang Zemin did this in 1995–96 regarding Taiwan. . . . Xi Jinping is following these lines—'tough with Japan and the United States, closer to Russia, and once he consolidates power he will be better to the U.S.—there is a learning curve.'"[56]

ROOM TO RUN FOR THE PLA

The highest organ of military decision making is the party's CMC, a body composed overwhelmingly of senior military personnel. Once he is chair of the CMC, the "supreme leader" finds that there is no analogue to the Office of the Secretary of Defense in the Pentagon or the National Security Council in the White House to institutionalize and create effective civilian oversight of the PLA on the leader's behalf. Thus an overwhelmed and often distracted civilian leader sits atop a specialized organization with which he has little personal expertise and few personal relationships born of shared experience. Over time, the civilian can appoint military officers and foster personal support and relationships, but it takes time. President Jiang Zemin appears to have been far more effective in this regard than his successor, Hu Jintao.

Complicating the life of the civilian/party chairman of the CMC is interservice rivalry—something familiar to American observers of their own defense establishment. Each branch of the PLA (the Second Artillery, the navy, the air force, the land army, and other specialized agencies) wants to boost its quota of high-ranking officers, complement of personnel, and expensive war-fighting platforms. As one long-experienced Chinese respondent in the foreign affairs system put it: "'Only in recent years, the services each have their own interests and bargain with the big bosses on the CMC, and the big guys try to keep balance among the services. If this were the Deng Xiaoping era, he didn't have this, but after him the services want to be somebody.'"[57]

Organizationally, there are few somewhat anemic horizontal, cross-system integrating structures that can help civilians monitor military behavior, apprise the civilian leadership of how military activity may affect other realms of policy, and make sure that civilian leadership decisions are implemented. The military basically has quite a lot of "room to run," since it has a direct channel to an overwhelmed leader at the top, and there is a dearth of coordinating and oversight mechanisms. In a 1999 group conversation with former senior American defense officials, President Jiang Zemin made what, at face value, seems a rather startling statement: "You mentioned missiles [potentially targeted on Taiwan] several times. . . . Actually, I am chairman of the Central Military Commission; [I] began this post in middle of my career. I am in charge of general policy but not in charge of actual deployments. 'I am not like your generals.' So I hope you won't be swayed by unfounded reports. You have good intelligence and know how many missiles—but I don't even know this information."[58]

The problem is not simply that the civilians are often ignorant of what the military is doing in detail, at least until it is too late. There is an added challenge—the entire foreign and security policy-making apparatus is fractured by institutional fault lines and personal rivalries and resentments. Some of this is quite normal, since politics is often about who has access to the top—a line of friction that, for example, sometimes separated Jiang Zemin's foreign policy adviser Wang Daohan (who had direct personal access to the president) and Foreign Minister and Vice-Premier Qian Qichen.[59] On the Politburo Standing Committee, each member has trusted allies in key positions below, opening up the possibility that different members of the supreme policy-making body get different information and perspectives from diverse subordinates and that policy coming from the supreme decision-making body is, in turn, implemented by a varied group of subordinates. This was the case when Jiang Zemin took advice from Vice Premier (and Foreign Minister) Qian Qichen, and Premier Li Peng tended to listen to his ally in the Foreign Affairs Office of the State Council, Liu Huaqiu (who happened to be a competitor to Qian). My notes of one meeting with a senior person in the Foreign Ministry system put it as follows:

> I asked about the difficulties having [Premier] Li in charge of the Foreign Affairs Small Group and Jiang as senior leader, with Qian Qichen, Jiang's man, in the Foreign Ministry ("Jiang always takes his advice from Qian") and Liu Huaqiu, [Premier] Li's man, in the Foreign Affairs Office of the State Council. He said that this "caused frictions, contradictions." [Premier] Li

could order someone in the office of North America and Oceania Affairs to do something and Qian might or might not know about it, and in any case the emphasis of what Li/Liu might direct the Bureau might be different from what Qian would prefer. It was not that the line was entirely different but simply that the tone, emphasis might be different—"Li was more rigid."[60]

This situation is a real problem: decision by committee at the top, with each committee member plugged into different parts of the sprawling bureaucracy, and woefully inadequate cross-system integration.

Some people in the Chinese military, foreign policy, and security structures have argued for years that Beijing needs a more effective staff coordinating apparatus that provides a check on the military greater than just the CMC chairman—a National Security Council (NSC) akin to that in the United States. This structure has never been created because, among other reasons, the Politburo Standing Committee considers itself to be that integrative body, even though it is overwhelmed with the problems of governing China across all issues, foreign and domestic, and because each Standing Committee member has a different functional coordinating responsibility. Someone senior in the national security analytic world in China explained:

> "For ten to fifteen years we have wanted an NSC, but it hasn't become a reality. Don't know. One reason is that we don't want to copy your IPR [intellectual property rights; joke!]. Another reason is that we have a different political system, we are a collective system, not a presidential system. Our head doesn't have the power of Obama. So with a collective system it is hard to have an NSC. Every leader [in the PBSC] is in charge of several departments, so if they can agree, we don't need to offset. So how to make the current system more effective [is the question.]"[61]

This creates an important, perhaps worrisome condition—the most senior civilian leader does not really see himself as "commander in chief" in the same way a U.S. president does. To the degree that there is an ultimate authority, it is the Communist Party's Standing Committee of the Politburo. One ranking member of the U.S. Senate, a recognized expert on foreign and security policy, met with President Hu Jintao in January 2011 and asked him, "Are you the commander in chief in China?" The legislator said that Hu had replied: "No, not really. The PLA reports to the party." The senator went on to observe that Hu's reply was not reassuring, asking: "Who is in charge?"[62] In short, the military makes its tactical and operational decisions in a bubble in which military officers are dominant. Although strategic decision power rests with the party and the Politburo Standing Committee, it is ill-equipped and insufficiently informed to manage the military minutely. China has no effective NSC staff (or equivalent), as one senior foreign policy adviser explained: "'The Full Politburo meets only once every few months or a couple of times a year in plenary session, though individuals get together more frequently. Beidaihe [the sometimes summer meeting place of the party elite] even is not so important. The Taiwan Affairs Leading Small Group is mostly short-term discussion, not operational, not what to do. The [U.S.] NSC gives the president direction each day. It is very difficult [for China] to change in a year.'"[63]

The PRC political structure is vastly different from the structure in the United States: China has about thirty or more politicians who are at the vice-premier level and above, each of whom wants a say and does not want to create some kind of foreign policy superagency. Creating a powerful, cross-system security, intelligence, and foreign policy integrator and coordinator will be difficult to politically engineer.[64] Consider the difficulties that the United States, even with its director of national intelligence, has had in getting its arms around the sixteen agencies of the U.S. "intelligence community."

Many of the considerations enumerated above simply boil down to leadership, command presence, or leadership style. Chinese leaders differ from one another. One Chinese scholar plugged into the PRC defense establishment explained to me in a 2011 conversation:

Lampton: Is it [the PLA] becoming more assertive and empowered in the policy process?

Chinese Scholar: I think it has to do with officers now feeling they can go to the media, like *Huan Qiu Shibao* [Global Times].

Lampton: But we just fired a general, Stanley McChrystal, for going to the press, admittedly criticizing our president, and Truman got rid of MacArthur. Some of us are wondering whether or not the current Chinese leadership, not having been in the military, feels able to exert the necessary control—or maybe they don't want to. Even Jiang Zemin seemed to have more visible interest in generating support in the military.

Chinese Scholar: This is a matter of "personal leadership style." Jiang Zemin's political style was to actively build support in the military and political structures. Hu's style is to find the consensus point in the existing structures and distribution of power.

Lampton: So Jiang actively tried to build supporters and support bases, and Hu is looking for the consensus that can be built assuming the current distribution of power?

Chinese Scholar: Yes, their personal political styles are different.[65]

The preceding considerations help explain where the PLA gets its "room to run." Often China's supreme leader appears to be responding to initiatives taken by the military that, while tactical in nature, have consequences (often negative) for Chinese foreign policy and for the PRC's standing in the world. It is this loose process of oversight, for instance, that may account for Hu Jintao's apparent surprise when he was told by visiting U.S. Secretary of Defense Robert Gates that the PLA had just unveiled its new stealth aircraft.[66] It may also be this process that accounts for the Foreign Ministry's apparent surprise to learn from the mass media about the PLA testing of an antisatellite weapon in early 2007. It is not that the PLA is making fundamental strategic decisions but rather that the PLA and defense industry move ahead to concretely implement general policy in ways that serve their separate or collective interests and exploit available room for maneuver. As the former senior U.S. intelligence official mentioned above put it, "I think there is a lot of local initiative in the PLA."[67] Upon occasion, the military has outright misled its senior leaders about what has transpired at lower echelons, as explained above, but the problems run deeper than misrepresentation.

The developments explained in this chapter have effects on domestic politics and on Chinese foreign and security policy; they also shape perceptions of the PRC abroad.

The PLA and associated industry are playing a larger role in the domestic economy and will do so in the future as they increase their capacity to innovate. As the military-industrial complex's domestic economic reach expands, so too will its political influence, even if the military remains only indirectly represented on the Politburo Standing Committee—as has been the case since 1997, when Admiral Liu Hua-qing was the last uniformed military officer on that august body as of 2013.

The fact that the PLA remains a party army means that China periodically can have a "two centers" problem. When there is division within the party there will be the danger that the military will align with one side or another in a domestic conflict or succession struggle. Even if this situation does not materialize, various fragments of the party will constantly be on alert for the danger or opportunity that military involvement may represent. Imagine, for instance, how different the situation would have been during the 1989 Tiananmen episode if the PLA had sided with Zhao Ziyang, not Deng Xiaoping.

To provide perspective, contrast the above possibility with the reality of a smooth transition in the United States when John F. Kennedy was assassinated in 1963. A smooth transition occurred even in a circumstance in which it was not clear whether foreign entities were involved in the president's murder—the U.S. military was not even a political consideration, as Robert A. Caro describes in his masterful biography of Lyndon Johnson: "It is, for example, not so much that the American military did not attempt to take control of the government; it is that no one even thought to ask where the military's support lay."[68] The military does not determine policy or succession in China, but the PLA matters, and where it puts its support will always make a difference until the system changes.

In terms of money, the PLA's budget deal has given it a modest, but relatively stable, percentage of China's rapidly growing GDP, in what was a relatively easy arrangement to maintain as long as China's GDP was growing at approximately 10 percent annually and the threat environment was relaxed. The civilian leadership could keep raising the PLA budget in absolute RMB without having to change overall budget priorities—indeed, the share of budget going to health, education, and social safety net expenditures could go up faster than military spending. If, however, Chinese economic growth slows, as is likely in the years ahead, it is predictable that the military's demands for a more advantageous budgetary deal will increase and the contradiction with domestic needs will become more acute. Military demands will become more strident and effectual if the external environment is perceived to be deteriorating. Expanding budgets are much easier to deal with than shrinking (or, in this case, less rapidly expanding) ones. How tame will the PLA be under these circumstances? What resource conflicts with other agencies will emerge?

Looking ahead, the PLA can be expected to lobby vigorously for more resources. One way to do so is to point to external security challenges for which PLA strengthening is the appropriate response and to identify ever more closely with Chinese nationalism. We see this phenomenon, with retired military officers speaking out in terms that mobilize domestic nationalism. Retired admiral Yang Yi, for instance, asks his fellow countrymen and foreigners alike: "Whenever there's a conflict, the first question U.S. leaders ask is where their nearest U.S. aircraft carrier is. The U.S. operates its warships worldwide, apparently as deterrence and to portray itself as the champion of freedom of navigation. One wonders what makes the U.S. navigation justified and China's disturbing."[69] The U.S. "rebalancing" or "pivot" policy is widely viewed in the PRC as scarcely disguised "containment"—whatever its strategic character, it has given added impetus to PLA pleas for more resources.

Another way to get resources is to invigorate revenue channels "outside the budget." A military that is insulated from effective civilian control, has significant independent sources of revenue, and is able to align itself with popular nationalism is of concern. No single reform would be of greater importance than ensuring effective and comprehensive civilian oversight of China's military so that all revenues flow through a transparent budget.

Finally, mechanisms for more effective cross-agency coordination in the foreign affairs and security policy areas must be developed. Too often China's Foreign Ministry is out of the loop. It is difficult for foreigners to be fully confident of the trajectory of a military of the character described above. Developing stronger constitutionally governed civilian control of the military, with more transparent revenue and expenditures and more effective interagency coordination, needs to be part of China's strategy if it is to reassure others. If China is to grow its "soft power," in part through a strategy of reassurance, institutional reform of the civil-military relationship must be part of that effort.

CHAPTER 7

Negotiation Chinese Style

You all understand China, but your new leaders don't [meaning the incoming Reagan administration]. It seems they do not regard China as a sovereign country. This represents a holdover of imperialism. It is out of step with the times. We should establish equal relations between two independent sovereign countries which respect each other. It is ridiculous to regard interference in China's internal affairs as their right. It is a political short sight. They aren't looking at it from the overall situation.

—Vice-Premier and Foreign Minister Huang Hua, November 20, 1980

We will have $350 to $400 billion in imports in this five-year plan [1991–95], so I am sure the United States will regard China's potential highly. For example, we have ordered twenty aircraft from Boeing and twelve from Airbus this year. President Clinton says his first priority is the economic revitalization of the American economy. If he misses out on the Chinese market, it won't help his efforts to revive the economy. So please convey this message when you return.

—Premier Li Peng, in talking about President Clinton's threat to not extend most-favored-nation tariff treatment to China, April 3, 1993, Beijing

[*Interviewee*]: "Taiwan must be resolved this century. We negotiated land borders because we were weak, but if [we are] stronger in the future [we] may not need to negotiate in the South China Sea."

[*Lampton*]: But you negotiated with Burma and Vietnam and they were weak, so it suggests that China made equitable arrangements even when it was stronger. And China recently concluded a border agreement with Russia when it [Russia]

was weaker, and it appears to have been an equitable solution.

[*Interviewee*]: "They [the deals with Russia] were concluded while Russia was weak. By yielding to Burma we got an ally to confront India. We don't want to push now on the South China Sea and have them oppose us on the Taiwan [issue]."

—Senior Chinese scholar, 2002

In this day and age China's comprehensive national strength is much greater, Beijing's negotiating resources and ploys are more robust, and the interlocutors with which the PRC must deal are far more numerous and varied than when Deng Xiaoping returned to the stage in mid-1977. More than thirty years ago, at the beginning of the reform era, China negotiated from a position of weakness—principally for more resources in order to modernize, to enhance its security, and to enter the principal organizations and regimes of international life from which it was absent. In the twenty-first century, China is now negotiating not only to obtain the resources it requires to further modernize and achieve middle-income status but also to deploy its growing resources and to protect its growing global interests.

Negotiation and diplomacy are related tools of statecraft by which one party induces the other to make decisions and reach agreements consistent with its preferences. Threats, inducements, and intellectual persuasion are the instruments used by Chinese negotiators—indeed, all negotiators. The skillful practitioner achieves optimal results with the least expenditure of power resources. Negotiation and diplomacy can be the means to achieve limited or expansive aims and to avoid conflict and war—or to prepare for it, sometimes providing partial insight into the opponent's intentions and capabilities. Negotiations can also be theater directed at outside audiences. As Zhou Enlai said in December 1946 of the then ongoing talks with Chiang Kai-shek's Kuomintang, "We turned the negotiations into a means of educating the people."[1]

Negotiation or bargaining is a central feature of Chinese governance and the policy-making process, as explained in chapter 3. How the PRC negotiates with *foreigners* is the topic of this chapter. As Henry Kissinger observes in his book *On China,* Mao Zedong, during his long rule of the PRC, dealt himself and China into the big-power game with a very weak hand—playing one superpower off against the other for nearly three decades.[2] "Mao," Kissinger tells us, "was able to draw on a long tradition in Chinese statecraft of accomplishing long-term goals from a position of relative weakness."[3]

Just how much attention the Chinese pay to the art of playing a weak hand was driven home to me in a conversation with a senior Chinese business leader about North Korea's modus operandi. Why, I asked, did China continue to send food and other material aid to a regime that repeatedly harmed China's interests? The more Pyongyang hurt Beijing, the more aid the Kim dynasty seemingly expected and often received. The Democratic People's Republic of Korea (DPRK) must have some pretty good negotiators, I observed. With a mix of admiration for the strategy he described, and frustration given its consequences for China, he explained that Kim Jong-Il, in fact, blackmailed Beijing: "'We can either send the food to North Korea or they will send the refugees to us—either way, we feed them. It is more convenient to feed them in North Korea than in China.'" Further, he added, "'Kim Jong-Il is not even grateful for the food. His view is that North Korea is the front line against the Americans and that North Korea serves China's interests by keeping the Americans away from the Chinese border. So China should pay for this service—it is not a favor Beijing does for Pyongyang.'"[4]

THE CHINESE APPROACH TO NEGOTIATION

Negotiation is a central feature of Chinese domestic and international behavior and is core to Chinese thinking. Whether in a domestic or international context, individuals, groups, organizations, and nations are intertwined in a complex web of interdependencies and relationships. One entity's actions affect many others. The Chinese are so attuned to networks and relationships that there is a specific vocabulary for this realm of human endeavor: *guanxi* (relationships); *lingdao guanxi* (leader relationships); *yewu guanxi* (professional or consultative relationships); *guanxiwang* (network of relationships); and *guanxixue* (the study of relationships). This brings us back to Joseph Needham's concept that Chinese thinking is "organismic," a cognitive approach in which thinking is not linear but premised on interconnection and mutual influence. For Chinese, networks exist in an ever changing environment in which the needs, capabilities, and intentions of all parties are in constant flux. Given the "situational ethics" calculus described in chapter 4, as the relative resources of parties wax and wane, as circumstances evolve, and/or as China's needs and interests change, relationships must be constantly adjusted. Such adjustment can occur through physical struggle or through explicit or tacit negotiation, with negotiated adjustment generally preferable to open conflict.

This emphasis on relationships, flexibility, and adjustment accounts for the ritual surrounding the start of every meeting with Chinese counterparts, namely a description of the character of the parties' relationship and its history—are you an "old friend," a "partner," an "adversary"? In foreign affairs, a conversation often starts with each party sharing its strategic perspectives—who is gaining in influence, who is losing it, what are the macrotrends and the broader context for the relationship? The character of the two parties' relationship directly affects the objectives of a negotiation, the calculations of costs and benefits, and the tools employed. If you are an "old friend," such status obligates you to be solicitous of Chinese interests. If you have been an adversary, you should prove your sincerity. The Chinese are far more process oriented than Americans, who tend to be more outcomes oriented. As an adviser to China's senior leaders aptly put it:

> Define the relationship. Are we friends? If we are friends, if you say you have concerns [about the sale of weapons-related things to, say, Pakistan], then I should say, sure we are friends, I will sell, yes, but I will sell less, and you should compromise too. The American way is to define interests, and then we'll define our relationship. We don't really look at an issue from the viewpoint of interest [e.g., proliferation]—our first concern is the relationship. We [Chinese] should define our interests more. You should pay more attention to relationships and we should pay more attention to interests.[5]

At the outset of a negotiation, the Chinese side may have several objectives, not all of which necessarily easily coexist with one another or are in a clear order of preference. The objective is often indeterminate, with the Chinese party seeking to obtain the optimal combination of outcomes given the varied possibilities that emerge in the course of the negotiations themselves. Americans often enter discussions with a clearer objective, thereafter judging their success or failure by the degree to which this objective is achieved. Lucian Pye attributed the absence of clear Chinese goals when negotiating to the following: "Once the Chinese have achieved their general principles, it is often hard to discern precisely what they are after because of their use of ploys, tactics, and gamesmanship, often of a subtle nature, but frequently crude and transparent."[6] I attribute the lack of clarity of objective(s) to (1) the search for the best deal after all possible permutations of gains and losses have been explored and considered, and (2) the need for the Chinese side to bargain among itself first, before accepting the final deal. Often the Chinese discover what they want in the course of negotiation. A good example of this process is given by a Chinese general who tried to explain China's varied objectives and negotiating posture concerning nuclear weapons programs in North Korea:

> [In dealing with the North Korea issue, we have] three principles: stability, nonproliferation, and cooperation with the U.S., but sometimes these are hard to balance, so China is cautious, prudent. We make it clear that we won't accept the DPRK with nukes, but on the other hand we want stability, and probably the United States and other powers too. Also, China wants stable and cooperative relations with the U.S. So we want to say, "The thinking of people in China and the West is different. You go from the concrete to strategy; we from strategy to the concrete. We always say, China, the city, the street, the number, but you do the opposite; number, street, city, state, and country."[7]

In the Chinese approach to negotiation, the power equation between parties is critical. At any moment, a specific relationship is characterized by a particular distribution of benefits and deprivations that reflects the comprehensive power balance among the parties. For Chinese, there is every expectation that as the power balance shifts the distribution of benefits and deprivations will adjust accordingly. A strong China should get a better deal than a weak China. A strong America needs to make fewer concessions than a weaker one. This is why Chinese postglobal financial crisis perceptions of American decline are so important and have ramifications throughout the relationship.

The broad and dramatic increase of China's comprehensive national power has been notable since 1977, whether in terms of coercive, economic, or ideational strength, though core elements of soft power are anemic[8]—What does China stand for in the realm of values that is globally attractive? What is "brand China" that will attract others? From the 1840s on, when China was weak and emasculated—a consequence of both its own inner decay and the rising industrial and military power of the West and Japan—its negotiating leverage was greatly diminished compared to what it had been historically, at the zeniths of the great dynasties. In the late twentieth century and into the new millennium, however, with mounting national strength, PRC leaders and citizens believe the time has come to renegotiate arrangements that were made when China was in a weak position (e.g., Hong Kong and Macau have already been brought under the wing of the PRC, and the process is under way with respect to Taiwan, at least in terms of economic integration). This likely is part of the dynamic of more assertive PRC claims in the South and East China Seas in the new millennium, though part also is a reaction to the activities of others.

A parallel Chinese objective is to make sure that China occupies its "rightful place" in global institutions that were formed and grew after World War II and during the Cold War, when China was much weaker and comparatively isolated. Incursions such as sending uninvited warships and reconnaissance vessels up to the PRC's Twelve-Mile Limit had to be accepted when China was weak (and the range of its shore batteries limited). Today Beijing is not so pliant or so poorly armed. China will not necessarily use force to effect these changes, but there will be continual negotiations with Beijing to see how old arrangements can be adjusted in light of this new power equation. This is an era bound to involve frictions, and, if these are not managed carefully, dangers lie ahead. The PRC leaders or populace could misjudge what their new power entitles them to, and the major post–World War II powers and those under the U.S. security umbrella could overestimate their capacities. The possibility of miscalculation is inherent in this situation.

In prior scholarly analyses of the Chinese communist negotiating modus operandi, a reified, timeless quality creeps into exposition—it can seem as if nothing about negotiating with Chinese has changed for decades, indeed centuries. Though evocative, this is not entirely true. When Deng reappeared on stage in mid-1977, there were few channels through which the outside world had authoritative contact with PRC organizations and citizens, in any domain. Every interaction was funneled through a minuscule number of government choke points: in commerce there were about a dozen foreign trade corporations, a ministry, and the Guangzhou Trade Fair; in education and culture, there were the Ministries of Education and Culture; and most other contacts were mediated through the foreign affairs bureaucracies in "units" or territorial administrations, all ultimately connected to the Foreign Ministry. By way of contrast, in the second decade of the new millennium, the number of Chinese entities with whom one negotiates is almost infinite. The PRC is far more permeable and pluralistic than it used to be; consequently, the negotiating problem, and the opportunities, are not entirely the same. For the non-Chinese party to the negotiation, for example, there are now opportunities to play localities off each other, local administrations off the central state apparatus, private entities off each other, and the private sector off the public sector. The central state and the party try to reduce these opportunities, but it is increasingly difficult the more permeable China becomes.

In 1977, the Communist Party maintained a unified message in single negotiations and across negotiations, to a remarkable degree. Now the diversity of messages, points of view, and interests being promoted in China has burgeoned, reflecting the expanding pluralism of bureaucracy and society that has been one recurring theme of this volume. As we emphasize the continuities of Chinese negotiation thinking and practice, therefore, we must keep in mind that today there are a far greater number of more diverse negotiating parties than ever before in China's long history.

It is of considerable importance, therefore, how China negotiates using all its instruments of comprehensive national power. Much has been written on the Chinese art of negotiation, most notably by Lucian Pye, Carolyn Blackman, Richard Solomon, and Kenneth Young.[9] Preceding their work and dating back to the early days of the Nixon administration, the U.S. Congress and executive branch devoted considerable effort to understanding Chinese negotiation approaches. This early work, given political leadership by Senator Henry M. Jackson, drew upon writings about England's early interactions with China in the 1830s, protracted negotiations with Beijing during the Korean War, and more recent negotiating experience.[10] Work by Fred Ikle summarized what had been learned about communist negotiating styles from dealing with both Moscow and Beijing.[11] The general orientation of all this work was that there was a Chinese (communist) style of negotiation and that America's diplomats had best be prepared for it. My purpose here is not to recapitulate their work but rather to examine how Chinese leaders have used negotiation to pursue state interests in the era of reform and to assess how, as China's power has grown, its approaches have evolved. Below we examine reform-era negotiating practices from a number of angles.

PREPARING FOR NEGOTIATION

Chinese negotiators do their homework. In every interaction, they have a command of the prior negotiating record that usually matches, and often exceeds, the knowledge of those across the table. In the U.S. political system, with its election-driven personnel turnover that penetrates down many layers in governmental bureaucracies, and with the defensive removal of many relevant executive branch records when one political party assumes power from the other in a transition, each new U.S. administration only gradually discovers what happened on its predecessor's watch. This reality contrasts with the promotion practices in the Chinese bureaucracy, which produce negotiators who spend most of their career in the same general bureaucratic silo. The American party to a negotiation is often disadvantaged by the Chinese side's level of preparation and continuity. Chinese negotiators also work to create a psychological setting that works to their advantage, and they do so by first learning as much as they can about the individuals with whom they are dealing—knowledge that becomes evident in the course of the interaction.

Chinese interlocutors pay attention to defining at least three key aspects of the negotiating context: the *moral matrix* for discussions; the *power relationship* between or among the parties; and *the arena* in which negotiation occurs.

Setting the Moral Matrix

The moral matrix involves the creation of a sense that the Chinese side is morally upright and united, that Beijing occupies the principled high ground, and that, therefore, moral rectitude requires any opposing party to concede, or at least compromise.

This emphasis in Chinese thinking was first given expression by Sun Tzu when, in talking of the tools of war, he said: "The first of these factors is moral influence. . . . By moral influence I mean that which causes the people to be in harmony with their leaders, so that they will accompany them in life and unto death without fear of mortal peril."[12] Yan Xuetong, a Tsinghua University international relations specialist, goes back to the pre-Qin era (prior to 221 BCE) in his recent work, arguing that Chinese thinking with respect to dealing with outsiders has always emphasized the independent power conferred by moral superiority.[13]

The underlying moral dimension that a Chinese negotiating team chooses to emphasize changes depending on the issue and the power relationships of the parties involved. In the 1970s, for example, with the Cultural Revolution decade still under way, America and China cautiously approached each other on the long road to normalization while Japan and the United States were allies. Initially, Beijing sought to drive a wedge between the two allies by emphasizing the discordance that

Washington's support for Japanese defense capability presented in the face of past Japanese World War II atrocities and its presumed future aggressive inclinations. In an August 1971 conversation with American scholars, Premier Zhou Enlai and Yao Wenyuan argued that it was a moral imperative to rein in the militarization of Japan. The underlying argument was an attempt to put Washington (and more particularly the anti–Vietnam War students with whom they were conversing) on the ethical defensive regarding the U.S. alliance with Japan.

> *Yao Wenyuan:* "The revival of Japanese militarism is being fostered single-handedly by U.S. imperialism. President Nixon also admitted this point in his public statements saying that they are fostering their former enemies. . . ."
>
> *Zhou Enlai:* "Yes, it is a fact that Japanese militarism is being revived because the Japanese economy is developing in a lop-sided way. They lack resources, they must import their natural resources and for markets too they depend on foreign countries. And after the war they were not burdened by paying reparations, and also for quite some time they spent very little on armaments. There is one characteristic of the development of their economy, that is, they made a fortune on wars fought by others, that is, the war of aggression against Korea and the war of aggression against Vietnam. . . . And so this lop-sided development of Japan, what will issue from it? She needs to carry out an economic expansion abroad. Otherwise, she cannot maintain her economy."[14]

Then, in the late 1970s, consistent with the "situational ethics" approach described in chapter 4, as China became more concerned about the Soviet Union and as Washington and Beijing moved toward normalization, Sino-American-Japanese military cooperation to offset Soviet expansionism became the new moral imperative. As President Jimmy Carter put it, "As our ties with the Chinese were strengthened, their concerns about a possible Japanese threat diminished, and they began to urge that Japan's defense capability be improved."[15] Chinese interlocutors did a moral about-face—suddenly Tokyo and Washington were not doing enough to oppose the "Soviet bear."

Setting the moral matrix can also apply to functional policy realms. Take the Copenhagen Conference on global climate change in December 2009, for instance. By trying to establish the ethical baseline for decision, Beijing sought to incline whatever eventual agreement there might be in the direction of its interests. The PRC argued that justice required the United States and other early industrializers to take greater responsibility, and assume greater burdens, in addressing the climate change issue in the twenty-first century because they had depleted the atmosphere's absorptive capacity with their emissions of greenhouse gases in the nineteenth and twentieth centuries. Basically, justice should not require the same burdens on today's poor, yet-to-industrialize countries as would be placed on those who had gotten rich by earlier environmental depredations.[16] In March 2009, China's ambassador to the climate change talks, Yu Qingtai, stated that there were different interpretations of responsibilities for "past problems they [the United States] [had] caused." "I expect harsh exchanges," he said of the United States and China at the Copenhagen Conference coming up at the end of that year.[17] Further, it was an issue of justice as to how contributors to the problem of climate change were defined—was per capita CO_2 emission the fair yardstick (in which case the United States had more than three times the Chinese emissions per capita in 2008), or was the absolute volume of CO_2 emission the just and appropriate standard (in which case China already had passed the United States)? Thus China frequently raises issues of justice, fairness, and equal treatment and uses them as instruments of global politics. Such discussions set the table for negotiation.

Defining the Power Relationship

Early on in a negotiation with a Chinese counterpart, one of the things that occurs is either an explicit or an implied definition of the power relationship (or trends in that relationship) existing between the two parties. A celebrated case of this was seen in Hanoi in July 2010 at the Regional Forum of the Association of Southeast Asian Nations (ASEAN), at which the Chinese foreign minister told the Singaporean foreign minister George Yeo that China was big and Singapore small and they would be well-advised not to forget it. Chinese negotiators are highly attuned to the strength of the other side's *domestic and foreign affairs* circumstances, believing that diminishing or fragmenting an opponent's domestic or international support can promote China's interests. "Sometimes" Sun Tzu said, "drive a wedge between a sovereign and his ministers; on other occasions separate his allies from him. Make them mutually suspicious so that they drift apart. Then you can plot against them."[18] In any case, the firmness of the interlocutor's domestic and foreign support is a key piece of information, as is Beijing's overall assessment of the adversary's comprehensive national power.

The Chinese use four power positions to portray themselves in the realm of international negotiations: (1) the stronger position, giving the other side little leverage to extract much, or playing the role of a solicitously helpful stronger partner; (2) the posture of the needy, weaker party, in which case the other "stronger" party has an obligation to help or rectify past injustice; (3) the posture that its power is growing, so that arriving at a deal earlier will be more advantageous to the other party than waiting (this scenario is a growing subtext in cross-Taiwan Strait interaction); (4) the posture that the two parties need each other reciprocally, requiring the flexibility and accommodation of both.

One approach to defining the power equation is to define a common opponent or problem, point out that the interlocutor's strength is insufficient to address that challenge alone, and suggest that under appropriate conditions China can cooperate to address that problem. Part of creating "appropriate conditions" is that the interlocutor must adjust policies in other domains salient to Beijing. In 2005, a very senior Ministry of Foreign Affairs official put it candidly in the context of being asked to boost pressure on North Korea to achieve nonproliferation objectives of great moment to Washington: "'China is ready to work with the U.S. for a peaceful, non-nuclear [Korean] peninsula. We want you to care as much about Taiwan as you want us to care about Korea.'"[19] On the same topic, a PRC university-based strategic analyst more recently put it even more bluntly: "'We hope that North Korea presents a threat to the United States and South Korea—this is in our interest. Only when we have stabilized the Taiwan Strait, then we abandon North Korea. North Korea knows this and knows now is their last chance to get nukes.'"[20]

Indeed, this strategy of identifying a common challenge and dangling possible Chinese cooperation as an inducement for progress on another issue was part of the logic that led to the normalization of relations between Beijing and Washington in the 1970s. In the second half of the 1970s, when Soviet power appeared to be growing unabated and Washington was not outwardly proceeding toward normalization with the PRC, Beijing told other countries that the United States was a declining power and needed Chinese cooperation to effectively oppose Moscow, the true threat to the West. In Foreign Minister Huang Hua's fall 1977 words:

> The world today is more tense and less relaxed than it was fifteen years ago. Why is this? It is because of the intensified rivalry between the USSR and the U.S. One can talk about a world climate and focus on food or human rights, but the real problem of "climate" is the position of the United States, which is one of steadily declining military power. The United States over the last

fifteen years has been going down in relative power. At the end of World War II the United States was supreme, but now that is no longer the case. In 1970 President Nixon said that the United States did not enjoy its previous status.

. . . The USSR, however, is unprecedentedly strong today, especially militarily. It is now successfully contending with the U.S. as it makes large appropriations for war preparations. Hua Guofeng has said that the U.S. has a defensive concern in protecting its interest while the USSR wants to attack. This is an objective fact which all people in the world recognize.[21]

In the new millennium, pointing out that Washington needs Beijing's help with Pyongyang, in stabilizing the global economy, or dealing with transnational issues such as climate change or infectious diseases, is de rigueur for Beijing. In the wake of the global economic crisis marked by the collapse of Lehman Brothers in late 2008, the Chinese debated among themselves the degree to which the United States was on the decline and the opportunities this might afford the PRC. The debate lasted in the media and Chinese society until at least 2012, at which time America's economy started growing again and the Chinese economic expansion slowed, forcing a recalibration of just how fast the United States was being eclipsed by a rising China. Indeed, a Pew poll released in late 2012 showed a 12-point drop in the percentage of Chinese seeing the PRC's economy as the world's "leading economic power" between the spring of 2009 and the spring of 2012.[22]

In negotiations, sometimes acknowledging its own weakness better serves Beijing's purposes. In the fifteen-year-long marathon negotiations with the United States and the GATT/WTO over accession to the global trade body (concluding with PRC entry in 2001), China argued that because of its still notable economic infirmities it merited "developing country" status that would entitle it to less onerous entry conditions than those imposed on more developed economies. Similarly, pleading lack of diplomatic clout can be a way to sidestep inconvenient demands. Beijing frequently argues that it lacks influence with countries that Washington wants Beijing to pressure—North Vietnam in the 1970s, North Korea in the 1990s and the new millennium, and Iran with respect to its presumed nuclear weapons program from 2000 on.

Sometimes China's incapacity is genuine. From Deng Xiaoping's earliest interaction with World Bank president Robert McNamara in April 1980, he used the PRC's genuine underdevelopment as a principal argument for early and massive World Bank engagement with China. McNamara was struck by Deng's open exposition on his country's disabilities, as recounted in chapter 1. I do not know whether Deng also knew that McNamara had been in China in World War II. The former defense secretary and the World Bank leader seemed to find redemption from his prosecution of the war in Vietnam by subsequently participating constructively in international development work generally, and especially in China, where he had positive World War II memories. Similarly, President Jimmy Carter, who was in Qingdao briefly in 1949 as a naval officer, was deeply affected by what he saw firsthand in the war-torn country—obvious weakness and great potential simultaneously. The combination of early exposure to a weak and war-torn China and a sense of moral obligation (from a strong Christian upbringing) can be a factor shaping negotiations; the Chinese often have played their cards well. Carter recounts: "Once when we were discussing the Far East, I remarked that the people of our country had a deep and natural affection for the people of China. When most of the group laughed, I was perplexed and a little embarrassed. It took me a few moments to realize that not everyone had looked upon Christian missionaries in China as the ultimate heroes and had not, as youngsters, contributed a penny or a nickel each week, year after year, toward schools and hospitals for little Chinese children."[23]

Akin to the "China is a developing country" line of argument is the "China is precariously weak" argument, which translates to "Pushing excessively for reform may destabilize everything, to the detriment of Chinese and foreigners alike." Vice-Premier Li Lanqing put it succinctly enough—"The development of China's economy will be important to world peace. Look at Yugoslavia. We don't want more Yugoslavias. Were we to fail we could bring trouble one hundred times that of Yugoslavia."[24] A very senior foreign affairs official used the same approach when speaking to American foreign policy journal editors in the late 1990s, saying, "Some talk of a China threat. Starving Chinese are a threat! North Korea doesn't have a big population and it wants assistance, but the international community cannot satisfy their requests. 'So, you can imagine if China were plunged into crisis—a real China threat.'"[25]

In short, how the power equation is framed at the outset of a negotiation is key. Sometimes one encounters the strong, united China; at other times it is China that needs assistance and to which one has an obligation to help by virtue of past injustice or benevolence. At still other times, China and the interlocutors may address a common problem as equals—a problem of a magnitude that neither can resolve alone but that both can manage together. How the power relationship is framed at the outset of the interaction can signal a great deal about possible scenarios and outcomes.

Specifying the Negotiation Arena

A third dimension of the context to which the Chinese attach great importance is the character of the arena in which negotiation is to occur. When specifying the arena, there are at least two aspects Beijing considers most conducive to achieving its objectives: setting the physical and psychological stage and defining the parties at the table.

There is a showmanship dimension to negotiations with Chinese. Usually the leader with whom one is dealing has obviously given forethought to where the meeting will occur—preferring the PRC as a rule. The actual location is usually grand in scale, opulent in detail, and extremely ordered with a kind of grace that envelops the visitor—elegantly tailored and coiffed tea ladies serve the visitors amid the wafting scent of jasmine. The decor of the room often seems selected to reinforce the message to be conveyed—discussing Taiwan in the Taiwan Room of the Great Hall of the People, for example. Leaders point to the paintings and murals on the walls to make points, such as referring to mountain scenes when urging the other side to "take a long-term strategic perspective" and to view things from lofty heights. The seemingly minimal security (though it is in fact pervasive) as you enter the leadership compound and approach the PRC leader with very little hint of security conveys absolute confidence. A meeting with China's president in the pavilion on Yingtai Island in Zhongnanhai in the middle of Beijing involves your driving a curved road to the elevated traditional building, with the president appearing like an apparition to greet you, an effect that goes some distance in conveying a clear sense of order, control, dominance, hierarchy, and, indeed, majesty that serves their purposes—perhaps to awe the visitor before discussions begin. For the Chinese, where you meet and what message is conveyed by the physical environment are part of setting the stage.

A second aspect of establishing the psychological setting that closely relates to the first is that against the background of splendor, indulgence, and hospitality there is an explicit or implicit expectation that such treatment calls for reciprocation, or at least deference, on the part of the visitor. As President Jiang Zemin put it to one senior group of American visitors that met with him on that island in Zhongnanhai,

"There is a saying of Mencius: since you have come from afar, you must have brought benefits to my country."[26] My introductory comments in my record of the meeting describe the impact of the physical setting: "President Jiang greeted us, emperor-like, at the front door—all in all, an ethereal physical context for the meeting."[27]

While the physical and psychological setting created by Chinese for meetings is distinctive, Beijing's preference to deal with weaker parties bilaterally and stronger parties multilaterally is not unique. China decries "internationalization" of the South China Sea issue, for instance, wishing to avoid a multilateral negotiation involving ASEAN (or any substantial subset of the group), much less an enlarged negotiation that might include "outside" powers. Dealing with individual small countries on its periphery one at a time, and thus isolating one claimant from the others, is far preferable from Beijing's perspective. Unsurprisingly, China's small neighbors prefer the opposite. Hanoi is very clear about this with respect to South China Sea claims. One senior member of Vietnam's National Assembly told me: "'China will try to go bilateral as much as possible.'"[28]

When the PRC wishes to constrain an equal or stronger power, however, then multilateral organizations may well serve Beijing's interests. For example, Beijing has joined with more than thirty countries (including India, Russia, *and* the United States) to oppose the European Union's effort to charge a carbon tax on airlines using EU airports, scheduled to start on January 1, 2012.[29] Beijing's expressed preference is to use the International Civil Aviation Organization (ICAO) to set whatever rules may eventually be adopted with respect to aircraft carbon emissions, rather than to have a regional organization of which it is not a member impose a standard. Incidentally, Beijing has consistently opposed granting membership or observer status in the ICAO to Taipei. In this example, we see Beijing's use of isolation from multilateral organizations as a way to apply pressure on Taiwan to adhere to Beijing's One China Principle.

A number of multilateral international organizations have decision rules that obscure accountability and give great weight to minorities, which is very helpful to the PRC when it is trying to stop international action while avoiding blame for the resulting stasis. In 2012, for instance, the UN Conference on the Arms Trade Treaty was convened in July in New York. One country could block any agreement that might be made. In this case, China, Russia, and the United States all found it expedient to indefinitely postpone agreement. Similarly, as of

July 2012, Beijing joined the Russians three times in vetoing various UN Security Council measures promoted by the United States, Europe, and others to try to put pressure on Syrian president Assad to stop killing his own people. In these organizations the PRC can stop, stall, sidetrack, or water down proposals to the point that it can sign on without major damage to its core interests and can often barely leave diplomatic fingerprints. In fairness, these same strategies also are employed by other big powers, not least the United States. One of the most notable changes in Chinese behavior in the new millennium has been its increasing willingness to more strongly assert its interests by using its capacity to block actions in the U.N. Security Council, even at the cost of considerable international criticism.

DEBATE

In thinking about the Chinese style of argumentation, the very first need is to get the vocabulary straight—there are "basic principles" (*jiben yuanze*), "policy" (*zhengce*), "goals" (*mudi*), and "proposals" (*jianyi*). Principles are presumably unwavering and non-negotiable; policies and goals can shift according to circumstances; and proposals are flexible, transient, and malleable, as long as they are relatively consistent with the principles involved. Of course, which "principle" is summoned to the debate can change. In general, the Chinese prefer to obtain agreement on broad principles before getting to a discussion of the more flexible elements of policies, goals, and proposals. A principal PRC official in Taiwan affairs put it this way with respect to the Taiwan issue in 2005: "'One China' is a basic principle, and we can't retreat, and firmly peaceful reunification is a goal, and we will try our best, but whether it is realized depends not only on us—Taiwan too—it is a policy, not a principle. 'One Country, Two Systems' is not a principle or a policy, it is a proposal. This can be discussed, [the PRC] won't force [Taiwan] to accept it. If Taiwan feels it is not good, it can suggest 'One Country, Three Systems,' or others."[30]

A recurring device in Chinese negotiating strategy is to anchor talks in the principle of respecting the differences among social and political systems. This strategy includes invoking respect for the more closed aspects of the Chinese political structure when the issue involves outside access to the PRC system, and simultaneously taking full advantage of the comparatively permeable and transparent nature of many external systems to maximize Chinese gains. The facade of equality is maintained because one standard is applied across the board—treating each system with equal respect, on its own terms. The outcomes, however, are unequal because the possibilities to exploit each system are radically different. The issue of "transparency" is a good example. With the U.S. freedom-of-information system and its open ethos, China (particularly the military) has less incentive to reciprocally provide information. As one senior Chinese academic put it: "The U.S. has the Freedom of Information Act. 'China gets a free lunch.'"[31]

The United States ran into this problem in the earliest days of the student exchange program, one of Deng Xiaoping's very first bilateral initiatives after his 1977 return. The number of U.S.-bound Chinese students grew much more rapidly than the number of Americans going to the mainland (for reasons beyond relative population size differences, disparate levels of education development, and the dearth of Chinese language-capable U.S. students). Moreover, research areas (both geographic and disciplinary) in the PRC were greatly limited for U.S. scholars, while Chinese students had access to almost every disciplinary field and physical location in America. A summarization of my rough field notes of a mid-1979 discussion between Fang Yi, Chinese minister of the State Scientific and Technological Commission, and Joseph Califano, U.S. secretary of Health, Education, and Welfare, explains that Beijing wanted China's Education Ministry to tightly control which Americans went where in China for what educational and research purposes, while PRC authorities wanted to deal individually with U.S. universities to maximize access and financial aid for Chinese students with a minimum of Washington oversight. Beijing wanted the benefits of centralism which its own system conferred on it when dealing with Americans, and the benefits of the U.S. federal, decentralized system when the issue was Chinese students going to America. President Carter and Secretary Califano were, I believe, very wise in accepting this inequality, but it was an inequality, except in the sense that each side was equally respecting the character of the other.[32]

Asking that a partner in debate respect the character of the Chinese system assumes other forms as well. It is common for Beijing to say that it agrees with the broad objectives of an interlocutor demanding change in China but to go on and explain that implementation of the desired policy is very complex and may require more time or may simply prove infeasible because of the complexities involved. For example, since the 1980s Washington has been pushing Beijing to control exports of dual-use technology and weapons to Iran, and in the second decade of the new millennium it wants the PRC's help with even more comprehensive and tighter sanctions. One senior PRC foreign affairs official explained the difficulties of doing everything Washington wanted:

> "Both are a priority, oil and nonproliferation. We have to have a balance in these things." We need to take all these entities and interests into account. Can we control these entities [the multitude of Chinese foreign policy actors]? We have export control, quite good and there is cooperation with the U.S., and we have an improving ability to implement. We sometimes worry whether these [Chinese] companies will have consequences for sanctions and they have a sense of risk. And we need to get provinces to implement. [They are] doing secret business with some countries. When we find companies doing business against UNSC [UN Security Council] sanctions.[33]

Over the reform era, Chinese interlocutors have increasingly invoked "public opinion" as a constraint on their latitude, as explained in chapter 4. The clincher rebuttal to a foreign demand is some version of "The Chinese people, all 1.3 billion of them, would dislodge leaders who agreed to that!" Defense Minister Chi Haotian explained why no Chinese leader could countenance Taiwan independence:

> As you know, my friends, in accordance with history, the 1895 Treaty of Shimonoseki, Taiwan was ceded to Japan. To us this is a national disgrace. At that time the whole people of China depended on Li Hongzhang [senior tutor to the heir apparent, senior grand secretary of state, minister superintendent of trade for the northern ports of China, viceroy of the province of Chili, and earl of the first rank, who negotiated the treaty,] and as a matter of fact Li Hongzhang is a disgraced name to the Chinese people. In 1945, [Taiwan] returned to the motherland. We can't allow Taiwan independence.[34]

Another device in the Chinese negotiation toolkit is to inoculate the Chinese side against threats by asserting that the threatening party (or third parties valued to the threatening party) will be hurt more grievously by the imposition of a threat than China. Good examples include post–June 4, 1989, attempts (particularly during the first Clinton administration) to hold the annual renewal of what was then called most-favored-nation (MFN) tariff treatment (it is now called Normal Trade Relations, or NTR) hostage to "whether China makes significant progress in improving its human rights record."[35] A key line of Chinese argumentation throughout the decade or so of trench warfare on this issue was that imposition of the threat not only would hurt U.S. economic interests, but also would hurt societies like Hong Kong and Taiwan—places the United States viewed as ideological or economic friends.[36] In 1991, vice-foreign minister and Xinhua director in Hong Kong Zhou Nan told the journalist David Gergen, "If MFN is rescinded, China will suffer but it will still survive. Hong Kong will be hurt even more."[37] A little more than two years later, Premier Li Peng spoke more bluntly: "Let me ask, if China's MFN status is revoked, who will lose the most? Surely the United States will not suffer the most because China's share of your trade is not that large. China will suffer, but not the most. We are not like Russia where people are suffering. We aren't begging for food. Hong Kong will suffer the most; the entrepot trade has given Hong Kong great opportunity for trade and profit. If you have any doubts, go ask the American consul general in Hong Kong. See if he agrees with my assessment."[38]

The tactic of arguing that unwelcome U.S. actions will hurt the ones Washington most cares about also applies to domestic constituencies within China itself. In a 1991 conversation with Foreign Minister Qian Qichen, he explained how the imposition of economic sanctions against the PRC would *not* particularly hurt state-owned enterprises (SOEs)—arms of the state that were the presumed target of U.S. economic reprisal for human rights abuses—but would hurt town and village enterprises (TVEs), which constituted the more nearly private, entrepreneurial, individual sector of the Chinese economy. This was the sector of the Chinese economy that Americans would want to nurture in most situations.[39] Likewise, Mayor Han Yulin of Zhangzhou City in Fujian argued that the imposition of U.S. economic sanctions would harm TVEs, foreign-invested enterprises, and wholly owned foreign enterprises in his city: "You are frank and enthusiastic, but you [Americans in general] have a defect. You make decisions rashly. The June Fourth incident [happened], then you put on sanctions [on China]. You should investigate things. All this affected TVEs, JVs, wholly owned enterprises. Americans don't want this, so listen to my suggestions and opinions. Second, the U.S. needs rapid economic growth; we are a 1.2 billion market. The U.S. ought not leave China. We buy Boeing aircraft, advanced equipment, [export] cheap goods."[40]

Similarly, from the beginning of reform until the present day, U.S. universities have found it difficult to deny access to increasingly large numbers of Chinese students and scholars coming to their campuses in order to persuade PRC authorities to stop blacklisting high-profile U.S. scholars (generally from the very same campuses that are accepting large numbers of PRC students and researchers). Why? In part, because the victims would be Chinese citizens who bear no responsibility for the offending policy and whom U.S. policy makers generally wish to assist. Of course, the quality of Chinese students, the tuition revenues they provide, and the central importance that PRC students play in many U.S. graduate programs are also critical considerations. Yet the essential issue remains—Chinese scholars have largely unfettered access to America, while U.S. scholars face more obstacles going to the PRC, even conceding enormous improvements in the situation since 1978. This has the patina of equality because each party is showing equal respect for the distinct qualities of the other's system, but things do not necessarily balance out.

LINKAGE

Beijing has been increasingly using "linkage" as a tactic against opponents—withholding cooperation on items important to the other side in order to push the opponent in the desired direction on another issue. The use of this tactic comes from China's increasing importance across an ever broader array of key global issues, and the growing need for Beijing's cooperation in their resolution or management. PRC Admiral Yang Yi explained the phenomenon subtly, but unmistakably, in 2010: "In America, there are some people who remark that China has previously tolerated U.S. sales of arms to Taiwan and ask why China is reacting so intensely this time. The reason for the Chinese reaction is that the Sino-U.S. relationship has grown beyond the bilateral domains and categories that were traditionally important and has become the kind of global partnership that responds to every kind of challenge. If one side lacks sincerity, then how will the other side retort?"[41]

"Retorts" may be seen in Beijing's policies toward North Korea, Iran, and Syria, and in many other behaviors. Basically, cooperation on pressuring North Korea (or Iran or Syria) may depend on Washington's policy toward Taiwan. Similarly in the wake of the U.S. rebalancing ("the pivot") policy of late 2011 and thereafter, the Chinese (quite predictably) may be inclined to be less cooperative on some third issues that Washington finds important.

Linkage, though decried by Beijing when Washington seeks to employ it (as it did in the first Clinton administration), is often used by China in the economic realm. The Chinese point to conflicts of interest between America and its allies, or to commercial competitors of U.S. companies—Japan, Germany, or Airbus. American negotiators often hear that if they adopt policies contrary to China's interests in one area,

U.S. firms will suffer while firms in Japan, Germany, and elsewhere will simply pick up the slack. Foreign Minister Qian Qichen explained to journalist and presidential advisor David Gergen: "Japan has many advantages [over the United States in dealing with the PRC]; nearer and better understanding of China. Japan provided us credits and loans; America also has conditions in its favor, but also domestic obstacles [meaning Congress, in part]. I believe it is not in the interest of the United States to resort to economic and trade means to pressure [others]. The U.S. stopped its grain exports to the Soviet Union, but it was American farmers who suffered."[42]

Sometimes this message is most effectively articulated by Chinese who have close and trusting relationships with the opposing side, as was the case in 1992 when a Chinese educational leader with a longtime American connection warned a visiting U.S. delegation that "most-favored-nation [tariff treatment] is not a favor just for China but also benefits this whole region and the United States. We hear daily of Japanese dominance and Germany, they'd welcome a U.S. so distanced from the Chinese market."[43]

In the 2010–13 period, Beijing sometimes practiced "linkage," without even announcing the policy, permitting action to do the talking. In late 2010 Beijing seemingly impeded the flow of strategic materials (rare earths) to Japan in retaliation for a maritime incident.[44] In 2012, it curtailed imports of Philippine bananas in retaliation for another maritime incident.[45] And in the wake of greatly heightened tensions over the Diaoyu/Senkaku Islands between Beijing and Tokyo in 2012–13, Chinese imports of Japanese products dropped, falling 14.5 percent in the single month of November 2012.[46] The China that decried economic linkage as practiced by Washington in the 1990s appears to be an ardent practitioner of the policy in the new millennium.

For Beijing, as Washington found out in its ill-fated efforts to tie the conferral of MFN status to Beijing's domestic human rights practices, linkage has a number of downsides. By taking a conflict in one zone and expanding it to another, other parties not directly involved are inevitably hurt, becoming collateral damage. Punishing Japan by slowing rare earth exports, for example, frightened the rest of the world about China's reliability as a strategic materials supplier. Immediately the world system began to adjust by seeking out and developing new, more reliable suppliers. In addition, enlarging the zone of conflict led to the loss of previously sympathetic constituencies in both the target country and the collateral damage areas. Finally, if Beijing punishes a supplier of components that it needs to manufacture its own exports, Chinese profits and employment levels are damaged by the PRC's own retaliation. Beijing is not oblivious to these realities.

An approach related to linkage is for the Chinese to try to induce the other side to reconsider the interests that might be served by accommodation. For instance, a point of contention with Beijing since June 4, 1989, has been Washington's prohibition against military sales and its restrictions on "dual-use" sales to Beijing. A particular sore point has been the Black Hawk helicopter that the United States sold China in the mid-1980s but since June 4, 1989, has refused to sell spare parts for, even to ensure airworthiness. Beyond Beijing's argument that America's allies (including Israel) manage to transfer technology to the PRC and thereby benefit because the Americans have unilaterally withdrawn from the China market, I was struck by the viewpoint of one ranking Chinese military officer. He argued that resuming dual-use technology sales to the PLA would provide Washington avenues of vision into China's technological development and that the PLA would become more dependent on the United States:

> Regarding technology exports. Would you welcome this thinking? If such technology is used by the PLA is it necessarily bad for the U.S.? "It is inconceivable that the U.S. and China should be at war with each other. Think of the vastness of the PLA as a market. If you would loosen up on technology to the PLA that doesn't bear on U.S. security, it would increase confidence. Take the Black Hawk helicopter—we need them at high elevations. For example, the Wenchuan earthquake, but the U.S. refused to provide parts [for the helicopters long ago sold to China prior to 1989]. Maybe our American friends need to think about technological cooperation with the PLA that could increase leverage over the PLA. You need to think about this."[47]

Last, when an incipient coalition is forming that needs China's cooperation on an issue—as in the stalled Doha Round of WTO talks in 2005, or intervention in Iraq in 2003, or Libya in 2011—and Beijing is either lukewarm or hesitant about having to take a stand, the PRC will simply wait to see what happens. In many situations, the PRC states something to the effect of "China will not stand in the way of a consensus reached by others, but Beijing will not take the lead in reaching that consensus." Beijing thereby avoids making enemies in what may prove to be a futile effort to reach a deal and leaves itself room to "sell" its support to the highest bidder in the end game.

This is what Beijing did in 1990 when it waited until the last possible moment before committing not to veto UN Resolution 678 authorizing the First Gulf War. In the negotiations immediately preceding that vote, the PRC extracted a Washington, D.C., visit for Foreign Minister Qian Qichen (which took place in March 1991), thereby breaking the post–June 4, 1989, ban on high-level official exchanges that Washington had imposed as reprisal for the June 4 violence. As President Bush Sr. and Brent Scowcroft later recounted concerning the run-up to the November UN resolution vote, Secretary of State James Baker was working to obtain Chinese support, or at least acquiescence for, UN Resolution 678. Qian "was noncommittal about backing the resolution and wanted something in return. He tried to get Baker to promise that either he or the President would visit Beijing. . . . Qian and Baker apparently agreed that Qian would come to Washington after the vote, to see the President if they gave a 'yes' vote and Baker if it was an abstention."[48] The Chinese abstained and Qian nonetheless saw the president early the following year after the Chinese ambassador in Washington called Scowcroft at 3:00 one morning to inform him that Minister Qian would cancel his trip if he didn't see the president.[49] It was a matter of face.

That the Chinese place great importance on "face" is a cliché. Nonetheless, they sometimes bet so much of their own face on an outcome—often for symbolism that will play well back home—that for the interlocutor to thwart a negotiation would produce consequences disproportionate to what seems at stake. In a game of chicken, the one who throws the steering wheel out the window first is likely to win. Often Beijing throws the steering wheel out the window over what seem to outsiders to be trivial issues. This suggests one of two things—either the issues are not trivial or this modus operandi is a Chinese tool of negotiation.

TOOLS

Effectively negotiating with the PRC requires understanding how Chinese view the relationship between coercive power (force) and softer power (persuasion). One high-level PRC central government official explained his view of hard and soft power and Deng Xiaoping's two-fisted negotiation style:

> "We are mobilizing hard and soft power. Soft power often is spontaneous, but hard power should be guided by the government. At some times it may be hard to balance the two types, but for those countries that have hard power, they may overemphasize and vice versa, and the danger is empty talk and no action, so we need a balance between the two." . . . If you use soft

power to resolve problems, it is better not to use hard power. The late Deng Xiaoping said once in analogy, "The right hand prepares to negotiate, the left hand to use force. But usually your right hand is stronger than the left hand."[50]

Words are used by the Chinese as a tool of negotiation. While Chinese interlocutors are capable of occupying time with either "short introductions" (*jiandan jieshao*), long explications of well-known facts, lengthy orations on the merits of China's positions, or the deficiencies of the other side's actions or stand, when they are serious about achieving an outcome from an interchange, they can listen attentively and be parsimonious. As one of China's premier diplomats in the 1970s and 1980s, Vice-Foreign Minister Zhang Wenjin, put it in a conversation with Ambassador Seignious of the Arms Control and Disarmament Agency in January 1980: "I intend to listen more than speak."[51]

For Americans, nature abhors a vacuum—which they often proceed to fill with conversation. For the Chinese side, this American proclivity toward chatter has its value—revealing motivations, supplying information, possibly revealing divergences of interest on the interlocutor's side, and giving the Chinese side an understanding of the possible outcomes of a negotiation. Negotiations in China almost always open with some version of the following statement: "Our guests have come from afar. It is Chinese custom to invite the guest to speak first." Interestingly, in negotiations that occur outside China, the opening gambit is quite similar in intent: "You are the host and we have come from afar to hear your views." In either case, Americans are usually happy to express their views first, often at length.

However, this is not to say that Chinese leaders do not enjoy talking; Chinese leaders vary greatly in their volubility. Jiang Zemin was loquacious, while Li Peng and Hu Jintao were more taciturn. Deng Xiaoping could be nearly monosyllabic but was always to the point. And, when the Chinese are dealing with a familiar interlocutor and have a clear objective, they may seize the initiative, seeking to set the agenda and make proposals.

There is also the art of what is *not* said or written. This art was practiced in virtuoso form in the 1972 Shanghai Communiqué in order to avoid overspecifying the "One China" concept—"The United States acknowledges that all Chinese on either side of the Taiwan Strait maintain there is but one China and that Taiwan is a part of China. The United States Government does not challenge that position." Along similar lines, in a 2008 conversation a very senior leader on Taiwan explained how Beijing and Taipei had decided to initiate cross-Strait charter flights and dealt with an issue that came up with the signing of the final agreement. The problem involved how each party wanted to write the date because Taipei (the Republic of China, or ROC) dates things from the 1911 revolution, whereas the PRC uses conventional Western dating. The PRC would not sign a document using the ROC dating system, and Taipei would not sign a document with only a Western date on it. This very senior Taiwan official explained the resolution. "When we reached agreement on charter [flight] agreements, the most difficult part was how to date the documents—the ninety-seventh year of the ROC. Both sides left blank the date and put it in later. So we were able to work around [the problem]. 'Chinese wisdom and a masterpiece of ambiguity.'"[52]

Another tool of Chinese negotiation is to try to divide, discredit, shame, intimidate, or upon occasion praise specific members of the interlocutor's team. If the Chinese perceive that there is a range of views among the opposing team, they sometimes seek to discredit the most vulnerable (usually lower-ranking) member of the opposing team, often by asserting that he or she "does not know China very well." The hope is that culling the weakest in the herd will inhibit others from expressing similar views and dampen nonconforming views on both the Chinese and foreign sides. A memorable instance of this occurred in Beijing when a senior PLA general took offense at an American scholar's remarks in the presence of senior U.S. defense leaders and gave him a tongue-lashing, seeking to tarnish his credentials in the eyes of his own countrymen:

> "Your [XX, U.S. scholar] assertion that China is in an arms race—not true! [*bu dui*]—twenty-six SU-27s, but no arms race. The idea that sovereignty is outdated is wrong! It cannot be violated by anyone—wrong! [*bu dui*]. It is rudeness to say our concept of sovereignty is outdated. This is hegemonistic. You don't understand China!" . . . Do you [XX, U.S. scholar] recognize Taiwan as a part of China? I am shocked, really shocked, about this. We cannot have repression under the pretext of stability. China emphasizes democracy. People should be involved in politics. There are 2,900 people's representatives in the National People's Congress—every nationality, representatives from the agriculture sector, every sector; this is a broad representation from all walks of life. How can it be said the PRC is not for democracy? I am shocked about the allegation. Political reform, I am shocked—[you] said political reform is behind economic reform. You should not point your finger at China. I am really shocked by all these allegations, so I asked for the chance to air my views. I would like to say I am really shocked—respect facts. What are the motives, if we don't respect the facts? . . . [XX, U.S. scholar] does not know well China, and fabrications.[53]

Another tool in the shaming repertoire is to throw interlocutors off balance by attributing sufficiently malicious motives so that they then feel compelled to reassure the Chinese side of their sincerity and good-will. In 2011 discussions with a very senior PRC foreign policy leader, for instance, I was struck that the U.S. party's expressed desire for stability on the Korean peninsula elicited the following rejoinder: "'Scholars in China are asking, Does the United States want tension on the peninsula because it serves U.S. interests?'"[54]

A reverse gambit, using praise, is for the Chinese side to make reference to people who "know China well," hoping that praise will elicit more thinking in that direction and turn the presumably erudite member of the opposing delegation into an even more effusive "friend." Yet another variant is to praise some uninvolved third party and to invoke his or her wisdom as a model for those present to emulate. In a meeting between NPC chairman Wu Bangguo and two members of the U.S. Congress in 2007, Wu used a combination approach, solicitously telling the congressmen: "In December I met Bill Gates and sat next to him for an hour and he said many members of Congress do not have much knowledge of China and he has less knowledge of China than I have of the U.S. You play an important role."[55]

In preceding chapters we have identified areas in which striking and important changes have occurred in the era of reform in China—the increase in comprehensive national strength, the rise of interdependence, less dominant leadership, and a more pluralized and empowered society notable among them. In the realm of negotiation, however, we have seen great continuity. What has changed, however, in negotiation with China is that the outside world now finds itself negotiating across a much wider range of topics, with a broader range of Chinese interlocutors who possess more resources—knowledge, information, and economic wherewithal—and who have a far more diversified set of interests than forty years ago. Considerably more emphasis is placed on soft power and the PRC's economic capacity than has ever been the case in modern times. In the twenty-first century the Chinese bring two more balanced and powerful "fists" to their negotiations with the external world than they did when Deng came to power in 1977.

Whether in diplomatic, commercial, or other settings, Chinese are extremely attuned to power relationships, both the current power relationship and the interlocutor's future power prospects. That is why the United States cannot be indifferent to a Chinese perception of American decline and why achieving a trajectory of growth in U.S. comprehensive national power is so important to healthy and balanced U.S.-China relations. At any given moment, depending on the context, China may pay particular attention to the coercive, economic, or ideational dimensions of another country's strength, but the economic trends are key because economic strength is convertible to other forms of power. One senior PRC professor put it as follows in the wake of the collapse of Lehman Brothers in fall 2008: "There is more realism, a new balance of power with the United States. The GDP of China is $4 trillion—the U.S. is $14 trillion. Now only 3.5 times [China's]. 'China enjoys a better bargaining position.'"[56] Another PRC strategic analyst explained it as follows: "The CCP doesn't think that the U.S. is reliable but needs to cooperate with the U.S. and tolerates weapons sales [to Taiwan], but it wants to change the status quo in twenty years; our GDP will be bigger, more influence, then the status quo would be changed."[57]

This chapter also highlights the degree to which China's increased power has moved it from being a negotiator that emphasized its weakness in many contexts and utilized the sense of obligation stemming from past mistreatment, to being a nearly equal negotiating partner that takes pride in its current interests and capabilities as well as its future potential. At the outset of reform, China was negotiating to get into the international system or to avoid being isolated within it. Now the issue is the size and potency of China's role in that system—with Beijing trying to increase its leverage without becoming overstretched by the resulting responsibilities it incurs. The key to China's comprehensive national power, its internal cohesion, its persuasive capabilities abroad, and its negotiating leverage is economic power. Sustained, rapid economic growth is not everything, but it is a great deal, and it cannot be taken for granted in the period ahead. Indeed, we can expect China's growth rate to fall over time, while remaining relatively high by the standards of developed countries for at least a decade or two longer.

Conclusion

Driving beyond the Headlights

The process of revolution in China and the Soviet Union was not the same. In 1917 Lenin mobilized workers to seize power. But we encircled urban areas by the rural [areas]—it took us twenty-eight years to achieve power. We couldn't have driven Chiang Kai-shek to Taiwan if we had listened to Stalin, who was in favor of armed struggle, and if we had listened to him we'd still have American concessions [in the treaty port cities] in China. Lenin never talked about a mixed economy.

—Premier Li Peng, February 1990, Beijing

We have become more diversified but less coordinated. . . . "It has taken us twenty years to recognize, to know that Congress and the executive [in the United States] sometimes are together and sometimes apart. It is time for you to see differences [in China]—so many departments, interest groups, voices. Harder to follow than in the past. You need to work harder."

—Chinese intelligence analyst, September 2011

"A Chinese pop song goes like this: 'May I ask where the path is? It is where you take your first step.'"

—Vice President Xi Jinping, U.S. Department of State, luncheon remarks, February 14, 2012

THE ROAD TRAVELED AND THE WAY FORWARD

Careers, revolutions, and research are similar in a few respects—each begins with the first step, their development follows logic not fully apparent at the outset, and the final destination is often unanticipated. I started this journey to better understand China, expecting a career in which I would never go to the PRC, much less meet citizens or leaders there. Instead, I supposed I would have a professional lifetime such as that I experienced in Hong Kong in the early 1970s, interviewing refugees and culling information from local mainland newspapers (*difang baozhi*) not intended for foreign eyes (*neibu faxing*) that had been used to wrap the produce imported from the mainland. These papers had been rescued from the municipal garbage by enterprising intelligence operatives and research organizations—some pages had tomato stains. The China I first encountered through the optics of this British crown colony clinging to the mainland's coast gave virtually no hint of what rapidly would emerge across the colony's border in Shenzhen and beyond.

From the vantage point of the second decade of the new millennium, China's second revolution of the communist era has reached a point that Deng and his compatriots could never have fully anticipated when they initiated it in the late 1970s. General Secretary Xi Jinping and his cohort of so-called fifth-generation leaders must now take further steps forward, without seeing the path ahead clearly or knowing the precise destination. The dangers of standing still outweigh those of forging ahead. If PRC leaders and the Chinese people do not continue to adapt creatively to the implications of preceding reform steps, things will go terribly wrong. Conversely, if they find a path to more humane, participatory, rules-based governance with a minimum of human anguish along the way, while simultaneously maintaining vigorous economic growth and becoming progressively more involved in providing global public goods, this Chinese revolution will have made enormous strides beyond those already achieved. China is at an inflection point, with the gains thus far achieved either providing the basis for a more stable and responsive future or signaling the appearance of a more pluralized, unmanageable polity and society.

As to research, the path taken by this work has led me to a greater, and to some degree unanticipated, appreciation of the fragility of the successes thus far achieved as well as the enormous challenges lying ahead. Among the challenges confronting China is the problem Plato addressed in *The Republic*—from where does the visionary, public-spirited leader arise in a society that tends to replicate what has preceded it? One could have asked this question at the time of Mao's death, yet Deng Xiaoping was the improbable answer—improbable because in many respects he was an almost indispensable instrument of Mao's flawed rule, yet after assuming power he became a leader who overturned much of the Chairman's handiwork. For that matter, Chiang Kai-shek's son, Chiang Ching-kuo, was an unlikely and unanticipated vehicle by which Taiwan would move toward a more democratic future in the 1980s—he came of age having been trained in the Soviet Union and having been a central player in the coercive apparatus. How does leadership that produces transformational results arise from a transactional system?

Whatever one thinks of the means Deng Xiaoping used to claw his way to power—his personal responsibility in the antirightist campaign and the Great Leap Forward that precipitated mass starvation of the late 1950s and early 1960s, or his responsibilities with respect to the June 1989 tragedy and its aftermath—the strategic decisions he made following his mid-1977 final return to power set China on a more productive course internally and externally than it had been on in more than 150 years. Whereas Mao became more erratic as he grew older, Deng made his greatest contributions in the last twenty years of his life.

Deng's revolution has produced a very different society and polity from the one in which he rose. The winners in the economic reform era have gained strength, yet many now resist the further changes necessary to bring the social structure and the governing system into greater harmony. Yesterday's successes have created today's intractable problems and resistance. This is normal—the robber barons and entrepreneurs of nineteenth- and twentieth-century America resisted the progressives, trustbusters, and regulators of their era.

The era of reform has brought China to a place with respect to governance it never has been before, as explained in chapter 2. Its leaders must govern collectively while the system grows increasingly complex, as power is diffusing, and as the bureaucracy and society continue to pluralize. Today, less dominant leaders seek to collectively govern an increasingly complex and empowered society with inadequate institutions to articulate interests, adjudicate conflicts, regulate and supervise political and societal actors, or ensure just and responsible policy implementation—all in the absence of robust legal or constitutional mechanisms of succession. Imagine, for instance, that Xi Jinping had become incapacitated in the period leading up to his ascension to power in 2012–13: What was "Plan B"? There was none, and one is sobered by the possibilities.

China is becoming vigorous in terms of economic and military power but brittle in terms of governance. Economic and social change have played midwife to a middle class that increasingly wants justice, respect, more voice—in a word, dignity. There is also a large urban underclass that has fueled relentless and fast-paced urbanization, and sooner or later China's leaders must address its demands for security and justice. Moreover, there are issues above either class or justice—as I write this sentence in February 2013 the China air quality monitoring website reports that Shijiazhuang is "severely polluted" at a reading of 401, with "protection recommended," and Xian, at a considerable distance from Shijiazhuang, is at 322, also "severely polluted" with "protection recommended."[1] Numbers higher than 50 carry health warnings. A government unable to protect its people from such conditions will soon need protection itself. Not to be overlooked, rural inhabitants are becoming more vocal, knowledgeable, and unwilling to passively accept what elite urbanites determine to be their lot in life.

Like an automobile driving at high speed on a moonless night in the desert, China is undergoing a rate of domestic change so rapid that the country's forward momentum cannot be stopped or the direction adequately adjusted in the existing zone of illumination—the PRC is driving too fast for the headlights to reveal what dangers lurk ahead. The rate of economic and social change is an indication of immense progress, but its pace has created perils, not least environmental, and at any moment China might hit a stationary object that was diffuse and unrecognized in the obscurity of the night.

If it is to be successful, China's strategy going forward must involve political changes different and greater than those to date. There must be movement away from almost single-minded economic performance-based legitimacy to *reform-based legitimacy*. Reform-based legitimacy is premised on bringing China's social, economic, and governing systems into greater harmony with one another in the very different PRC that has evolved since mid-1977. It is legitimacy anchored in procedural justice and participation, as well as continued economic and quality-of-life improvements. This means that China must find ways to manage pluralization constructively. This will prove to be Xi Jinping's greatest hurdle.

This political change needs to increase system responsiveness, even though compared to the ossified system of Leonid Brezhnev in the Soviet

Union the CCP has demonstrated considerable capacities in this regard. A principal legacy of the Soviet model in China was that it was a "supply system." In other words, the political center determined what the state, society, and individuals needed and undertook to supply them with it or to ignore those needs entirely. Civic society, to the degree it existed, was not an actor but rather acted upon. The initiative was top down. Deng's reform was about moving toward a "demand-driven system" in the economic sphere, but he left the political system in the top-down, supply-system mode.

Over the years of reform, a "responsive authoritarian" capacity has evolved piecemeal, enabling PRC leaders to hold things together, thus far. However, in the twenty-first century, the broadly encompassing change Deng unleashed in the economic realm must be matched to a far greater extent in the political domain—building institutions of interest articulation, adjudication, and implementation that are the political equivalents to the economic marketplace. The government must move from the role of participant to that of referee. It would be best if this political reform happened in a gradual, controlled manner, but it needs to happen, and the course needs to be set by leaders who bring the vision to this era that Deng brought to his.

As this book goes to press, Xi Jinping's era is just beginning, and it is too early to say whether his experience stewarding China's most modernized, cosmopolitan, and globally interdependent areas (Fujian, Zhejiang, and Shanghai), and his limited but important experience in the military, have endowed him with the necessary authority and vision. Surrounding Xi in 2013 are six individuals on the Standing Committee of the Politburo, a group that is far more educationally diverse than its predecessors. This diversity could presage a period of creativity and experimentalism, or the diversity of the group itself could signal immobilization in the face of crushing problems.

In short, there is a new leadership in China, with somewhat different characteristics from its predecessors, which create the possibility for a next wave of advancing reform. To a considerable extent, the era of Hu Jintao was focused on consolidation, while the preceding era of Jiang Zemin has been insufficiently credited for the dynamism that was its hallmark. Preliminary indications in mid-2013 are that the forces that favor tackling long-deferred economic and political reform bottlenecks have gained strength. The story, indeed the legacy, of the so-called fifth generation will be the degree to which the dynamic impulse in China can prevail over the interests resistant to further change—and whether a proud generation of beneficiaries of Deng's reforms will be able to resist the siren song of assertive nationalism.

GOVERNANCE CHALLENGES

The Rise of a Middle Class

For Americans, all good things have traditionally been thought to come from having a strong middle class. China is building a huge middle class, already around the magnitude of the entire population of the United States, even though this still leaves around a billion Chinese people who remain in much less secure economic circumstances. In *the long run,* the middle class may become a force for more responsive, humane, and predictable governance. Much happens before you get to *the long run,* however. Today's middle class is still a comparatively small island, floating in a sea of relative poverty, and it may, therefore, continue to ally with the elite in the quest to protect what it has struggled to achieve—the work of Bruce Dickson and Margaret Pearson, among others, suggest this is the current predisposition of many in the middle class, particularly its business components.[2] However, when this social stratum constitutes a greater proportion of society, less fearful of the underclass, it may challenge the elite, setting off instability or going in policy directions that could inflict terrible costs on many, both within and outside the PRC. Only when the middle class has become the ascendant political force is there a center of gravity adequate to solidify rule of law and build a society in which one sees a shift from "survival" to "self-expression" values.

Moreover, gains made in modernization can be lost—political development is not a one-way conveyor to an ever more humane and secure future. While having a fully institutionalized, middle-class-centric system can foster stability, the pathway to that place is rocky. The middle class also is a vehicle for the more effective expression of popular passions, and, as America's Federalist forefathers knew, popular passions are not always enlightened or compassionate. This was driven home to me by the stunning remarks of one senior Chinese academic about what the rise of a PRC middle class would mean for Taiwan:

> "The first priority is to put the [Taiwan] issue under control. Put a boundary as no independence. For Beijing, resolution means reunification; only unsure when—twenty years? And the starting point is a middle class that is half the Chinese population. Then China will pay more attention to individual rights. So governance will be changed in China and the nature of the middle class

changes. The starting of democratization on the mainland will never allow an independent Taiwan. We will pass a referendum [on the mainland on the Taiwan issue], inform you when [Taiwan] is reunified, and we will take over. Democracy in China is the end of the current situation [with regard to Taiwan]."[3]

There are other PRC views about Taiwan, to be sure, but what is described above is one possible course of future events. My sense is that most middle-class Chinese would resonate with the above sentiment.

The interviews that form the bedrock of this volume indicate that Chinese citizens and leaders alike believe that their country's economic power now entitles them to more leverage in negotiations and more favorable outcomes in the world system. The biggest change in this respect can be dated from China's relatively unscathed emergence from the Asian financial crisis of 1997–98 and then accelerated by China's continued growth in the face of the global economic downturn in 2008 and thereafter. As one senior adviser to China's top leaders explained in late 2009, in China there is " 'a common understanding that the United States is not in good shape. . . . Power is shifting and [China is] more confident.' "[4]

This premature discounting of the United States will prove mistaken, I believe, but my analysis does not diminish the force of this widely shared Chinese conviction.[5] This middle-class and hair-trigger nationalist empowerment was on full display in September 2012, when thousands of predominantly middle-class citizens took to the streets in fifty or more cities throughout China, carrying placards, in some cases perpetrating vandalism, and shouting vehement anti-Japanese slogans, calling for retaliation on Japan for infringements on what they saw as Chinese sovereignty over the small outcroppings in the East China Sea called the Diaoyu or Senkaku Islands. At least one placard (printed in *China Daily* as a cover story) went so far as to display what appeared to be a burning Japan ignited by nuclear weapons.[6] Moving into early 2013, this conflict was assuming worrying military dimensions, with the intrusion of Chinese military, paramilitary, and civilian aircraft and maritime vessels into Japanese defense zones holding out the possibilities of conscious escalation, miscalculation, or accident.

Thus the rise of a middle class offers the longer-term hope of more humane, participatory, and predictable governance, but it also carries within it the seeds of instability, extremism, and the tyranny of assertive nationalism. Mature middle-class democratic states may possess the attributes democracy promoters attribute to them, but getting to such a state is an altogether more tumultuous process. The PRC now faces dilemmas similar to those that confronted the founders of the United States in developing a constitutional architecture. How does one build a system of governance with sufficient strength to regulate society in essential areas, without citizens losing control over the leviathan that has been created? How does one prevent democracy from becoming a tyranny of the majority? How does a constitutional order constrain popular passion while liberating the citizen to act responsibly? How does one define responsible behavior? Today's China has no effective constitution—one is needed. However, the question is: "How can a constitution be written and embedded in the hearts of the Chinese people?" And will the beneficiaries of the current order find ways to incorporate, peacefully, the new, more assertive societal groups that the vision and policies of Deng's generation spawned?

Corruption: A Cancer on the Regime

In his report to the Eighteenth Party Congress, outgoing general secretary Hu Jintao, in speaking of corruption, said: "If we fail to handle this issue well, it could prove fatal to the Party, and even cause the collapse of the Party and the fall of the state."[7] A few days later, in addressing the new Politburo, incoming general secretary Xi Jinping similarly minced no words, saying: "A mass of facts tells us that if corruption becomes increasingly serious, it will inevitably doom the party and the state."[8]

The regime of Mao Zedong was profoundly corrupt in the sense that one man and a small coterie around him had unspeakable power over China's people that they exercised with minimal regard to consequences. In relative comfort this privileged clique, whose children grew up in hermetically sealed communities behind high walls, formed networks that gave them and their progeny great advantage when China turned toward the "socialist market economy." The hypocrisy of a Jiang Qing (Mao's fourth wife) who harangued on behalf of proletarian equality in public and lived in palatial residences, wearing Western clothing and watching Hollywood films with her cronies in private—all indulgences denied the Chinese people at the time of the Chairman's demise—is a profound testament to the moral rot of the Mao regime. Nonetheless, at that time, most Chinese were materially and politically equal—equally impoverished and powerless.

Something very profound has happened in China's reform era. As Robert Dahl and Charles Lindblom explained in the 1950s, societies have three basic ways to achieve control beyond spontaneous self-limitation imbued through indoctrination (ethics): hierarchies, bargaining (markets), and preference counting systems (voting).[9] The reform era has brought the weakening of hierarchies in the PRC, while voting has remained unacceptable to the party as an alternative way to exercise legitimate control, forcing the system to fall back upon bargaining (and markets) to a considerable extent. Markets have brought enormous material and social liberation benefits to China's people since the late 1970s, but without the constraints of effective and impartial legal, regulatory, and judicial systems, without shared moral norms, and without accountability through preference counting methods, nothing stands in the way of bargaining activity mutating into an ever widening spiral of corruption.

Whether corruption accounts for about 4 percent of GDP (as Minxin Pei estimated for the late 1990s), 13.3 to 16.9 percent, as Wang Shaoguang, Hu Angang, and Ding Yuanzhu have asserted (also for the late 1990s), or the much higher range of numbers that other scholars have estimated, the magnitude of "take" in the world's second largest economy is staggering—corroding the elite's right to rule and greatly reducing domestic and global confidence.[10] The revelations concerning former Chongqing party secretary Bo Xilai and others (such as Ao Man Long, the Macau transport secretary taking kickbacks totaling more than a hundred million U.S. dollars) in the spring and summer of 2012 only shone a light on what everyone in China knows: corruption among the elite is rampant.[11] In an era of widespread information availability and a rising middle class looking for some measure of justice and respect, corruption is a time bomb ticking at the regime's clay feet.

The Military-Civilian Balance

The danger of the relationship between the civilian and military leadership is unlikely to be the actual replacement of civilians by uniformed officers in a couplike development. Indeed, under Xi Jinping, the practice of having no uniformed military officer on the Standing Committee of the Politburo has continued, and the norm of having the CMC chaired by the individual simultaneously holding the other paramount civilian positions has also been strengthened. The more profound dangers in the civil-military relationship are fourfold. First, the military-industrial complex is likely to become progressively more central to the

Chinese economy, and hence more influential. Second, the military may become an increasingly potent symbol of China's nationalist aspirations in the minds of the public, and China's civilian political leaders could become progressively more reluctant to tangle with the military on highly charged nationalistic issues. Third, the military may simply expand its "room to run" in the system, as it has demonstrated the capability to do from time to time, presenting civilians with faits accomplis from which they find it difficult to extract themselves. In the aggregate, these first three dangers could give rise to a fourth, in which the fear should be less a military takeover than a situation in which military-related personalities and interests become so strong that moderating civilian control is inhibited.

This fourth danger in part materialized in the 2002–4 period when Jiang Zemin retired from his posts as general secretary and president while retaining the chairmanship of the CMC for two additional years. As explained in chapter 6, this development created the potential dilemma that the head of state and the party general secretary (then Hu Jintao) did not control the military—the "two centers" or "two headquarters" problem. As it so happened, there was no circumstance in which the two centers (Jiang Zemin and Hu Jintao) wanted to go in radically different directions in any important situation (so far as we know); hence no crisis ensued. The fact that in the 2012 party transition there again was an argument over whether the predecessor (Hu Jintao) should for a time retain control of the military rather than hand it over to the successor (Xi Jinping) is disquieting, though in the end Xi was appointed. It is not desirable to have ambiguity as to who is in charge in a crisis.

An area of debate (starting in the 1980s) that is likely to assume greater importance in the future is the degree to which the military should remain an instrument of the Communist Party or become an instrument of the state, irrespective of the political coloration of the regime. Any meaningful liberalization and constitutional development will involve a redefinition of the PLA's relationship to the Communist Party.

CHINA AND THE WORLD
Impulses Shaping Chinese Global Behavior

Beijing now deals with the outside world from a position of greater strength, more interdependence, and more confidence than at any time in the modern era. Accompanying this newfound strength has been and will be a degree of "realism" and "pragmatism" in China's dealings with the outside world that is disconcerting to many in the West. This will be particularly so to an America seeing itself in search of shared global norms to govern the conduct of international affairs and the internal behavior of individual states—though, it should be noted, Washington often is no more willing to delegate decisions about its vital interests or internal affairs to others than is Beijing. The West starts its thinking about international affairs with the search for norms and formal constraints and then accommodates its principles to the stubborn realities of limited resources and vital interests.

On the other hand, Beijing's thinking on international affairs does not derive from the vision of universal norms. Rather, the starting point for China is fluid process—the endless accommodation to dynamic reality, the ceaseless endeavor of adjusting relationships, and the quest for an ever shifting pathway that maximizes its interests. This reality notwithstanding, however, in 2013 there are high-ranking people and opinion leaders in and out of government in the PRC who argue that China's future global status and role rest on aligning the country more closely with global norms and who do not simply dismiss the call for universal values as capitulation to "westernization."[12] China still is debating whether and how to adopt universal values—something America did long ago, asserting that its own values *were* universal values. As the U.S. Declaration of Independence put it, "We hold these truths to be self-evident . . . " China's different starting point, its very different historical experience and self-conception, its distinctive resource endowments and economic circumstances, and its far different geostrategic setting all result in distinctive Chinese leadership and popular perceptions and behavior. Conflicts of interest, value, and policy will be enduring fixtures of the West's interaction with China.

PRC political leaders and many of its citizens have concluded that the global balance of power is tilting away from the established post–World War II powers (the United States, the European Union, Japan, and the Soviet Union/Russia), that America has lost the moral legitimacy to be the default global leader, and that China has gained sufficient strength to be less deferential to the preexisting international power hierarchy.[13] If this assessment means that the United States will be less dominant in the global system in the future than in the past, along important dimensions this is proving true, but I sense a widespread tendency in China to underestimate the resilience of the U.S. cultural, economic, and political system.[14]

It is not that Beijing wishes to overturn the international system (particularly the global economic apparatus) from which it has gained so much, but it most assuredly wants more influence in that system and wants to "rectify" some of the perceived injustices of prior arrangements. Among those injustices is the separation of Taiwan and American challenges to Beijing's desire for a wider security buffer in all security dimensions—land, air, sea, space, and cyber. For two centuries China, believing that power is the principal coin in the realm of international affairs, has been determined to augment its comprehensive national power. As one Chinese foreign policy analyst put it to me: "'When China has more power, the U.S. will pay more attention.'"[15] China is not comfortable with a U.S.-led international security order, one reliant on alliances born of the Cold War, and instead feels more comfortable working within the United Nations system, which requires Beijing's assent before collective security action can be taken.

Throughout history, China has viewed itself in several different relationships to what we may loosely call the international system. In the dynastic period, the Middle Kingdom thought of itself as the center of a cultural universe in which peripheral states at progressively greater distance from China had less salience and fewer obligations—this was a China that was basically self-reliant, with its borders expanding or contracting as central power waxed and waned. The tone and substance of relations with its regional neighbors were at once variable and reciprocal. Speaking of China's traditional relations with neighbors, Ren Xiao explains: "The more distant they were from the center, the weaker the political link between them. For those remote areas, what was left often was simply an empty shell that only existed in theory."[16] Then, in the middle and second half of the nineteenth century, China became a victim of a predatory industrialized West and aggressive Japan. By virtue of internal political disorder and weakness, as well as foreign encroachment, China lost control of both its internal circumstances and its external relations.

Upon the communist victory in 1949, a new page was turned, with China regaining its full sovereignty and, for a time, aligning itself with the Soviet Union in the ideological and armed conflicts of the Cold War. In the late 1960s and early 1970s, as Sino-Soviet relations dramatically deteriorated, Beijing sensed the danger of having conflicts with two superpowers simultaneously and tilted toward Washington to offset the greater threat from Moscow.

Now, in the second decade of the twenty-first century, for the first time in its modern history China sees itself as a strong independent actor in a world of nominally equal sovereign states. Accepting the basic structure of international economic and cultural institutions, Beijing wishes to contribute to them but rejects the American dominance that has typically characterized those structures. This is to say, China accepts the economic and social structures of the international system and the universalistic character of the UN-oriented international security system, as well as the regimes in which it has negotiated membership. However, Beijing rejects the U.S.-dominated alliance system (particularly in East Asia), and even more the right of Washington to act unilaterally (or through ad hoc coalitions it creates) on a global basis.

A core question for the future is: "Can the United States work with the PRC and others to develop a shared vision of international security architecture, first in East Asia and then globally?" The West has already gone quite far in accommodating Beijing's economic and cultural participation on a global basis. But China's still powerful "victim mentality," its fear of "bullying," its aversion to being sucked into international obligations it can ill afford, and its anxiety about the West's proclivity to involve itself in the PRC's internal political evolution will make it a prickly partner on the security side. Mounting frictions in East and Southeast Asia do not look promising for a new, shared vision of an inclusive regional security order, but this should be the objective.

There is another powerful impulse at work in China as its leaders and people think about their relationship to the world, particularly America, and Washington's ceaseless effort to get Beijing to use its growing power for U.S. purposes. As one adviser to China's senior leaders put it to me amid the anti-Japanese demonstrations sweeping the PRC in September 2012, "'We think about China, not the U.S. We tell the U.S. to do its thing and China will do its peaceful development. . . . Do your own thing and leave us alone.'"[17]

The United States and China in the Years Ahead

While there is much that strains the fabric of U.S.-China relations, at least two strands help knit the two countries together. First, a number of critical problems that the planet and individual nations face cannot be adequately addressed without Sino-American collaboration, among them global economic growth, world health, and environmental issues. This does not mean the two countries can resolve global challenges without others, but it does mean that not much will be accomplished if they do not cooperate. Second, both societies face the fundamental and long-term task of rebuilding themselves for a new age—economically, socially, and institutionally. Neither the United States nor China needs the diversion of having to deal with the other as a principal external problem.

A central question therefore is: Will the centripetal forces of interdependence, the gains to be made through cooperation, and the need of each nation to recreate itself for a new age prove stronger than the combined forces of different philosophical starting points, often divergent national interests, distinctive national narratives, and increasingly fragmented societies and polities? Several forces are contending for primacy in China and for that matter in the United States—domestic politics, interdependence, big-power realist thinking, and the technological action-reaction cycle. Given these contending impulses, the way forward is to construct an inclusive balance of forces in Asia that restrains assertive impulses, build inclusive multilateral economic and security institutions, and reinforce interdependence, thereby raising the costs of unrestrained conflict.

Two things seem blindingly obvious to me after more than forty years of interaction with a multitude of leaders in the PRC and those around the world who deal with them. First, crude external pressure applied to accelerate internal change in China and crude external pressure designed to produce a more congenial PRC foreign policy generally backfire. As one of China's premier analysts of public opinion put it in late 2012 in speaking of Secretary of State Hillary Clinton's trips to China: "'She is a guest, but gives the Chinese no face. So I don't give you face. We don't have friendship, we have policy.'"[18] Second, excessive accommodation to PRC demands feeds an image in Beijing of weakness in the outside world that, itself, invites further attempts to push. The way out of this dilemma is the combined power of example, opportunity, comprehensive national power carefully sheathed, and dialogue—never forgetting that resolving our own problems can be more effective than coercing others to solve theirs.

Appendix

The Interviews and Interviewing in China

This appendix provides additional detail and explanation concerning the interview set and data management system used in this volume. A brief consideration of where this research fits into the broader methodological firmament of contemporary China studies is the appropriate place to begin. For a thorough *tour d'horizon* of the research methods currently employed in the quest to understand China in comparative perspective, I recommend *Contemporary Chinese Politics: New Sources, Methods, and Field Strategies.*[1] In terms of understanding the specific challenges of fieldwork in the PRC, see *Doing Fieldwork in China.*[2] An indispensable tool for basic biographical work on the PRC is *China Vitae* at www.chinavitae.org. Finally, the Hoover Institution's *China Leadership Monitor* at www.chinaleadershipmonitor.org is a unique source on a broad variety of PRC leadership-related topics.

WHERE THIS RESEARCH FITS INTO THE POLITICAL AND SOCIAL SCIENCE FIELDS

This research is in what Calvin Chen and Benjamin Read would broadly term the "ethnographic" tradition of interviewing, supplemented by rich contextual detail drawn from primary and secondary documents, statistical compilations, and contemporary scholarly and journalistic accounts. With respect to the interviews, in a few cases (e.g., my 1982 interviews in the Yangzi River Basin) I was embedded in a Chinese bureaucratic system and a particular organization within that system long enough to get to know people and get a feel for the overall circumstance in which they found themselves. In other cases, I interviewed or met with the same people periodically over a substantial span, sometimes decades, episodically cutting into their lives as their careers unfolded (e.g., Zhu Rongji as Shanghai mayor, vice-premier, and premier). My approach is ethnographic in its attempt to understand how people perceived their situation and the society and organizations in which they were involved. Over more than four decades, I have perpetually sought to understand what drove individual and organizational behavior. This is a bottom-up, inductive approach, the purpose of which is to produce generalizations and propositions about the system and specific policy issues that others can test using a broader array of methodologies. I have always viewed Philip Selznick's *TVA and the Grass Roots: A Study in the Sociology of Formal Organization* as an exemplary piece of work in this regard.[3] In the "ethnographic" tradition there is an objective both to understand subjects as they understand the world and simultaneously to protect them as human subjects. An ethnographic approach is most useful and appropriate, as Benjamin Read says, "when what we are studying is *subtle* . . . , and when what we are studying is *hidden,* sensitive, or otherwise kept behind barriers that require building trust."[4] As explained below, in my interviews I used what Lily Tsai calls "conversational or flexible interviewing," not standardized interviewing techniques.[5]

This work clearly would be categorized as elite studies within the broad field of Chinese politics and political science more generally, though it does not rely, for the most part, on aggregate attribute data that are important sources for many scholars, including Robert Scalapino's early work on elites, Cheng Li's more recent contributions, and the contemporary work of Victor Shih, Wei Shan, and Mingxing Liu.[6] This research focuses on leaders at various levels throughout the functional and territorial systems of the PRC because in an authoritarian system such individuals exert outsized influence over policy and because, generally speaking, they constitute the selectorate that perpetuates the elite and political apparatus.

THE DATA SET

To elaborate on what already has been said in the Introduction to this volume, the respondents are a diverse group in terms of functional field,

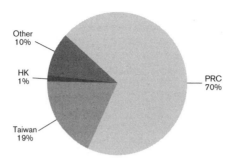

FIGURE 4. Nationality of interviewees.

level in the system, citizenship, personal characteristics, era encountered, and the length of time I have known them—some interviewees I
have known for decades, while others I met only once. Seventy percent
of my interviews were from the PRC (not including Hong Kong), 19
percent from Taiwan, 1 percent from Hong Kong, and 10 percent
"other" (see figure 4). Each interview was systematically coded along
several dimensions, as explained below.[7]

Rank

Rank (nine categories) refers to the level of the interviewee within party,
state, military, and societal hierarchies. In the PRC's bureaucratic system, every official has a precise rank, but these internal designations
were not always made known to me. Further, rank systems are not the
same in the various administrative jurisdictions and localities from
which my interviews are drawn—differing between Hong Kong, Taiwan, Macau, and the PRC, not to mention among non–Greater China
governments and organizations (e.g., the World Bank, the International
Monetary Fund, or the United Nations, where Chinese nationals now
often are employed). Consequently, I have assigned my own, standardized rankings based on the individual's title, available biographic material, and his or her own description where available. The interview set
includes 25 supreme leader interviews, 10 from the PRC and 15 on
Taiwan; 58 Politburo-level interviews, of which 45 were in the PRC;
113 governor and ministerial-level interviews, of which 49 were in the
PRC; 91 vice-governor and vice-ministerial-level interviews, of which
89 were in the PRC; 85 Bureau-level or equivalent interviews, of which
77 were in the PRC; 65 lower-level and miscellaneous interviews, of
which 60 were in the PRC;[8] 17 ambassadorial-level interviews, 17 of

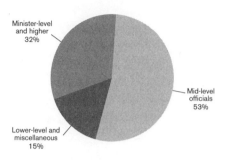

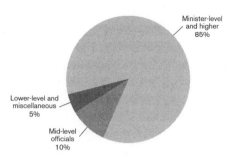

FIGURE 5. Rank of PRC and HK interviewees. Note: "Minister-level and higher" refers to supreme leaders, Politburo members, vice-premiers, state councilors, CMC vice-chairmen, governors, ministers, municipality mayors, and ambassadors.

FIGURE 6. Rank of Taiwan interviewees. Note: "Minister-level and higher" refers to Taiwan equivalents to PRC ranks in figure 5.

which were with PRC individuals;[9] 32 department director–level interviews, all of which were in the PRC; and 11 CEO or chairman of the board–level interviews, 8 of which were in the PRC, though in reality there were additional interviews in this category in Taiwan because the CEOs involved (e.g., Koo Chen-foo) had other governmental titles and ranks that were employed. Much more detail on the ranking data can be found in the note.[10]

Concerning the frequency of high-level, midlevel, and lower-level interviews on China's mainland versus Taiwan, the island has over the last four decades made a greater effort to expose visitors to people who, on average, are of higher formal rank than the individuals to whom one is given entrée on the mainland—over the years, 32 percent of my interviews in the PRC were with ministerial-level and higher officials, while the corresponding figure for Taiwan was 85 percent (see figures 5 and 6).

Domain

Domain refers to the location of the interviewee in the hierarchy of central places, in this case "center" (meaning the apex of the political system in the capital), 395 total interviewees, of which 296 were in the PRC; "province," 85 interviewees, of which 75 were in the PRC; and "local," 16 interviewees, of which 14 were in the PRC (see figures 7 and 8). The PRC data set is top-heavy, with well over a majority of respondents at or near the pinnacle of the hierarchy of central places (75 percent of interviewees were at the "central" level, and only

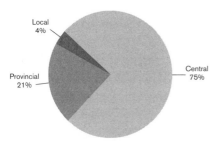

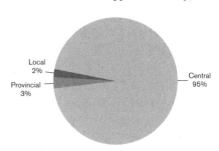

FIGURE 7. Domain of PRC and HK interviewees. Note: Provincial-level interviewees include provincial-level cities and Hong Kong.

FIGURE 8. Domain of Taiwan interviewees.

4 percent at the "local" level)—there is very little direct representation of China's rural or small- and medium-sized city leaders among those interviewed. This bias in the data is even more pronounced in the interviews with Taiwan respondents, with 95 percent of interviews at the "central" level. This fact limits what can, and what cannot, be concluded from this body of information. Though provincial-level leaders in the PRC may seem to be "local" actors by some reckonings, in fact, provincial-level officials there are responsible for geographic units with populations and land areas that would constitute a medium to large nation-state in much of the world. In short, this data set provides only indirect and circumscribed insight into small-town, much less rural, China.[11] Rural and local China is an enormous part of the challenge of governing the PRC, and grassroots perspectives shape what Daniel Yankelovich memorably called "the boundaries of the permissible" in both domestic and foreign policy. As one senior academic put it in 2013, "The leaders are afraid of silent farmers."[12] To the extent that the interviews used in this study provide insight into rural and local Chinese society, it is generally through the eyes of leaders at the apex of the system—an important perspective, albeit one with major blind spots.

Status

Status refers to the *self-defined* functional hierarchy in which the interviewee places him or herself—the three most important of which are "military," "party," and "state." Many leaders in the PRC are in two of these vertical, systemically central hierarchies simultaneously; an exalted few are in all three simultaneously, most notably the PRC's

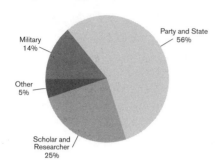

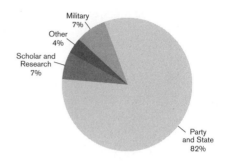

FIGURE 9. Status of PRC and HK interviewees.

FIGURE 10. Status of Taiwan interviewees.

"supreme" or (what used to be called) "core" (*hexin*) leader, but also individuals such as some senior military officers on the Party's Central Military Commission, for instance.[13] Indeed, the definition of supreme or "core" leader has traditionally been the one who is simultaneously the head of all three systemically central hierarchies—party, state, and military. The outside world, as well as the Chinese people, will know that political system transformation has occurred in the PRC when membership in a single party is not the overwhelming criterion for holding positions of authority in all systemically central hierarchies and when a constitution effectively divides at least some components of executive, legislative, and judicial power.[14]

Among the PRC interviewees in this data set, 56 percent were "party and state," 14 percent "military," 25 percent "scholar and researcher," and 5 percent "other" (see figure 9). Most senior PRC interviewees were very likely in the Communist Party—however, the CCP membership status of many academics and researchers was often unknown or uncertain to me. With respect to the Taiwan interviewees (figure 10), the "party and state" category is even more prominent, reflecting the higher level of attention that the authorities on the island have been willing to provide visiting academics and others. Ironically, in Taiwan one can easily get a more party- and state-dominated view of things than on the mainland, though it is importantly true that it has been much easier to gain access to Taiwan society over much of the last decades than has been the case on the mainland.

These three systemically central hierarchies (party, state, and military) dominate my interview set. Thus the people I have predominantly interviewed and interacted with over the years in Greater China are significant players in the "system," not common citizens, much less dissidents. The number of dissidents I have spoken with over the years is small, though I have interacted with a few high-profile individuals.[15] Further, though the interviews as a whole are dominated by members of the systemically central hierarchies, there are deep recesses of those hierarchies that foreigners rarely see up close—Public Security comes to mind, as does the Communist Party's Organization Department (which handles personnel). It was not until 2011, for instance, that I had a meaningful conversation with senior officials of the Chinese Communist Party's "International Liaison Department" (Zhonglianbu), the department historically responsible for connecting the CCP to communist parties abroad. In more recent times, that department has broadened its portfolio of those with whom it conducts exchanges (including the Republican and Democratic parties of the United States) as the number of ruling communist parties abroad has dwindled to near the vanishing point. In English it is known as the "International Department," with a large, modern headquarters on Beijing's west side that increasingly hosts noncommunist foreigners. Therefore, I do not claim to represent every Chinese organizational perspective in this volume; rather, I point out a number of blind spots obviously circumscribing findings.

Another important aspect of my interview set is the fact that there are other statuses (which are not mutually exclusive with the above three) that I have encountered with increasing frequency as we have entered the second decade of the new millennium: "corporate" personalities and "nongovernmental organization (NGO)" individuals are two of these statuses.[16] Another sector represented in my data set is the rapidly growing nonstate sector. In short, the proportion of interviewees who may not be involved in the party, state, or military apparatuses has climbed over time (while remaining modest), suggesting that China's leadership and society are becoming more diverse, pluralized, and transparent—a reality that is having dramatic consequences for governance in the PRC, as seen in chapter 2 and throughout this volume.[17] Also, the frequency of foreign interaction with China's academics and researchers has dramatically increased since the turn of the millennium, as has the less inhibited nature of those interactions.

Gender

Gender distribution among interviewees is interesting and revealing in both the PRC and Taiwan subsets. Among the PRC interviewees, about 5 percent were female, while the Taiwan subset was about 17 percent

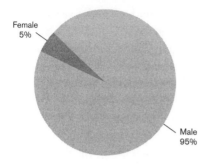

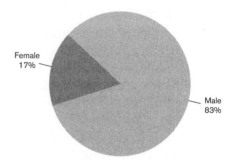

FIGURE 11. Gender of PRC and HK interviewees.

FIGURE 12. Gender of Taiwan interviewees.

female (see figures 11 and 12). The percentage in the Taiwan group is even more notable given that these interviewees include women who have been political party leaders (Tsai Ing-wen), presidential candidates (Lu Hsiu-lien and Tsai Ing-wen), legislators (Bi-khim Hsiao), ministers (Lai Shin-yuan), and a vice president (Lu Hsiu-lien/Annette Lu). In the PRC, on the other hand, while overall rights and status of women have improved and women have made great strides in many walks of life, their presence at the upper reaches of the policy and political system remains very small—Cheng Li reports that in 2007 only two out of twenty-nine PRC ministers were female.[18] Indeed, in the run-up to the Eighteenth Party Congress of November 2012, just one woman was known to have been considered for membership on the Standing Committee of the Politburo (Liu Yandong), but she was not selected, instead being placed on the lower-ranking twenty-five-person Politburo, along with Sun Chunlan, Tianjin's female first party secretary. Comparatively, Taiwan has made considerably more progress in this arena of female representation at the top of the political system.

Distribution of Interviews over Time

This data set contains interviews spanning 1971–2013, with the distribution over time reflecting the explosion of access to all levels of Chinese society over the forty-plus-year period covered in this volume. The temporal distribution of interviews in the PRC is a relatively good, albeit imperfect, indicator of the expanding openness, access, and transparency of post-Mao Chinese society. About 1.4 percent of the PRC interviews were conducted in the 1971–76 period when Mao was alive. Even after the Chairman's death, the PRC remained relatively closed to outsiders throughout the rest of the 1970s—only 2.3 percent of these interviews occurred in the period from Mao's September 1976 death until the end of that decade. The 1980s account for about 9 percent of my interviews; the 1990s nearly 22 percent; and the new millennium (2000–2013) 65 percent. My interview rate has more than doubled every decade, reflecting both increased travel to China in general and the increased capacity of Chinese to go abroad. This distribution of interviews, of course, also reflects my own career development and wider range of contacts in China over time, but the basic point remains. In the early days of reform, even the most senior people in the China studies field were not meeting with many Chinese leaders, not to mention then junior scholars in the field, such as myself.

This temporal distribution of interviews is an imperfect but important indicator of access to, and openness of, China for many reasons. Whereas in the 1970s three to four weeks were required at a minimum to make a productive trip to China, in 2013 air transportation to China (and all forms of travel within the country) has so improved that it is easy to make more numerous, shorter, and highly productive trips to the PRC. In China, for example, it usually is about equally quick to take the high-speed train (Gao Tie) from central China's Nanjing to Beijing in the north as it is to fly. Moreover, in the earlier years, once one finally arrived at a location in the PRC for research, things moved at a glacial rate. Simply making an appointment was a laborious undertaking, an adventure that began with trying to use the telephone system for which there was no publicly available phone directory. City maps were practically classified documents, and, oh yes, there were no taxicabs, even if one had an address—one had to rely on transportation provided by a designated unit host (*jiedai danwei*). And I remember sometimes asking my assigned guide on the way to an interview, "Where are we?" only to be told that they were "unclear" (*wo bu qingchu*). Finally, even if one cleared these hurdles, any interview or conversation usually involved a *peitong*, or minder, assigned by the local Foreign Affairs Office—whose presence generally exerted a chilling effect on respondent and interviewer alike. Interview sessions sometimes actually involved rather large numbers of extraneous Chinese in the room, for what purposes one could only imagine.

Often it seems that today's foreign demands for openness, transparency, and access to Chinese people, organizations, and information are made without a full appreciation of how far China has come since 1971 or, for that matter, how far the country has come in the new millennium. Chinese leaders having news conferences, bureaucracies having spokesmen, and ministries having online chats with citizens are very recent sociopolitical "innovations," as is the fact that the Foreign Ministry would begin to open its archives to foreigners. As the outside world loses any memory of a truly closed, indeed reclusive, China (a recollection that might help temper foreign demands), Beijing will face an increasingly impatient and insistent outside world. The more open the PRC becomes, the more it will face demands for additional openness and transparency.

A FEW IMPORTANT ASIDES

Protecting Respondents

The 558 interviews constituting this data set contain remarks by many more than 558 individuals—multiple respondents (and groups of visitors asking questions) participated in numerous conversations. This requires explanation as to the terms on which the data were obtained, the responsibilities of the interviewer, and the human subject safeguards that have governed this research and publication.

I have not released material in which a respondent could be identified if we had agreed to any permutation of "off the record." Further, in meetings with very senior leaders (in Beijing, Taipei, and Washington, D.C.) multiples of people often took notes (on both the foreign and Chinese sides), and only in a few instances did leaders explicitly say that their remarks were off the record—though the unspoken expectation was (and is) in meeting with Chinese leaders that those having the opportunity to interact with these figures will exercise prudence. "Prudence" means that if you hope to have access in the future you should be mindful of what you attribute to leaders by name. Using vaguer identifiers such as "a very senior leader said," is what is expected.

In terms of concerns about human subjects, most individuals in this data set would be categorized as "public personalities" or "public officials," and therefore we were operating in the realm of the historical record. While academic and think tank respondents are in a grayer zone, when interviewing them, I either asked them how they wished to be identified if I thought I might wish to use their name, or I cited them in a nonidentifiable way. Throughout the forty-plus years covered by these interviews, there were only a handful of times when the respondent asked for absolute protection and confidentiality. Consequently, I will not place in a publicly accessible archive the entire set of original interviews and related documents until a number of years after my death—and presumed passing on of the respondents as well. As a practical matter, however, in many meetings with officials, there were note takers from the Chinese government or party (and often the American government as well) recording what was said.

Interviewing

Interviewing in China or in Chinese communities elsewhere is not *sui generis,* meaning that the commonsense and ethical approaches that work elsewhere are generally applicable.[19] While the PRC is no longer the far side of the moon, one must exercise delicacy in posing politically sensitive questions and disseminating any replies for which the respondent might conceivably suffer negative consequences in the present or the unpredictable political future. Building and maintaining trust with respondents is the coin of the realm. To my knowledge, no interviewee has ever been harmed as a result of speaking with me. For one-time interviewees, of course, there is no preexistent record of personal trust (beyond your general reputation), but when you repeatedly return to the same locality, organization, or individual, this record of trust is slowly built and becomes indispensable. Without such a record, repeated access is not likely to be gained. An unobtrusive indicator of trust, therefore, is whether the researcher repeatedly gains access to localities, organizations, and individuals. In China, being trustworthy is not only an ethical imperative but a research necessity.

Related to trust, I believe, is another issue—I have never used audio recording devices, even when the Chinese side has a stenographer there presumably recording every word said. Moreover, it is likely that many conversations were recorded by devices that remained out of sight, feeding information directly into the security, foreign policy, and intelligence bureaucracies. Nonetheless, I have felt it is essential to the "atmosphere" that the interviewee always be able to say to his or her compatriots, as a last resort, "The foreigner misunderstood what I said," without fear of definitive refutation.

The hardest work of an interview occurs before you walk into the meeting place. The interviewer should learn as much as possible beforehand about the subject(s) he or she is exploring for several reasons, one of which is that time is too valuable to waste learning what already is known, or knowable, from the publicly available record. An essential dimension of preinterview research and preparation is to familiarize oneself with the vocabulary that is specific to the area of concern. Using the correct, technical vocabulary indicates to the interviewee that you are knowledgeable, and technical vocabulary is more precise than a layperson's phraseology, gently pushing the interviewee to see you as a member of his or her guild rather than as an "outsider."

When I engaged in extensive interviews in the Ministry of Water Conservancy and Electric Power "system" (*xitong*) in 1982, for instance, I used the bureaucratic and engineering vocabulary employed in that functional domain because many interlocutors were engineers. Using the appropriate technical vocabulary was more precise and efficient, and it helped move the discussion from the unstable terrain of politics toward the far safer territory of a "technical discussion." I recall asking one division-level Ministry of Water Conservancy and Electric Power official, for instance, about the *shiyefei* (operational or program funds) in his ministry, a subject about which I had read in a ministry publication. From the prior reading it was clear that these kinds of funds were problematic, but I did not understand exactly what they were and where the problems arose. The mere use of the correct term, *shiyefei,* elicited a long, detailed, and illuminating discussion by the interviewee that explained how discretionary operational funds had originated, how they had evolved into large reservoirs of unaccounted money, how corruption and inability to control investment by the center had resulted, and how all this also had to do with an absence of law. This illuminating conversation occurred in 1982, a period of generally tight political discipline. A section of my notes from that meeting recounts:

> I then asked what the *shiyefei* was and why it was a problem. XX said it was originally to be "operations" money (like phone, etc.), but it has grown over the years and is used in "illegal ways" (*buhefa*), but the legal system was so chaotic that these funds had been diverted to all sorts of capital construction and miscellaneous uses such as furniture, buildings, land acquisition, etc. He said it was a problem of great importance and that while he didn't know the precise size of the *shiye* funds in the 1950s, the size of the *shiyefei* had grown greatly in recent times. I asked what the *qiekuai banfa* (the method of cutting up the lump, literally) is, and he said it is slicing up the *shiyefei* among provinces (basically on fixed percentages) and then not having any accounting or control over how these monies are subsequently spent and they don't have to be returned to the center if unspent. In short, the *shiyefei* had become a large pool of discretionary money for provinces. The *shiyefei ceng ceng* (or the *shiyefei* level by level) is the division of the *shiyefei* in the MWCEP [Ministry of Water Conservancy and Electric Power] "system," level by level on a

basically fixed percentage with no returns and no accountability or control on the funds' use. All this, XX said, led to abuses and illegal behavior, except it was difficult to say it was illegal because [of] the disrepair of the legal system.[20]

A related point is that even if the interlocutor's English language is better than the interviewer's Chinese, I have found it preferable to conduct the interview in Chinese. This builds trust, shows respect, and drives the researcher to use the terms in which the Chinese system operates and your interviewee thinks. Moreover (to be frank), your interviewee will generally try to make his points exceedingly clear and provide the essentials out of consideration of the linguistic inequality. Nonetheless, it is essential to learn the technical vocabulary dominant in the field in which one is interviewing.

Part of "getting to know your subject" does not simply mean the functional area one is exploring, it also means the interviewee as well. Establishing a human connection helps establish a professional connection—personal connection and professionalism are not necessarily mutually opposed. The easiest way to do this is to find a point or points in common, which may be mutual acquaintances, school or geographic ties, or experiences. Starting a conversation with someone from Hubei Province (particularly Wuhan), for instance, by talking about local dishes (*doupi* or *tangbao*) can provide an expedited path to a comfortable and productive interview. But the starting point is to know something about your subject, and he/she knowing something about you. An admittedly unusual example would be an interview I had with then-retired vice-premier Gu Mu, a man about whom I had written a biographic study some years before we met. Before I met with him, I conveyed to his staff the book I had written in which his life was one chapter. I walked into Building 15 at the Diaoyutai State Guest House with a colleague, and my notes record the following as we sat down, neither having met the other before: "I walked into a large, beautifully decorated reception room with Jan Berris and met a smiling Gu Mu, with sparse teeth beaming with much gold. He is a bit frail but appeared in good health for a man of about eighty. I told him in Chinese that 'though this is the first time we have actually met, I feel that we are old friends from my research about your life.'"[21] This meeting proved to be one of the most comfortable and enlightening that I have had.

In terms of interview technique, I have found it most productive to use an open-ended style—"conversational or flexible interviewing." The interviewer approaches the respondent from the vantage point of wishing to know many things, realizing that there will be insufficient time to cover everything and pragmatically selecting a subset of subjects on the basis of where the interviewee demonstrates the greatest interest and knowledge and the least apprehension. I have a long list of possible questions in mind, but I let the actual questions posed flow from the conversation's logic to the fullest extent possible.

A practice that has served me well is to stay away from loaded words such as *politics*—I focus instead on how things work, letting the explanation of the process lead the discussion into the underlying views and conflicts. For instance, a common word used to describe bureaucratic processes in China is *xietiao* ("to coordinate," to resolve divergences among people, organizations, and territories). Exploring who needs to be "coordinated," why they need to be coordinated, and how they are coordinated gets you to the heart of politics without ever using the word itself.

Notes

In these notes I cite each interview in my data set by a document number specifically assigned to it; where others have taken the interview notes and I have not been present, I have given their name (e.g., "notes by Jan Berris"), and where I have taken the interview notes, I have used the abbreviation "DML" (David M. Lampton). In each citation I provide as much information as to the identity/category of the respondent, the place and time of interview, and other useful information as I have judged in each case to be consistent with prudence and the protection of my subjects. Where I have used notes by others (except government documents or interviews by journalists), I have treated them as "near verbatim" rather than exact wording.

INTRODUCTION

The epigraph from the secretary-general is Doc. 346 (DML). For the use of quotation marks here and with other interview material from my files, see the discussion below at the end of the section entitled "The Information Base."

1. I start the era of reform with the restoration of Deng Xiaoping to the positions stripped from him in 1976 in the wake of Premier Zhou Enlai's death and the first Tiananmen incident shortly thereafter. See also Li Lanqing, *Breaking Through: The Birth of China's Opening-Up Policy* (Oxford: Oxford University Press; Hong Kong: Foreign Language Teaching and Research Press, 2009), p. 397. I use the date of July 1977 as the nominal start of Deng's revolution because the Chinese people knew from his prior policy initiatives after the Great Leap Forward and from his brief return to power in 1974–76 what his policy proclivities were, even though formal adoption of his initial domestic and foreign policies had to await the Third Plenum of the Eleventh Central Committee of December 1978 and the nearly simultaneous formal, mutual diplomatic rec-

ognition between the United States and China. Even after these landmark events, Deng acquired power gradually.

2. Guo Liang, *Surveying Internet Usage and Its Impact in Seven Chinese Cities* (Beijing: Center for Social Development, Chinese Academy of Social Sciences, November 2007), p. iv, www.worldinternetproject.com/_files/_Published/_oldis/_China%20Internet%20Project%20Survey%20Report%202007.pdf.

3. Deng Xiaoping, interview by Mike Wallace of CBS News, September 2, 1986, Beijing, Doc. 860, p. 5.

4. Crane Brinton, *The Anatomy of Revolution* (New York: Vintage Books, 1965).

5. Communiqué of the Third Plenum of the Eleventh Central Committee of CPC, adopted December 22, 1978, and published December 29, 1978, www.bjreview.com.cn/90th/2011–04/26/content_357494_3.htm.

6. Cheng Li, "China's Fifth Generation: Is Diversity a Source of Strength or Weakness?," *Asia Policy*, no. 6 (July 2008): 53–93.

7. See David Shambaugh, *China's Communist Party: Atrophy and Adaptation* (Berkeley: University of California Press, 2008).

8. John J. Mearsheimer, *The Tragedy of Great Power Politics* (New York: W.W. Norton, 2001).

9. See Yan Xuetong, *Ancient Chinese Thought, Modern Chinese Power,* ed. Daniel A. Bell and Sun Zhe (Princeton: Princeton University Press, 2011); see also Zhang Wenmu, "Back to Yalta: A Roadmap for Sino-US Relations," *China Security*, no. 19 (2011): 49–56, ZhangWenmu2011_CS19_Ch4–2.pdf.

10. Quoted in Nicholas Thompson, *Hawk and Dove* (New York: Henry Holt, 2009), p. 272.

11. Some other sources of interviews and memoranda of conversation generally have not been used here simply because they are widely available and have been studied by others; also, I mainly drew on interviews, conversations, and meetings in which I was personally involved, so that my knowledge of the setting, my observation of the body language, and my hearing of the discussion in both Chinese and English (often with consecutive interpretation) all inform my sense of what was being said. Moreover, in many instances I met with interlocutors periodically over several decades, and therefore our sense of mutual trust and ability to pick up one conversation where the prior one had left off gave me a sense of knowledge, confidence, and continuity that would have been lacking had I primarily relied on interviews conducted by others. Other sources available currently include the National Security Archives at George Washington University; *The Kissinger Transcripts: The Top-Secret Talks with Beijing and Moscow,* ed. William Burr (New York: New Press, 1998); and the U.S. Department of State series entitled *The Foreign Relations of the United States.* In addition, because of the number of agreements between agencies of the U.S. government and Chinese counterparts, the archival holdings of individual U.S. government departments undoubtedly also possess extensive notes and memoranda of conversations that gradually will be declassified and become available to scholars. Further, the Ford Presidential Library holds the oral history of Michel Oksenberg during his years in the Carter administration. And the archives of China's Foreign Ministry also gradually are opening (with a sub-

stantial time lag for declassification and an unknown degree of selectivity in documents being made available).

12. I have been careful in citing my interviews to take into account the possible sensitivities and vulnerabilities of the delegation members meeting with a Chinese interlocutor, as well as those of the interlocutor him- or herself. Given that I am speaking from the viewpoint of the Chinese interviewee or informant, when I say "foreigner" I am referring to the non-Chinese participant.

13. This interview, because of its early date, was conducted by a delegation from the Committee of Concerned Asian Scholars (CCAS). See CCAS, "Interview with Chou En-lai" [July 19, 1971], *Bulletin of Concerned Asian Scholars* 3, nos. 3–4 (1971): 31–59, http://criticalasianstudies.org/assets/files/bcas/v03n03 .pdf, abstracted in DML, Doc. 812.

1. EVOLUTION IN THE REVOLUTION

The second epigraph to this chapter (quote from Deng Xiaoping) is from a meeting with National Committee Board of Directors, October 23, 1977, notes by Lucian Pye, Doc. 709. The mayor's remarks in the third epigraph are from DML, Doc. 380, p. 2. The article by Li Shenzhi cited in the fourth epigraph is in *Selected Writings of Li Shenzhi,* ed. Ilse Tebbetts and Libby Kingseed (Dayton, OH: Kettering Foundation Press, 2010), p. 128. And the senior academic's comment in the fifth epigraph is from DML, Doc. 838, p. 1.

1. Cheng Li, ed., *China's Emerging Middle Class: Beyond Economic Transformation* (Washington, DC: Brookings Institution Press, 2010).

2. Ezra F. Vogel, *Deng Xiaoping and the Transformation of China* (Cambridge, MA: Harvard University Press, 2011), ch. 6.

3. I say "yet again" because on two prior occasions Mao had turned on Deng (once in the 1930s in the base areas and again in the second half of the 1960s during the opening stages of the Cultural Revolution), only to recall him on each of these two prior occasions—finding Deng just too capable to throw on the scrap heap.

4. Hua Guofeng was eased out of power gradually, first being replaced as premier by Zhao Ziyang in September 1980; then being demoted to Communist Party vice-chairman from chairman in 1981 (replaced as chairman by Hu Yaobang); then having his post as vice-chairman of the party abolished in 1982, so that he was left with only the modestly dignified position of member of the Central Committee until November 2002. Hua died in August 2008, powerless, but with widespread gratitude for having exited gracefully.

5. The most thorough and scholarly account of Deng Xiaoping's transformation of China is Vogel's *Deng Xiaoping.*

6. Deng Xiaoping, "Heping he fazhan shi dangdai shijie de liang da wenti" [Peace and development are the contemporary world's two big issues], *Deng Xiaoping wenxuan* [Selected Works of Deng Xiaoping], vol. 3 (Beijing: Renmin chubanshe, 1993), pp. 104–6.

7. It is of course true that this era was not entirely peaceful, with the Soviet Union's invasion of Afghanistan in the late 1970s stirring up conflict to China's

west, and Deng's own high-cost "defensive counterattack" against Vietnam in 1979.

8. Deng Xiaoping, meeting with the National Committee Board of Directors, October 23, 1977, notes by Lucian Pye, Doc. 709, p. 2.

9. There is a meaningful debate over the actual size of the Chinese military budget and how much spending may occur either off budget entirely and/or under other budget categories. But there is little dispute over the shape of the curves and trends.

10. Deng Xiaoping, meeting with U.S. governors, October 17, 1979, notes by Jan Berris, Doc. 776, p. 5.

11. Amitai Etzioni, *A Comparative Analysis of Complex Organizations* (New York: Free Press, 1961), ch. 1.

12. Deng Xiaoping, meeting with U.S. governors, October 17, 1979, notes by Jan Berris, Doc. 776, p. 5.

13. Deng Xiaoping, meeting with the National Committee Board of Directors, October 23, 1977, notes by Lucian Pye, Doc. 709, p. 3.

14. Unsurprisingly, Deng Xiaoping played a key role in pulling China out of its early 1960s economic slide—a calamity in which perhaps thirty (one source says forty) million people had perished. The policies he employed then to a considerable extent became the template for his efforts once he was the supreme leader nearly two decades later. See Frank Dikötter, *Mao's Great Famine: The History of China's Most Devastating Catastrophe, 1958–1962* (New York: Walker, 2010).

15. Deng Xiaoping, meeting with U.S. governors, October 17, 1979, notes by Jan Berris, Doc. 776, p. 3.

16. For the definitive study on China's one-child policy as an ongoing campaign and preoccupation of Chinese leaders, see Tyrene White, *China's Longest Campaign: Birth Planning in the People's Republic, 1949–2005* (Ithaca: Cornell University Press, 2006), particularly p. 248. For a discussion of possible changes in population policy in 2013, see, Ted Alcorn, "China's New Leaders Cut Off One-Child Policy at the Root," *Lancet* 381 (March 23, 2013): 983.

17. Deng Xiaoping, meeting with the National Committee Board of Directors, October 23, 1977, notes by Lucian Pye, Doc. 709, p. 3.

18. For example, one of Deng's two sons, Deng Pufang, was pushed, fell, or jumped from a building in the Cultural Revolution at a time when he was under heavy Red Guard pressure. He became gravely disabled.

19. Deng Xiaoping, meeting with U.S. governors, October 17, 1979, notes by Jan Berris, Doc. 776, p. 3.

20. For the number of Chinese students in the United States in 1978 and 1984, see David M. Lampton with Joyce A. Madancy and Kristen M. Williams, *A Relationship Restored: Trends in U.S.-China Educational Exchanges, 1978–1984* (Washington, DC: National Academy Press, 1986), p. 30; for later numbers, see Institute of International Education, "Open Doors 2011: International Student Enrollment Increased by 5 Percent in 2010/11, Led by Strong Increase in Students from China," press release, November 14, 2011, www.iie.org/Who-We-Are/News-and-Events/Press-Center/Press-Releases/2011/2011-11-14-Open-Doors-International-Students; Institute of International Education, "International Stu-

dent Enrollments Rose Modestly in 2009/10, Led by Strong Increase in Students from China," press release, November 15, 2010, www.iie.org/Who-We-Are/News-and-Events/Press-Center/Press-Releases/2010/2010–11–15-Open-Doors-International-Students-In-The-US. See also Institute of International Education, "Open Doors Fact Sheet: China," 2012, www.iie.org/Research-and-Publications/Open-Doors/Data/Fact-Sheets-by-Country/2012.

21. *Zhongguo tongji nianjian 1990* [China statistics yearbook, 1990] (Beijing: Zhongguo tongji chubanshe, 1990), p. 721; and *Zhongguo tongji nianjian 2009* [China statistical yearbook, 2009] (Beijing: Zhongguo tongji chubanshe, 2009), p. 805. These figures are cited in Thomas G. Rawski's "Human Resources and China's Long Economic Boom," *Asia Policy*, no. 12 (July 2011): 53.

22. "China's Higher Education Students Exceed 30 Million," *People's Daily Online*, March 11, 2011, http://english.peopledaily.com.cn/90001/98649/7315789.html.

23. World Bank and Development Research Center of the State Council, *China 2030: Building a Modern, Harmonious, and Creative High-Income Society*, Conference ed. (Washington, DC: World Bank, 2012), pp. 36–37; an original source is Center for World-Class Universities, Shanghai Jiaotong University, "Academic Ranking of World Universities," www.arwu.org/.

24. Deng Xiaoping, "Senior Cadres Should Take the Lead in Maintaining and Enriching the Party's Fine Traditions," in *Selected Works of Deng Xiaoping (1975–1982)* (Beijing: Foreign Languages Press, 1984), pp. 213–14.

25. Ibid., p. 218.

26. Wei Jingsheng, "The Fifth Modernization: Democracy (1978)," in *Sources of Chinese Tradition: From 1600 through the Twentieth Century*, 2nd ed., vol. 2, ed. W.M. Theodore de Bary and Richard Lufrano (New York: Columbia University Press, 2000), pp. 497–500.

27. Deng Xiaoping, "Uphold the Four Cardinal Principles," *People's Daily Online*, March 30, 1979, p. 4/15, http://english.peopledaily.com.cn/dengxp/vol2/text/b1290.html.

28. Deng Xiaoping, meeting with U.S. governors, October 17, 1979, notes by Jan Berris, Doc. 776, p. 4.

29. Deng would have been concerned because in 1976 deliveries of oil fell short of the contracted amounts with Japan. For a thorough discussion of the role petroleum was to play in China's development and turn outward, see Kenneth Lieberthal and Michel Oksenberg, *Policy Making In China: Leaders, Structures, and Processes* (Princeton: Princeton University Press, 1988), ch. 5, esp. p. 205.

30. Deng Xiaoping, meeting with the National Committee Board of Directors, October 23, 1977, notes by Lucian Pye, Doc. 709, p. 4.

31. Li Lanqing, *Breaking Through* (Hong Kong: Oxford University Press, 2009), particularly ch. 2.

32. Ibid., pp. 89–91.

33. Ibid., p. 93.

34. Robert S. McNamara, "Transcript of Interview with Robert S. McNamara," interview by John Lewis, Richard Webb, and Devesh Kapur, April 1, 1991, World Bank History Project, Brookings Institution, Washington, DC,

http://siteresources.worldbank.org/EXTARCHIVES/Resources/Robert_
McNamara_Oral_History_Transcript_04_01_and_10_03_1991.pdf. In one
March 4, 1997, interview, Premier Li Peng acknowledged the importance of
World Bank advice, saying, "Generally, World Bank projects have good return
rates. At the same time, China has learned a lot about management and construction from the World Bank. For instance, feasibility studies, we adopted the
capital system in China, and the practice of bids and tenders. We learned all this
from the World Bank, so we hope our cooperation will continue." Premier Li
Peng, interview by author, March 4, 1997, DML, Doc. 414, p. 3.

35. Robert S. McNamara, speaking during comments by participants at
Kettering-Chinese Academy of Social Sciences Sustained Dialogue, Peace Hotel,
Beijing, September 27, 2005, DML, Doc. 459, p. 1.

36. David M. Lampton, *Paths to Power: Elite Mobility in Contemporary
China* (1986; repr., Ann Arbor: University of Michigan, Center for Chinese
Studies, 1989).

37. Party secretary, District Party Committee, Shanghai, September 1, 2007,
DML, Doc. 429, p. 1.

38. James MacGregor Burns, *Leadership* (New York: Harper and Row, 1978).

39. For a fascinating study of one transformational leader, see Jonathan D.
Spence, *God's Chinese Son: The Taiping Heavenly Kingdom of Hong Xiuquan*
(New York: W. W. Norton, 1996).

40. Cheng Li, "China's Fifth Generation: Is Diversity a Source of Strength or
Weakness?" *Asia Policy,* no. 6 (July 2008): 59–77.

41. World Bank, "Overview: China's Challenge: Building a Modern, Harmonious, and Creative High-Income Society," draft document, August 2011,
p. 17. This document was informally circulated for review; hence it is not publicly available and a complete citation for it is not possible. The subsequently
published version of this draft report had negotiated language that dropped and
revised language in the earlier draft document, including the figures cited here.
The subsequently published version of this report is World Bank and Development Research Center of the State Council, People's Republic of China, *China
2030: Building a Modern, Harmonious, and Creative High-Income Society,*
Conference ed. (Washington, DC: International Bank for Reconstruction and
Development/International Development Association and World Bank, 2012).

42. "GDP Growth in China, 1952–2011," information drawn from National
Bureau of Statistics [PRC], China Statistical Yearbooks; National Bureau of
Statistics Plan Report; and National Bureau of Statistics Communiqués, at
Chinability, November 5, 2011, www.chinability.com/GDP.htm; for 2012 ser-
vices percentage, see "China's Non-manufacturing Sector Growth Picks Up
Pace," BBC, July 2, 2012, www.bbc.co.uk/news/business-18684519.

43. David M. Lampton, "Presentation to National Academy of Sciences,"
Washington, DC, February 7, 1977, based on data obtained from Steroid
Chemistry Group to China, October 1976, DML, Doc. 623; see also David M.
Lampton, "Administration of the Pharmaceutical Research, Public Health, and
Population Bureaucracies," *China Quarterly,* no. 74 (June 1978): 392.

44. Barry Naughton, *The Chinese Economy: Transitions and Growth* (Cambridge, MA: MIT Press, 2007), pp. 102–5.

45. Charles Duhigg and David Barboza, "In China, Human Costs Are Built into an iPad," *New York Times,* January 25, 2012, www.nytimes.com/2012/01/26 /business/ieconomy-apples-ipad-and-the-human-costs-for-workers-in-china. html?pagewanted=all&_r=0.

46. Deng Xiaoping in a meeting with the National Committee on U.S.-China Relations Board of Directors, October 23, 1977, notes by Lucian Pye, Doc. 709, p. 2.

47. New annual commitments to loans from the World Bank to China peaked in 1994 at $2.94 billion. World Bank, *World Development Indicators 2012* (Washington, DC: World Bank, 2012), http://data.worldbank.org/sites/ default/files/wdi-2012-ebook.pdf.

48. U.S. Treasury, "Major Foreign Holders of Treasury Securities," www. treasury.gov/resource-center/data-chart-center/tic/Documents/mfhhis01.txt; also U.S. Treasury, "Major Foreign Holders of Treasury Securities," www .treasury.gov/resource-center/data-chart-center/tic/Documents/mfh.txt.

49. Xiaotian Wang, "External Debt Highest since 1985: SAFE Report," *China Daily,* March 22, 2003, www.chinadaily.com.cn/china/2012–03/22 /content_14893609.htm.

50. U.S. Department of Agriculture, Economic Research Service, "China /Trade," www.ers.usda.gov/topics/international-markets-trade/countries-regions /china/trade.aspx (accessed October 12, 2012).

51. Kevin Jianjun Tu and Sabine Johnson-Reiser, *Understanding China's Rising Coal Imports,* Policy Outlook (Washington, DC: Carnegie Endowment for International Peace, February 16, 2012), Summary, www.carnegieendowment .org/files/china_coal.pdf.

52. Jonathan Anderson, "Is China Export-Led?," *UBS Investment Research: Asian Focus,* September 27, 2007, p. 4, http://allroadsleadtochina.com/reports/ prc_270907.pdf.

53. Mayor Xu Kuangdi, dinner conversation, January 14, 1998, DML, Doc. 319, p. 1.

54. First Party Secretary Li Yuanchao, Provincial Guest House, Nanjing, June 23, 2007, DML, Doc. 431, p. 2.

55. See "Revenues of China's Customs Duties Top 1.6t Yuan," *China Daily,* January 13, 2012, www.chinadaily.com.cn/business/2012–01/13/content_ 14438069.htm; also "China's 2011 Fiscal Revenue up 24.8% to 10 Trillion Yuan," *Xinhua Wang News,* January 20, 2012, http://news.xinhuanet.com /english/china/2012–01/20/c_131370457.htm.

56. "China Urban Dwellers Exceed Rural Population," National Health and Family Planning Commission, People's Republic of China, January 19, 2012, www.npfpc.gov.cn/data/201202/t20120220_381737.html.

57. From Chinese Academy of Social Sciences, *Blue Book on Macro Economy,* cited in Chen Chen, "China's Urbanization Rate to Peak Soon," China .org, April 15, 2010, China.org.cn/china/2010–04/15/content_19823645.htm; see also Clarence Kwan, "Urbanization in China: Another 280 Million People by 2030," *China Issues* (Deloitte, Chinese Services Group), May-June 2010, www.deloitte.com/view/en_US/us/Services/additional-services/chinese-services- group/8ad3bdb92e119210VgnVCM200000bb42f00aRCRD.htm.

58. Homi Kharas, "The Emerging Middle Class in Developing Countries," Working Paper No. 285 (Paris: Organisation for Economic Co-operation and Development, Development Centre, January 2010), p. 30. There are, however, many other estimates of the size of China's middle class, some quite large, with definitional issues accounting for the variance. I have used one of the lowest estimates here. For another figure, see Li Chunling, *Duanlie yu suipian—Dangdai Zhongguo shehui jieceng fenhua shizheng fenxi* [Cleavage and fragmentation: An empirical analysis of social stratification in contemporary China] (Beijing: Shehui kexue wenxian chubanshe, 2005), cited in Cheng Li, ed., *China's Emerging Middle Class: Beyond Economic Transformation* (Washington, DC: Brookings Institution, 2010), p. 16.

59. World Bank and Development Research Center, *China 2030*, p. 34.

60. "China's Urbanization Rate Expected to Reach 48 Percent in 2010," *People's Daily Online*, December 22, 2009, http://english.peopledaily.com.cn/90001/90778/90862/6848826.html.

61. On the change over time in the Gini coefficient, see World Bank and Development Research Center, *China 2030*, p. 13. The accuracy of Gini coefficient calculations in China may be distorted by the household registration system. On the urban-to-rural income ratio and the Gini coefficient, see Martin K. Whyte, lecture, to the seminar "China Briefings for Mid-career Military Officers," February 12, 2013, transcript, p. 11. The statistics are from the China Household Income Project, not counting migrants; Terry Sicular, "Inequality in China: Recent Trends," PowerPoint presented at the Rural Education Action Program's conference "Will China Fall into a Middle-Income Trap? Growth, Inequality, and Future Instability," December 2011, Stanford, CA, http://iis-db.stanford.edu/evnts/6930/China_inequality_Sicular.pdf.

62. Martin Whyte, *Myth of the Social Volcano: Perceptions of Inequality and Distributive Injustice in Contemporary China* (Stanford: Stanford University Press, 2010).

63. Yi Fuxian, "The Great Urgency to Scrap the Family Planning Policy," *China-US Focus*, May 13, 2011, www.chinafocus.com/political-social-develop ment/the-great-urgency-to-scrap-the-family-planning-policy/.

64. Ibid.

65. "Statistics on Social Organizations," *China Statistical Yearbook 2011*, table 21–35.

66. Information Office of the State Council, People's Republic of China, "China's Foreign Aid," April 21, 2011, http://english.gov.cn/official/2011–04/21 /content_1849913.htm.

67. See, for example, Daniel H. Rosen and Thilo Hanemann, *China's Changing Outbound Direct Investment Profile: Drivers and Policy Implications*, Peterson Institute for International Economics, Policy Brief No. PB09–14 (Washington, DC: Peterson Institute, June 2009), www.iie.com/publications/ interstitial.cfm?ResearchID=1245; see also Daniel H. Rosen and Thilo Hanemann, "An American Open Door? Maximizing the Benefits of Chinese Direct Foreign Investment," Special Report, Center on U.S.-China Relations of the Asia Society and the Kissinger Institute on China and the United States, May 2011, www.ogilvypr.com/files/anamericanopendoor_china_fdi_study.pdf.

68. Ibid., Executive Summary, p. 8.

69. Evan S. Medeiros, Roger Cliff, Keith Crane, and James C. Mulvenon, *A New Direction for China's Defense Industry* (Santa Monica, CA: RAND, 2005).

70. "35,860 Chinese Evacuated from Unrest-Torn Libya," Xinhua, March 3, 2011, http://news.xinhuanet.com/english2010/china/2011-03/03/c_13759456. htm. It is appropriate to note that China received some outside assistance in this endeavor.

71. On foreign students in China, see "Total Number Foreign Students," www.sinograduate.com/international-student-statistics (accessed May 30, 2012); Chen Jia, "Expat Student Numbers Rise," March 4, 2011, www.chinadaily .com.cn/cndy/2011-03/04/content_12112597.htm.

72. Miscellaneous notes, April 12, 2011, Alexandria, VA, DML, Doc. 779, p. 2.

73. Pew Global, "China Seen Overtaking U.S. as Global Superpower," July 13, 2011, p. 1, http://pewglobal.org/2011/07/13/china-seen-overtaking-us-as-global-superpower/.

74. Lydia Saad, "U.S. Surpasses China in Forecast for Economic Power-house," Gallup Poll, February 16, 2009, www.gallup.com/poll/114658 /Surpasses-China-Forecast-Economic-Powerhouse.aspx.

75. Senior Chinese foreign policy analyst, April 26, 2010, DML, Doc. 694, pp. 2–3.

76. Vogel, *Deng Xiaoping*.

2. GOVERNANCE AND LEADERSHIP

The first epigraph, by Deng Xiaoping, is from Doc. 776 (notes by Jan Berris), p. 4. The second epigraph, by the bureau director, is from Doc. 728 (DML), p. 2. The third epigraph, by the governor of Sichuan, is from Doc. 766 (notes by Jan Berris), p. 1. The fourth epigraph, by President Jiang Zemin, is from Doc. 394 (DML), p. 2.

1. C.H. Tung, "Remarks at Carnegie Endowment in Washington, DC," September 29, 2011, DML, Doc. 846, p. 1.

2. Senior Chinese economic leader paraphrasing Yao Yilin, August 2, 2010, Washington, DC, DML, Doc. 705, p. 1.

3. Vice-Premier Li Xiannian, June 24, 1979, Great Hall of the People, Beijing, DML, Doc. 427, p. 3.

4. Vice-Premier Qian Qichen, January 11, 2000, Beijing, Zhongnanhai, DML, Doc. 589, p. 2.

5. Senior Chinese academic, September 20, 1999, Beijing, DML, Doc. 577, p. 1.

6. I want to thank School of Advanced International Studies PhD student Ms. Lily Chen for this comment in reading an early draft of this chapter in April 2012.

7. Premier Wen Jiabao, April 1, 2005, Beijing, Zhongnanhai, Purple Pavilion, DML, Doc. 454, p. 3.

8. Sun Yafu, director of the Taiwan Affairs Office of the State Council, January 12, 2010, Beijing, DML, Doc. 672, p. 1.

9. Former senior official in State Council, July 16, 2012, DML, Doc. 862, p. 2.

10. For a good academic overview of these changes, see Peter Hays Gries and Stanley Rosen, eds., *Chinese Politics: State, Society and Market* (London: Routledge, 2010).

11. Committee of Concerned Asian Scholars (CCAS), "Interview with Chou En-lai" [July 19, 1971], *Bulletin of Concerned Asian Scholars* 3, nos. 3–4 (1971): 31–59, http://criticalasianstudies.org/assets/files/bcas/v03n03.pdf, abstracted in DML, Doc. 812. An image of Zhou Enlai, the terrified underling in the Chairman's presence, is clearly seen in Dr. Li Zhisui's book, with the editorial assistance of Anne F. Thurston, *The Private Life of Chairman Mao* (New York: Random House, 1994), especially pp. 508–11. One of the more memorable descriptions of Mao's relations with Zhou in this volume was "Mao demanded Zhou's absolute loyalty, and had he not received it, Zhou would no doubt have been overthrown. But because Zhou was so subservient and loyal, Mao held the premier in contempt" (p. 510).

12. Dr. Susan L. Shirk, remarks at the symposium "The Week That Changed the World," March 7, 2012, U.S. Institute of Peace, Washington, DC.

13. Deng Xiaoping (Teng Hsiao-ping), November 14, 1974, Beijing, Great Hall of the People, notes taken by National Committee (Jan Berris?), American University Presidents Delegation, DML, Doc. 769.

14. Ibid., p. 4.

15. Vice-Premier Deng Xiaoping, October 23, 1977, notes by Lucian Pye, Doc. 709, pp. 1–2.

16. Senior policy adviser, June 10, 2007, China, DML, Doc. 433, p. 1.

17. Tabitha Grace Mallory, "The Sea's Harvest: China and Global Fisheries," *SAISPHERE*, 2011–2012, p. 40, http://media.sais-jhu.edu/saisphere2011/article/sea's-harvest-china-and-global-fisheries.

18. Denis Fred Simon, "Gradual Shift in S&T Funding," draft paper presented at the Conference on the Structure, Process, and Leadership of the Chinese Science and Technology System, July 16–17, 2012, La Jolla, CA, graph 15.

19. Richard P. Suttmeier and Shi Bing, "A Frog on Steroids? The Chinese Academic Research System and the Challenges of Innovation," working paper, Conference on the Structure, Process, and Leadership of the Chinese Science and Technology System, July 16–17, 2012, La Jolla, CA, p. 20. Note that the word *business* does not denote quite the autonomy the word may convey to a non-Chinese audience.

20. Former senior official in State Council, July 16–17, 2012, DML, Doc. 862, p. 2.

21. Department director, July 16–17, 2012, DML, Doc. 862, p. 1.

22. Huang Zhiling and Xin Dingding, "Air Traffic Grounded by Sky-High Towers," *China Daily*, July 3, 2012, p. 3.

23. Sharon LaFraniere, "A Chinese Official Tests a New Political Approach," *New York Times*, December 31, 2011, p. A5.

24. "Wukan Protesters End Action after Chinese Government Offers Concessions," December 21, 2011, www.guardian.co.uk/world/2011/dec/21/wukan-protesters-chinese-government-concessions.

25. Yan Xuetong, *Ancient Chinese Thought, Modern Chinese Power,* ed. Daniel A. Bell and Sun Zhe, trans. Edmund Ryden (Princeton: Princeton University Press, 2011).

26. Feng Tianyu, He Xiaoming, and Zhou Jiming, eds., *Zhonghua wenhua shi* [Chinese cultural history] (Shanghai: Shanghai renmin chubanshe, 1994), p. 184.

27. Yan, *Ancient Chinese Thought,* p. 6.

28. Wang Daohan, meeting with the editorial board of the *Christian Science Monitor,* January 9, 1997, Boston, DML, Doc. 371, p. 2.

29. Minister in Taiwan, July 6, 2011, DML, Doc. 830, p. 3.

30. Premier Wen Jiabao, press conference, March 16, 2007, Doc. 443, p. 4.

31. Zhou Enlai, meeting, June 15, 1973, Beijing, notes by Jan Berris, Doc. 750, p. 1.

32. President Jiang Zemin, November 22, 2002, Beijing, Great Hall of the People, DML, Doc. 521, p. 2.

33. David M. Lampton, with the assistance of Yeung Sai-cheung, *Paths to Power: Elite Mobility in Contemporary China,* No. 55 (Ann Arbor: Center for Chinese Studies, University of Michigan, 1989).

34. Policy analysts and advisers, June 20, 1998, Shanghai, DML, Doc. 807, p. 3.

35. Deng Mao Mao, *Deng Xiaoping: My Father* (New York: Basic Books, 1995), ch. 30.

36. Premier Zhao Ziyang, meeting with U.S. governors, National Governors Association trip to China, December 5–18, 1983, notes by Jan Berris, Doc. 763, p. 1.

37. First party secretary and mayor of Shanghai, Chen Liangyu, November 20, 2002, Jin Jiang Hotel, Central Banquet Building, Shanghai, November 20, 2002, DML, Doc. 517, p. 2.

38. Figures from Alice Miller, "China's New Party Leadership," *China Leadership Monitor,* no. 23 (Winter 2008), p. 4, www.chinaleadershipmonitor.org. For additional data and analysis on elite change, see H. Lyman Miller and Liu Xiaohong, "The Foreign Policy Outlook of China's 'Third Generation' Elite," in *The Making of Chinese Foreign and Security Policy in the Era of Reform,* ed. David M. Lampton (Stanford: Stanford University Press, 2001), p. 127.

39. Alice Miller, "The New Party Politburo Leadership," *China Leadership Monitor,* no. 40 (Winter 2013), p. 3, www.chinaleadershipmonitor.org.

40. White House, "Memorandum of Conversation," Zhou Enlai [Chou Enlai] and Dr. Henry Kissinger, October 20, 1971, Beijing, Great Hall of the People, synopsis in Doc. 701.

41. James MacGregor Burns, *Leadership* (New York: Harper and Row, 1978).

42. Max Weber, "The Profession and Vocation of Politics," in *Weber: Political Writings,* ed. Peter Lassman and Ronald Speirs, Cambridge Texts in the History of Political Thought (Cambridge: Cambridge University Press, 2007), pp. 311–13.

43. "Highlights—China Premier Wen Jiabao's Comments at NPC Press Conference," March 14, 2012, www.reuters.com/article/2012/03/14/china-npc-highlights-idUSL4E8EE11K20120314.

44. Cheng Li, "Shaping China's Foreign Policy: The Paradoxical Role of Foreign-Educated Returnees," *Asia Policy,* no. 10 (July 2010), p. 71.

45. Zhang Liang, comp., and Andrew J. Nathan and Perry Link, eds., *The Tiananmen Papers: The Chinese Leadership's Decision to Use Force against Their Own People—In Their Own Words* (New York: Public Affairs, 2001), p. 191.

46. Ezra F. Vogel, *Deng Xiaoping and the Transformation of China* (Cambridge, MA: Harvard University Press, 2011), p. 17.

47. Deng Xiaoping, October 17, 1979, Beijing, Great Hall of the People, notes by Jan Berris, Doc. 776, p. 4.

48. Ibid., p. 3.

49. Senior Taiwan academic, June 30, 2000, DML, Doc. 598, pp. 1–2.

50. Senior Chinese professor, July 8, 2011, DML, Doc. 827, p. 1.

51. Senior Chinese diplomat, August 16, 2002, Beijing, DML, Doc. 538, p. 4.

52. Alexander V. Pantsov and Steven I. Levine, *Mao: The Real Story* (New York: Simon and Schuster, 2012).

53. Vice-Premier Deng Xiaoping, October 17, 1979, notes by Jan Berris, Doc. 776, p. 5.

54. Vice-minister, November 6, 2002, United States, DML, Doc. 751, p. 2.

55. Former Shanghai mayor Wang Daohan, conversation with *Christian Science Monitor* editorial board, January 9, 1997, Boston, DML, Doc. 371, p. 2.

56. Senior Chinese policy analysts, June 20, 1998, China, DML, Doc. 807, p. 4.

57. Calculated from the World Trade Organization Statistics Database using total merchandise trade in current U.S. dollars, http://stat.wto.org/Home/WSDBHome.aspx?Language.

58. Calculated from the World Trade Organization Statistics Database using total merchandise trade in current U.S. dollars, http://stat.wto.org/Home/WSDBHome.aspx?Language.

59. "The Communist Party of China (CPC, CCP)," China Today.com (official party website), n.d., www.chinatoday.com/org/cpc/ (accessed August 20, 2012).

60. Barry Naughton, "State Enterprise Restructuring: Renegotiating the Social Contract in Urban China," in *China Today: Economic Reforms, Social Cohesion and Collective Identities,* ed. Taciana Fisac and Lelia Fernandez-Stembridge (New York: Routledge Curzon, 2003), pp. 3–27.

61. Table 2–13, "Contribution of the Three Strata of Industry to GDP Growth," in *China Statistical Yearbook 2011* (Beijing: China Statistics Press, 2011); see also, for slightly different figures, Economist Intelligence Unit Data Services, www.eiu.com (accessed June 3, 2012).

62. Jiang Zemin to the National Committee on U.S.-China Relations Board of Directors, May 9, 1992, Beijing, DML, Doc. 403, p. 2.

63. Ibid., p. 3.

64. Senior Chinese diplomat, August 15, 2002, Beijing, DML, Doc. 550, p. 1.

65. CCAS, "Interview with Chou En-lai," 32–33, 35, 36, abstracted in DML, Doc. 812, pp. 3–4.

66. Cheng Li, "The Battle for China's Top Nine Leadership Posts," *Washington Quarterly* 35 (Winter 2012): 131–45.

67. R&D official, July 16–17, 2012, DML, Doc. 862, p. 2.

68. Chinese diplomat, December 21, 1998, Washington, DC, DML, Doc. 579, p. 1.

69. Remarks of department director, July 16–17, 2012, DML, Doc. 862, p. 1.

70. Li Lanqing, *Breaking Through: The Birth of China's Opening-Up Policy* (Oxford: Oxford University Press; Hong Kong: Foreign Language Teaching and Research Press, 2009), p. 371.

71. Secretary, Minhang District Party Committee, September 1, 2007, Shanghai, DML, Doc. 429, p. 1.

72. Susan L. Shirk, *The Political Logic of Economic Reform in China* (Berkeley: University of California Press, 1993).

73. Even if one corrects for the fewer interviews in the earlier period, the frequency remains overwhelmingly in the direction described.

74. Zhang Laicheng, Tong Xunyuan, and Zhang Meiwen, "Market Information Survey Industry: Maturing Rapidly," *Zhongguo Xinxibao,* August 2, 2011, www.zgxxb.com/cn/xwzx/201108010008.shtml. Much opinion polling is aimed at market research germane to consumer preferences and marketing.

75. Chinese pollster, November 19, 2012, DML, Doc. 879, p. 1.

76. Adviser to nuclear power corporation, July 21, 2009, DML, Doc. 649, p. 4.

77. Niu Xinchun, "Eight Myths about Sino-U.S. Relations," *Contemporary International Relations* 21, no. 4 (July/August 2011): 10.

78. Very senior person in foreign affairs system, August 15, 2002, Beijing, DML, Doc. 549, pp. 2–3.

79. Table 8–4, "National Government Expenditure and Ratio of Central and Local Governments," in *China Statistical Yearbook 2011* (Beijing: China Statistics Press, 2011).

80. For the 1978 figure, see Yang Jing, "Development of the Non-state Sector in China: An Update," EAI [East Asian Institute] Background Brief, no. 606, March 10, 2011, www.eai.nus.edu.sg/BB606.pdf; for the 2009 figure, see Andrew Szamosszegi and Cole Kyle, *An Analysis of State-Owned Enterprises and State Capitalism in China,* U.S.-China Economic and Security Review Commission (Washington, DC: Capital Trade, 2011), p. 13.

81. Ibid.

82. Regarding the corruption of military leaders, see "Crime Clubs: Clamping Down on Criminal Networks in China," *Jane's Intelligence Review,* 24, no. 5 (April 12, 2012): 46–49; and John Garnaut, "Rotting from Within: Investigating the Massive Corruption of the Chinese Military," *Foreign Policy,* April 16, 2012, www.foreignpolicy.com/articles/2012/04/16/rotting_from_within.

83. Table 20–7, "Number of New Students Enrollment by Level and Type of School," in *China Statistical Yearbook 2011,* www.stats.gov.cn/tjsj/ndsj/2011/html/U2007E.HTM.

84. Table 20–2, "Basic Statistics by Level and Type of Education (2010)," in *China Statistical Yearbook 2011,* www.stats.gov.cn/tjsj/ndsj/2011/indexeh.htm.

85. Cheng Li, "Shaping China's Foreign Policy: The Paradoxical Role of Foreign-Educated Returnees," *Asia Policy,* no. 10 (July 2010): 69.

86. Institute of International Education, "Open Doors Data: Top 25 Places of Origin of International Students, 2009/10–2010/11," www.iie.org/Research-and-Publications/Open-Doors/Data/International-Students//Leading-Places-of-Origin/2009–11.

87. Cheng Li, "Shaping China's Foreign Policy," 69.

88. Secretary, Minhang District Party Committee, September 1, 2007, Shanghai, DML, Doc. 429, p. 1.

89. Ma Jun, "NGOs and Environmental Governance in China: An Interview with Ma Jun," *Yale Journal of International Affairs* 4 (Winter 2009): 87.

90. PLA senior officers, January 23, 2010, Washington, DC, DML, Doc. 679, p. 3.

91. Ibid., p. 3.

92. Zbigniew Brzezinski, *Strategic Vision: America and the Crisis of Global Power* (New York: Basic Books, 2012), pp. 26–36.

93. Very senior Chinese economist, August 2, 2010, Washington, DC, DML, Doc. 705, p. 2.

94. First party secretary and mayor, November 20, 2002, major Chinese city, DML, Doc. 517, p. 1.

95. Senior Chinese scholar, August 2, 2010, Washington, DC, DML, Doc. 705, p. 3.

3. POLICY MAKING

The first epigraph (the quote by the state planning commissioner) is from Doc. 741 (DML), pp. 2–3. The second epigraph (the quote by the trade negotiator) is from Doc. 802 (DML), p. 2.

1. Former mayor of Shanghai Wang Daohan, January 16, 1997, Washington, DC, DML, Doc. 382, p. 2.

2. Principal leader of major Chinese university, April 9, 2012, Washington, DC, DML, Doc. 859, p. 1.

3. The World Bank and Development Research Center of the State Council, People's Republic of China, *China 2030: Building a Modern, Harmonious, and Creative High-Income Society* (Washington, DC: World Bank, 2012), pp. 55–56. Levels of government below the center account for 80 percent of total budgetary expenditure, but only 40–50 percent of their expenditure burdens are financed from centrally derived monies. Looking lower in the system, to counties/townships, where the revenue expenditure gap is greatest, particularly in poorer areas, David Bulman explains that "counties/townships only take in ~20% of total revenue, but they are responsible for ~40% of total expenditure." See David J. Bulman, "Leaders and Economic Growth in China's Counties: Characteristics and Consequences of Constrained Development," dissertation prospectus (draft), Johns Hopkins—School of Advanced International Studies, May 29, 2012, p. 6, n. 19.

4. Richard L. Walker, *China under Communism: The First Five Years* (New Haven: Yale University Press, 1955), p. 27.

5. Carl J. Friedrich and Zbigniew K. Brzezinski, *Totalitarian Dictatorship and Autocracy* (Cambridge, MA: Harvard University Press, 1956), p. 4.

6. David M. Lampton, "Chinese Politics: The Bargaining Treadmill," *Issues and Studies* 23, no. 3 (March 1987): 11–41; David M. Lampton, "Water: Challenge to a Fragmented Political System," in *Policy Implementation in Post-Mao China,* ed. David M. Lampton (Berkeley: University of California Press, 1987), pp. 157–89; Kenneth Lieberthal and Michel Oksenberg, *Policy Making in China: Leaders, Structures, and Processes* (Princeton: Princeton University Press, 1988); and Kenneth G. Lieberthal and David M. Lampton, eds., *Bureaucracy, Politics, and Decision Making in Post-Mao China* (Berkeley: University of California Press, 1992).

7. A. Doak Barnett, *The Making of Foreign Policy in China* (Boulder, CO: Westview Press, 1985).

8. One tends to see a resurgence of the factional model when elite strife becomes increasingly pronounced. In the run-up to the Eighteenth Party Congress in 2012, for example, factional-type analysis emerged in the work of Cheng Li and others.

9. Aaron Wildavsky, *The Politics of the Budgetary Process,* 2nd ed. (Boston: Little, Brown, 1974).

10. Robert A. Dahl and Charles E. Lindblom, *Politics, Economics, and Welfare* (New York: Harper Torchbooks, 1963).

11. Yu Qing, YQ.People.com.cn, http://yq.people.com.cn, cited in Da Wei, "Has China Become 'Tough'?," *China Security* 6, no. 3 (2010): 99–100; see also James Reilly, *Strong Society, Smart State: The Rise of Public Opinion in China's Japan Policy* (New York: Columbia University Press, 2012), pp. 35–37, 220–26.

12. Andrew Mertha, "'Fragmented Authoritarianism 2.0': Political Pluralization in the Chinese Policy Process," *China Quarterly,* no. 200 (2009): 995–1012; also Andrew C. Mertha, *China's Water Warriors: Citizen Action and Policy Change* (Ithaca: Cornell University Press, 2008).

13. Yun Zhou, "China Responds to Fukushima," *Bulletin of Atomic Scientists,* June 28, 2012, http://thebulletin.org/china-responds-fukushima.

14. Nuclear law expert, August 5, 2011, Beijing, DML, Doc. 835, p. 2.

15. Bo Kong and David M. Lampton, "Whither the Atomic Energy Law in China?," unpublished report prepared for U.S. National Nuclear Safety Administration, February 2012 (Report 6), p. 5.

16. For a detailed report on the story of the Atomic Energy Law, see ibid.

17. Nuclear law expert, August 5, 2011, Beijing, DML, Doc. 835, p. 3.

18. Central People's Government of the People's Republic of China, "The State Council," October 25, 2005, http://english.gov.cn/links/statecouncil.htm. Note that in the spring of 2013 there was a modest reconfiguration of State Council organizations at the Twelfth National People's Congress. These adjustments were rather unobtrusive in comparison to prior expectations for change, and the alterations do not materially affect the situation described here.

19. Senior official of the State Nuclear Power Technology Corporation (SNPTC), July 28, 2009, DML, Doc. 641, p. 3.

20. Senior MOFTEC official, August 16, 2002, DML, Doc. 541, p. 2.

21. Senior security-related official, January 6, 2012, Beijing, DML, Doc. 856, p. 4.

22. Nicholas R. Lardy, *Sustaining China's Economic Growth: After the Global Financial Crisis* (Washington, DC: Peter G. Peterson Institute for International Economics, 2012), p. 145.

23. Shanxi planning and transport officials, Shanxi Province, May 16, 1985, Shanxi Province, DML, Doc. 721, p. 2.

24. Arms control expert, July 15, 2009, Beijing, DML, Doc. 642, p. 4.

25. Wen Jin Yuan, "China's Export Lobbying Groups and the Politics of the Renminbi," Freeman Briefing Report, Center for Strategic and International Studies, February 2012, p. 2, http://csis.org/files/publication/fr12no102.pdf; see also He Xingqiang, "The RMB Exchange Rate: Interest Groups in China's Economic Policymaking," *China Security*, no. 19 (2011): 23–36.

26. Wen Jin Yuan, "China's Export Lobbying Groups"; see also He Xingqiang, "RMB Exchange Rate."

27. Lardy, *Sustaining China's Economic Growth*, pp. 148–49.

28. Benjamin L. Read, "Benjamin Read on Homeowners' Protests in Shanghai," February 28, 2008, http://chinadigitaltimes.net/2008/02/benjamin-read-on-homeowners-protests-in-shanghai/.

29. "Citizens Challenge New Maglev Route in Shanghai," China.org, citing *China Youth Daily*, January 14, 2008, www.china.org.cn/english/China/239667.htm.

30. "Shanghai Residents Protest Controversial Maglev Project on Jan. 6," *China Digital Times*, January 13, 2008, http://chinadigitaltimes.net/2008/01/shanghai-residents-protest-controversial-maglev-project-on-jan6/. See also Chenzhong Xiaolu, "Shanghai Suspends Maglev Project," *Caijing*, March 6, 2009, http://english.caijing.com.cn/2009-03-10/110116802.html.

31. Zha Minjie, "Maglev Extension Given Green Light," *Shanghai Daily*, March 14, 2010, www.shanghaidaily.com/article/print.asp?id=431107; see also "Shanghai-Hangzhou Maglev Plans," *Shanghaiist*, January 19, 2011, www.shanghaiist.com/2011/01/19/shanghai-hangzhou_maglev_plans_swit.php; "Maglev Link Plan Is Suspended," *China Business News*, January 19, 2011, http://cnbusinessnews.com/maglev-link-plan-is-suspended/#axzz2aSnQ8M2e; Geoff Dyer, "Protests Suspend Work on Shanghai Maglev," *Financial Times*, March 6, 2008, www.ft.com/cms/s/0/1f2e3fc8-ebae-11dc-9493-0000779fd2ac.html.

32. Geoff Dyer, "Protests Suspend Work on Shanghai Maglev," *Financial Times*, March 6, 2008, www.ft.com/intl/cms/s/0/1f2e3fc8-ebae-11dc-9493-0000779fd2ac.html#axzz29mCfybKi.

33. President Jiang Zemin, March 20, 2001, Great Hall of the People, Beijing, DML, Doc. 772, p. 1.

34. "Top 20 Internet Countries By Users—2012 Q2," Internet World Stats, www.internetworldstats.com/top20.htm (accessed October 14, 2012).

35. Senior military officer, June 27, 1999, DML, Doc. 757, pp. 2–3.

36. Vice-Minister of Foreign Affairs Wang Hairong, July 28, 1976, U.S. Liaison Office, Beijing, notes by Jan Berris, Doc. 748, p. 5.

37. Earthquake Geospatial Research Portal, "Overview of the Wenchuan Earthquake," n.d., http://cegrp.cga.harvard.edu/content/overview-wenchuan-earthquake (accessed October 14, 2012).

38. "Former Head of China's Drug Watchdog Executed," Xinhuanet.com, July 10, 2007, http://news.xinhuanet.com/english/2007–07/10/content_6353536.htm.

39. David M. Lampton, "Presentation to National Academy of Sciences, Washington, DC," February 7, 1977 (based on October 1976 trip to the PRC), Doc. 623, p. 1.

40. Premier Wen Jiabao, December 7, 2003, New York City, Waldorf-Astoria Towers, DML, Doc. 505, p. 1.

41. Senior Chinese economist, March 29, 2005, China, DML, Doc. 663, p. 1.

42. Jamil Anderlini, "Word on the Tweet Forces Bo Crisis into the Open," *Financial Times,* April 12, 2012, p. 6.

43. Xiamen business leader, January 15, 2010, Xiamen, Fujian, DML, Doc. 671, p. 4.

44. Wu Lengxi, November 12, 1982, Beijing, DML, Doc. 734, p. 2. Parenthetically, *Garrison's Gorillas* was the first American TV series to be shown in the PRC in the 1970s—it was wildly popular, and reportedly the crime rate nationwide dropped on nights it was broadcast.

45. Secretary-general of special project, July 14, 2003, DML, Doc. 346, p. 2.

46. Senior official of nuclear organization, August 5, 2011, Beijing, DML, Doc. 836, p. 3.

47. Senior trade official, April 12, 2002, Beijing, DML, Doc. 661, p. 2.

48. Chinese government researchers, December 6, 2011, Washington, DC, DML, Doc. 853, p. 1.

49. David M. Lampton, "The Policy Implementation Problem in Post-Mao China," in Lampton, *Policy Implementation,* pp. 3–24.

50. Senior Chinese economist, March 29, 2005, China, DML, Doc. 663, p. 2.

4. THE WORLD

The first epigraph (quote by General Jiang Youshu) is from Doc. 736 (DML), p. 2. The second epigraph (quote by high-ranking Chinese economic official) is from Doc. 738 (DML), p. 3. The third epigraph (quote by Wang Xuebing) is from Doc. 358 (DML), p. 2. The fourth epigraph (quote by senior Foreign Ministry official) is from Doc. 526 (DML), p. 1. The fifth epigraph (quote by senior foreign policy think tank leader) is from Doc. 695 (DML), p. 2. The sixth epigraph (quote by State Councilor Dai Bingguo) is from Doc. 819 (DML), p. 4.

1. Senior Chinese intelligence official, October 2, 2003, DML, Doc. 506, p. 1.

2. Ren Xiao, "Traditional Chinese Theory and Practice of Foreign Relations: A Reassessment," in *China and International Relations: The Chinese View and the Contribution of Wang Gungwu,* ed. Zheng Yongnian (London: Routledge, 2010), pp. 102–16.

3. In speaking of Chinese thought in the realms of science and philosophy, Joseph Needham, in his *Science and Civilization in China,* called this "organismic" thought, arguing that Western science made progress by simplifying reality into linear, causal models but that in China there was an aversion to this

simplification because it was difficult to assert straight-line causality when one started from the premise that everything influenced everything else in a single seamless, mutually influencing reality.

4. Vice-Minister of Foreign Affairs Qiao Guanhua, June 8, 1973, Beijing, notes by Jan Berris, Doc. 778, p. 5.

5. "Interview of Mike Wallace with Deng Xiaoping," CBS News, Beijing, September 2, 1986, in *Deng Xiaoping wen xuan,* Di San Juan (Beijing: Renmin chubanshe, 1993), pp. 167–75, http://english.peopledaily.com.cn/dengxp/vol3/text/c1560.html.

6. Henry Kissinger and Premier Zhou Enlai, classified "Memorandum of Conversation" ("Exclusively Eyes Only"), White House, October 20, 1971, Beijing, Great Hall of the People, pp. 5–6, released by the U.S. National Archives and Records Administration (no date of release or other information).

7. In 2008, after a successful Olympics and the crash of Lehman Brothers, 41 percent of Chinese saw China as "the world's leading economic power." Four years later, after slowing growth, domestic scandal, and a not entirely smooth generational transition among leaders in Beijing, only 29 percent of Chinese saw the PRC in this light. Alarmingly from a U.S. point of view, 58 percent of British and 62 percent of Germans saw China "as the world's leading economic power" in 2012. Pew Research Center, Global Attitudes Project, "Growing Concerns in China about Inequality, Corruption" (Issued October 16, 2012), pp. 5, 14, www.pewglobal.org/files/2012/10/Pew-Global-Attitudes-China-Report-FINAL-October-10-2012.pdf.

8. Ibid., p. 4.

9. Premier Li Peng, April 3, 1993, Great Hall of the People, Beijing, DML, Doc. 396, p. 3.

10. Ambassador Seignious (U.S. Arms Control and Disarmament Agency) and Vice-Minister of Foreign Affairs Zhang Wenjin, January 8, 1980, Zhongnanhai, Beijing, declassified U.S. government document, DML, Doc. 696.

11. Carl E. Walter and Fraser J.T. Howie, *Red Capitalism: The Fragile Financial Foundation of China's Extraordinary Rise* (Singapore: John Wiley and Sons [Asia], 2011), pp. 21–24.

12. Henny Sender, "Dug In Too Deep," *Financial Times,* June 25, 2012, p. 7.

13. David M. Lampton, *Same Bed, Different Dreams: Managing U.S.-China Relations, 1989–2000* (Berkeley: University of California Press, 2001), p. 330; see also Alice Miller, "The CCP Central Committee's Leading Small Groups," *China Leadership Monitor,* no. 26 (2008): 8–10, http://media.hoover.org/sites/default/files/documents/CLM26AM.pdf. Miller indicates uncertainty about when there was a shift in the leadership of the Foreign Affairs Leading Small Group.

14. The eight points from Jiang Zemin's speech "Continuing to Strive toward Reunification of China," January 30, 1995, are republished in "Jiang Zemin's Eight-Point Proposal," Bridging the Straits, January 11, 2007, http://english.cri.cn/4426/2007/01/11/167@184028.htm.

15. Senior Chinese foreign policy analyst, December 1, 1998, DML, Doc. 580, p. 1.

16. PLA officer, June 27, 1999, Beijing, DML, Doc. 757, p. 3.

17. Director Xu Jiatun, September 20, 1989, Hong Kong, DML, Doc. 404, p. 2.

18. Vice-Foreign Minister Zhou Nan with David Gergen, April 1991, Hong Kong, notes by Jan Berris, Doc. 767, p. 3.

19. On April 16, 1988, an American delegation of which I was a member met with Vice-Foreign Minister Zhou Nan, who spoke about Hong Kong, among other things. He was dismissive of the idea that there were any reasons for the people of Hong Kong to be concerned about the 1997 reversion of Hong Kong to the PRC. "Why would we hurt it? There should be no problem with confidence." Vice-Foreign Minister Zhou Nan, April 16, 1988, Foreign Ministry, Beijing, DML, Doc. 397, p. 1.

20. Governor Christopher Patten, September 1992, DML, Doc. 739, p. 1.

21. Zhao Ziyang, *Prisoner of the State: The Secret Journal of Premier Zhao Ziyang*, trans. Bao Pu, Renee Chiang, and Adi Ignatius (New York: Simon and Schuster, 2009).

22. Notes in interview file, May 2, 1992, DML, Doc. 599, p. 1.

23. Vice-foreign minister, June 28, 1999, Beijing, DML, Doc. 351, p. 2.

24. "DCI Statement on the Belgrade Chinese Embassy Bombing," House Permanent Select Committee on Intelligence Open Hearing, July 22 1999, https://www.cia.gov/news-information/speeches-testimony/1999/dci_speech_072299.html.

25. Chinese vice-minister, June 28, 1999, Beijing, DML, Doc. 352, p. 2. This was a retrospective comment, given that Clinton had been acquitted in his Senate trial the previous February.

26. Chinese office director, June 29, 1999, Beijing, DML, Doc. 353, p. 2.

27. Michael D. Swaine and Zhang Tuosheng, eds., with Danielle F. S. Cohen, *Managing Sino-American Crises: Case Studies and Analysis* (Washington, DC: Carnegie Endowment for International Peace, 2006), pp. 327–75.

28. PLA officer, June 27, 1999, Beijing, DML, Doc. 757, p. 2.

29. Ibid., p. 3.

30. Chinese scholar, June 29, 1998, DML, Doc. 807, p. 7.

31. Senior Foreign Ministry figure, May 6, 1999, DML, Doc. 578, p. 2.

32. Premier Zhu Rongji, March 31, 1999, Great Hall of the People, Xinjiang Room, Beijing, DML, Doc. 369, p. 3.

33. Senior Chinese economist, March 29, 2005, Xian, China, DML, Doc. 663, p. 3.

34. PLA officer, June 27, 1999, Beijing, DML, Doc. 757, p. 2.

35. Senior Chinese bank official, March 19, 2009, Beijing, DML, Doc. 635, p. 1.

36. Zhangzhou mayor Han Yulin, July 27, 1993, Zhangzhou, Fujian, DML, Doc. 610, p. 1.

37. Professor Pieter Bottelier, pers. comm., October 24, 2012.

38. Mayor Xu Kuangdi, January 14, 1998, Shanghai, DML, Doc. 319, p. 1.

39. Think tankers, June 27, 1999, DML, Doc. 707, p. 2.

40. Vice-Foreign Minister Qiao Guanhua, June 8, 1973, Beijing, notes by Jan Berris, Doc. 778, p. 6.

41. Ibid, p. 5.

42. Lu Chang, "A Lot on the Plate," Chinadaily.com, March 30, 2012, http://europe.chinadaily.com.cn/epaper/2012–03/30/content_14950430.htm.

43. Senior adviser, August 19, 2002, DML, Doc. 547, p. 1.

44. Ibid.

45. Senior adviser to Hu Jintao, December 13, 2002, DML, Doc. 331, p. 2.

46. Chinese minister of finance Xiang Huaicheng, September 8, 2002, Washington, DC, DML, Doc. 340, p. 3.

47. Senior Chinese economist, March 29, 2005, Xian, China, DML, Doc. 663, p. 3.

48. "US Will Never Default, Vice-President Biden Tells China," BBC News, August 21, 2011, www.bbc.co.uk/news/world-asia-pacific-14605974?print=true.

49. AFP, "Clinton Wraps Up Asia Trip by Asking China to Buy US Debt," Breitbart.com, February 22, 2009, http://www.breitbart.com/print.php?id=CNG.42a44b0f5d9cf5c9762e80574e79a3d5.831.

50. Senior adviser, August 19, 2002, DML, Doc. 547, p. 1.

51. President Jiang Zemin, January 13, 1998, Office 202, Zhongnanhai, Beijing, DML, Doc. 582, p. 2.

52. Vice-Chairman Zhang Wannian, September 6, 1996, Beijing, DML, Doc. 417, p. 3.

53. "David Gergen and Foreign Minister Qian Qichen," April 1991, notes by Jan Berris, Doc. 765, p. 5.

54. Foreign Minister Qian Qichen, August 26, 1992, DML, Doc. 381, p. 2.

55. For an extensive discussion of "comprehensive national power," see David M. Lampton, *The Three Faces of Chinese Power: Might, Money, and Minds* (Berkeley: University of California Press, 2008), pp. 20–25.

56. Pew Research Center, "Growing Concerns in China," p. 14, www.pewglobal.org/files/2012/10/Pew-Global-Attitudes-China-Report-FINAL-October-10–2012.pdf.

57. Premier Zhou Enlai, late-night conversation with Michael Blumenthal, June 15, 1973, Beijing, notes by Jan Berris, Doc. 750, pp. 5–6.

58. Premier Zhao Ziyang, meeting with U.S. governors, National Governors Association trip to China, December 5–18, 1983, Beijing, notes by Jan Berris, Doc. 763, p. 3.

59. Deng Xiaoping, October 17, 1979, Beijing, Great Hall of the People, notes by Jan Berris, Doc. 776, p. 2.

60. Vice-Premier and Foreign Minister Huang Hua, November 20, 1980, (Old) Ministry of Foreign Affairs, Beijing, notes by Jan Berris, Doc. 715, p. 6.

61. Senior PRC intelligence official, October 2, 2003, DML, Doc. 506, p. 1.

62. Chinese academics, July 21, 2009, DML, Doc. 651, p. 4.

63. Vice-Chairman Zhang Wannian, September 6, 1996, Beijing, DML, Doc. 417, p. 2.

64. Senior Chinese scholar, August 19, 2002, DML, Doc. 535, p. 1.

65. Jianmin Qi, "The Debate over 'Universal Values' in China," *Journal of Contemporary China* 20, no. 72 (2011): 881–90.

66. Senior Chinese scholar, August 19, 2002, DML, Doc. 535, p. 2.

67. Pew Research Center, "Growing Concerns in China," p. 4.

68. Vice-Chairman Li Xiannian, June 1979, Beijing, notes by Jan Berris, doc. 775, p. 4.

69. Li Juqian, "Legality and Legitimacy: China's ASAT Test," *China Security* 5, no. 1 (Winter 2009): 51.

70. Chinese general, 2011, DML, Doc. 833, p. 3.

71. Keith Bradsher, "China Said to Bolster Missile Capabilities," *New York Times,* August 25, 2012, p. A5.

72. Chinese strategic analyst, August 19, 2002, DML, Doc. 535, p. 2.

73. John Hickman, "Red Moon Rising," *Foreign Policy,* no. 194, June 18, 2012, www.foreignpolicy.com/articles/2012/06/18/red_moon_rising (accessed June 28, 2012).

74. Katharina Hesse, "Interview with China's Vice Minister of Foreign Affairs: 'The West Has Become Very Conceited,'" *Der Spiegel,* August 22, 2011, www.spiegel.de/international/world/0,1518,781597,00.html. On another website, Susanne Koelbl is listed as the interviewer. See also DML, Doc. 840.

5. NIGHTMARES

The first epigraph (quote by Liu Binyan) is from Doc. 768 (Jan Berris), p. 1. The second epigraph (quote by Xiang Nan) is from Doc. 618 (DML), p. 2. The third epigraph (quote by Premier Zhu Rongji) is from Doc. 561 (DML), p. 2. The final epigraph (quote by director general) is from Doc. 456 (DML), p. 2.

1. "Missteps" does not quite capture the enormity of the tragedies Mao Zedong created. In *Xin Shijie Shibao* [New World Times], in an apparently signed article dated March 27, 2012, and carried in the paper July 13, 2012, under the title "'Wen ge' fansi yu zhengzhi tizhi gai ge," Jiang Zemin's onetime political adviser, Wang Huning, was reported to have revealed that three million persons had been "knocked down" as "rightists" in 1957; forty million had died of starvation in the late 1950s and early 1960s; and twenty-plus million had died in the Cultural Revolution. My efforts to verify the authenticity of this alleged Wang Huning article have been inconclusive.

2. Premier Zhao Ziyang, September 27, 1987, Beijing, Zhongnanhai, interview by Tom Brokaw, Doc. 803, p. 3.

3. "Portrait of Vice President Xi Jinping: 'Ambitious Survivor' of the Cultural Revolution," confidential U.S. Embassy Beijing cable, November 16, 2009, reference ID 09Beijing3128, http://wikileaks.org/cable/2009/11/09BEIJING3128 .html.

4. Ibid.; see also Xi Jinping, interview by Carsten Boyer Thogersen and Susanne Posborg, *Zhonghua Ernu* [Sons and Daughters of China], summer 2000, DML, Doc. 866, pp. 6–7. For a compendium of short pieces written from 2003 to 2007 by Xi Jinping and published under his own name, see Xi Jinping, *Zhi Jiang xin yu* (Zhejiang: Zhejiang renmin chubanshe, August 2007).

5. DML, Doc. 838, p. 2.

6. Premier Wen Jiabao, meeting with members of U.S. Congress, April 1, 2005, DML, Doc. 454, p. 3.

7. Sichuan governor Yang Xizong, December 1983, notes by Jan Berris, Doc. 766, p. 2.

8. "Income Gap between China's Urban, Rural Residents Narrows in 2011," Xinhuanet, January 20, 2012, http://news.xinhuanet.com/english/china/2012–01/20/c_131371091.htm.

9. Senior U.S. statesman, May 8, 2012, DML, Doc. 858, p. 1.

10. He Qinglian, "Why Have China's Peasants Become the Major Force in Social Resistance?," *China Rights Forum*, no. 2 (2009), www.hrichina.org/print/content/3790.

11. Jiangnan Zhu, "The Shadow of Skyscrapers: Real Estate Corruption in China," *Journal of Contemporary China* 21, no. 74 (March 2012): 243–60.

12. He Qinglian, "Why Have China's Peasants."

13. Ibid.

14. Ministry of Finance, "Report on the Implementation of the Central and Local Budgets for 2010 and on the Draft Central and Local Budgets for 2011," March 5, 2011, p. 11, http://english.gov.cn/official/2011–03/17/content_1826516.htm.

15. Wang Hairong, July 28, 1976, Beijing, U.S. Liaison Office, notes by Jan Berris, Doc. 748, pp. 3–4.

16. Secretary Hu Qili, October 16, 1985, Beijing, Great Hall of the People, notes by Jan Berris, Doc. 800, p. 2.

17. *Bulletin of Activities* [*Gongzuo Tongxun*], ed. J. Chester Cheng (Stanford, CA: Hoover Institution on War, Revolution, and Peace, Stanford University, 1966).

18. Vice-Premier Geng Biao, November 25, 1978, Beijing, notes by Jan Berris, Doc. 761, p. 2.

19. Xi Jinping, interview by Thogersen and Posborg, DML, Doc. 866, pp. 7–8.

20. Senior U.S. diplomat, May 8, 2012, DML, Doc. 858, p. 1.

21. "China's Male-to-Female Ratio Declines for the First Time," *People's Daily Online,* June 4, 2010, http://english.peopledaily.com.cn/90001/90776/90882/7012887.html.

22. Vice-Chairman Li Xiannian, June 1979, Beijing, notes by Jan Berris, Doc. 775, p. 3.

23. Senior Chinese economist, March 29, 2005, China, DML, Doc. 663, p. 2.

24. For background, see Anita Chan, *Wal-Mart in China* (Ithaca: Cornell University Press, 2011); Tim Pringle, *Trade Unions in China: The Challenge of Labor Unrest* (New York: Routledge, 2011); David Barboza, "In Chinese Factories, Lost Fingers and Low Pay," *New York Times,* January 5, 2008, www.nytimes.com/2008/01/05/business/worldbusiness/05sweatshop.html? pagewanted=all&_r=0; see also "Trade Unions in China: Membership Required," *Economist,* July 31, 2008, www.economist.com/node/11848496/print.

25. David Barboza and Charles Duhigg, "China Contractor Again Faces Labor Issue on iPhones," *New York Times,* September 10, 2012, www.nytimes.com/2012/09/11/technology/foxconn-said-to-use-forced-student-labor-to-make-iphones.html?pagewanted=all.

26. Premier Zhu Rongji, April 5, 2002, Beijing, Zhongnanhai, DML, Doc. 561, pp. 1–2. In this interview, Zhu mentions Han Dongfang being in the United States. Han's organization, China Labour Bulletin, was founded in Hong Kong in 1994.

27. Andrew Jacobs, "Protests over Chemical Plant Force Chinese Officials to Back Down," *New York Times,* October 29, 2012, p. A4; "Ningbo Defends Chemical Plant after Protests," Xinhua, October 24, 2012, www.china.org.cn/china/2012–10/24/content_26896978.htm.

28. Engineers, September 9, 1982, Wuhan, Yangzi River Valley Planning Authority, DML, Doc. 785, p. 1.

29. *The Twelfth Five-Year Plan for National Economic and Social Development of the People's Republic of China* (Beijing: Central Document Translation Department of the Central Compilation and Translation Bureau, July 2011), p. 12.

30. State Councilor Song Jian, Chairman, SSTC, April 15, 1994, DML, Doc. 664, p. 2.

31. Hu Qili, secretary, Central Committee, October 16, 1985, Beijing, Great Hall of the People, notes by Jan Berris, Doc. 800, p. 3.

32. U.S. Department of State Reporting Cable, Foley and NPC Standing Committee Head Wan Li, May 23, 1989, Washington, DC, U.S. Capitol, DML, Doc. 698; Reuters, "China Inflation Slows," *New York Times,* December 29, 1989, www.nytimes.com/1989/12/29/business/china-s-inflation-slows.html; Marcus Noland, *Pacific Basin Developing Countries* (Washington, DC: Institute for International Economics, 1990), p. 151.

33. "China Inflation Rate," *Trading Economics,* n.d., www.tradingeconomics.com/china/inflation-cpi (accessed July 26, 2012).

34. Vice-Premier Zhu Rongji, June 12, 1996, Beijing, DML, Doc. 395, p. 2.

35. Wen Jiabao, premier, March 16, 2007, Beijing, Great Hall of the People, premier's press conference, Doc. 443, p. 6.

36. President Jiang Zemin, May 9, 1992, Beijing, DML, Doc. 403, p. 2.

37. Vice-Premier Zhu Rongji, June 12, 1996, Beijing, DML, Doc. 395, p. 2.

38. Yi-En Tso and David A. McEntire, "Emergency Management in Taiwan: Learning from Past and Current Experiences," unpublished paper, p. 8.

39. "President Ma Ying-jeou's Popularity Plunges to New Low, TVBS Poll Shows," *Taipei Times,* July 6, 2012, p. 1, www.taipeitimes.com/News/front/archives/2012/07/06/2003537070; "Survey on President Ma Ying-jeou's Approval Rating and People's Views on the Unification-Independence Issue," Global Views Survey Research Center, conducted April 13–17, 2011.

40. Ko Shu-ling, "Morakot: The Aftermath: Ma, Liu Approval Ratings Plummet in Morakot's Wake," *Taipei Times,* August 20, 2009, p. 1.

41. Keith Bradsher, "Collapse of New Bridge Underscores Worries about China Infrastructure," *New York Times,* August 25, 2012, p. A4.

42. U.S. Geological Survey (USGS), "Earthquakes with 1,000 or More Deaths since 1900," n.d., http://earthquake.usgs.gov/earthquakes/world/world_deaths.php (accessed July 28, 2012).

43. National Climate Data Center (NCDC), "Flooding in China, Summer 1998," November 20, 1998, http://lwf.ncdc.noaa.gov/oa/reports/chinaflooding/chinaflooding.html.

44. "The World's Worst Floods by Death Toll," n.d., www.epicdisasters. com/index.php/site/comments/the_worlds_worst_floods_by_death_toll/ (accessed July 28, 2012); Yi Si, "The World's Most Catastrophic Dam Failures," in *The Dragon River Has Come! The Three Gorges Dam and the Fate of China's Yangtze River and Its People*, ed. Dai Qing (Armonk, NY: M. E. Sharpe, 1998), p. 38.

45. United Nations Environment Programme, "The Songhua River Spill, China, December 2005," field mission report, December 5, 2005, p. 7, http:// unep.org/PDF/China_Songhua_River_Spill_draft_7_301205.pdf.

46. Ibid, p. 14.

47. Centers for Disease Control and Prevention, "Global SARS Outbreak, 2003," in "Frequently Asked Questions about SARS," July 2, 2012, www.cdc. gov/sars/about/faq.html. The CDC numbers on both total deaths and total cases are slightly lower than WHO figures, which are used for the country-specific data. World Health Organization, "Cumulative Number of Reported Probable Cases of SARS," www.who.int/csr/sars/country/2003_07_11/en/# (accessed November 2, 2012).

48. President Chen Shui-bian, June 6, 2007, Taipei, Presidential Building, DML, Doc. 428, p. 2.

49. Meeting with senior Chinese analyst, February 24, 2009, DML, Doc. 632, p. 2.

50. Ibid.

51. Vice-Chairman Li Xiannian, June 1979, notes by Jan Berris, Doc. 775, p. 3.

52. President Jiang Zemin, June 14, 1996, Beijing, Zhongnanhai, DML, Doc. 394, pp. 4–5.

53. Vice-minister, Beijing, Ministry of XX, June 28, 1999, DML, Doc. 352, p. 2.

54. "35,860 Chinese Evacuated from Unrest-Torn Libya," Xinhua, March 3, 2011, http://news.xinhuanet.com/english2010/china/2011–03/03/c_13759456. htm.

55. Jane Perlez, "Chinese Plan to Kill Drug Lord with Drone Highlights Military Advances," *New York Times*, February 21, 2013, p. A5.

56. Premier Wen Jiabao, April 1, 2005, Beijing, Purple Pavilion, DML, Doc. 454, pp. 3–4.

57. "Xi Jinping's Explanation of the Chinese People's Dream," Chinadaily. com.cn, January 16, 2013.

58. Senior foreign affairs figure, June 27, 2011, Beijing, DML, Doc. 833, p. 2.

6. SOLDIERS AND CIVILIANS

For the first epigraph (Eisenhower's farewell address), see http://mcadams.posc. mu.edu/ike.htm. The second epigraph (quote from think tank analyst) is from Doc. 807 (DML), pp. 4–5. The third epigraph (quote from senior Chinese diplomat) is from Doc. 550 (DML), p. 1. The fourth epigraph, from *China's National Defense in 2010*, white paper (Beijing: Information Office of the State

Council, 2011), can be accessed at www.china.org.cn/government/whitepaper/node_7114675.htm.

1. Division-level officer, July-August 1976, notes by Jan Berris, Doc. 797, p. 1.

2. Chiou Yi-jen, March 28, 2000, Washington, DC, DML, Doc. 628, p. 2.

3. PLA major general, January 10, 2005, China, DML, Doc. 489, p. 2.

4. Senior Chinese scholar, August 15, 2005, Tokyo, Japan, DML, Doc. 758, p. 2.

5. David Shambaugh, *Modernizing China's Military: Progress, Problems, and Prospects* (Berkeley: University of California Press, 2002), p. 13.

6. PLA general, January 11, 2005, China, DML, Doc. 334, p. 3.

7. International Institute for Strategic Studies, *The Military Balance* (London: IISS), annual volumes published in 1993, 2001, and 2012.

8. Tai Ming Cheung, ed., *New Perspectives on Assessing the Chinese Defense Economy* (La Jolla: University of California, Institute on Global Conflict and Cooperation, 2011); Evan S. Medeiros, Roger Cliff, Keith Crane, and James C. Mulvenon, *A New Direction for China's Defense Industry* (Santa Monica, CA: RAND Corporation, 2005).

9. Li Cheng and Scott W. Harold, "China's New Military Elite," *China Security* 3, no. 4 (Autumn 2007): 72–73.

10. Chinese general-grade officer, June 26, 2011, DML, Doc. 820, p. 5.

11. Tai Ming Cheung, *New Perspectives;* also senior think tank scholars, December 6, 2011, DML, Doc. 853, p. 1.

12. Hu Jintao, "Full Text of Hu Jintao's Report at the 18th Party Congress," Xinhua, November 17, 2012, http://news.xinhuanet.com/english/special/18cpcnc/2012-11/17/c_131981259_10.htm (accessed February 16, 2013).

13. Li Cheng and Scott W. Harold, "China's New Military Elite," *China Security* 3, no. 4 (Autumn 2007): 69.

14. Kenji Minemura, "China's Senkakus Operations Overseen by Party Task Force Led by Xi," February 4, 2013, *Asahi Shimbun*, http://ajw.asahi.com/article/asia/china/AJ201302040089.

15. John Garnaut, "Rotting from Within: Investigating the Massive Corruption of the Chinese Military," *Foreign Policy*, April 16, 2012, www.foreignpolicy.com/articles/2012/04/16/rotting_from_within.

16. Li Cheng and Harold, "China's New Military Elite," pp. 65–70.

17. PLA colonel, September 2005, China, DML, Doc. 459, p. 3.

18. Senior Chinese scholar, August 19, 2004, China, DML, Doc. 502, pp. 1–2.

19. Senior Chinese scholar, August 19, 2004, China, DML, Doc. 500, p. 1.

20. Strategic analyst, August 19, 2004, DML, Doc. 502, p. 2.

21. PRC senior strategic analyst and others, January 18–22, 2003, United States, DML, Doc. 754, p. 2.

22. President Jiang Zemin, November 22, 2002, Hebei Room, Great Hall of the People, Beijing, DML, Doc. 521, p. 2.

23. Ibid., p. 3.

24. Senior military officer, January 6, 2012, China, DML, Doc. 856, p. 4.

25. Jeremy Page and Lingling Wei, "Bo's Ties to Army Alarmed Beijing," *Wall Street Journal*, May 17, 2012, p. A1, http://online.wsj.com/article/SB10001424052702304203604577398034072800836.html.

26. Yin Fanglong, "Er pao zhengzhibu zhuren: Geren de xiaoqing xiaoyi fu cong dang de daqing dayi" [An individual's emotions and causes must be subordinate to the party's righteous cause], *Renmin Ribao* [People's Daily], April 13, 2012, http://news.ifeng.com/mainland/detail_2012_04/13/13850516_0.shtml.

27. James Mulvenon, "The Bo Xilai Affair and the PLA," *China Leadership Monitor,* no. 38 (August 6, 2012), www.chinaleadershipmonitor.org.

28. General-grade Chinese officer, May 9, 2001, DML, Doc. 564, p. 1.

29. Senior foreign affairs system official, August 20, 2002, China, DML, Doc. 536, p. 3.

30. Shirley A. Kan et al., "China-U.S. Aircraft Collision Incident of April 2001: Assessments and Policy Implications," Congressional Research Service, RL30946, October 10, 2001, www.fas.org/sgp/crs/row/RL30946.pdf.

31. Senior PLA officer, May 9, 2001, DML, Doc. 564, p. 1.

32. Chinese senior officer, January 6, 2012, DML, Doc. 856, pp. 2–3.

33. Senior Chinese foreign and security analyst, September 21, 2011, DML, Doc. 847, p. 3.

34. First vice-chairman, Central Military Commission, Liu Huaqing, May 26, 1994, Diaoyutai State Guest House, Beijing, DML, Doc. 612, p. 3.

35. Discussions of the PLA budget are tricky, and one needs to differentiate among measures. Here we are using the measure of defense spending as a percentage of GDP. Because of China's rapidly growing GDP, one can have the phenomenon of rising absolute defense expenditures occupying a declining share of GDP. Another measure is defense spending as a percentage of total central government expenditure. By this measure, China's defense expenditure in the Deng era never again reached the 17.7 percent it was the year Deng returned to power in 1977—by 2001, the percentage was 8.2 percent. See Shambaugh, *Modernizing China's Military,* pp. 188–89. Since 1989, there have been briskly rising absolute defense expenditures and a declining, and then generally low, defense expenditure-to-GDP ratio and a declining percentage of defense expenditure in total central government expenditure. This discussion pertains to official government figures; there is debate over the magnitude of spending occurring beyond the acknowledged figures.

36. James Mulvenon, *Soldiers of Fortune: The Rise and Fall of the Chinese Military-Business Complex, 1978–1998* (Armonk, NY: M.E. Sharpe, 2001), particularly ch. 3.

37. "GDP Growth (Annual %)," World Bank, World Development Indicators, http://data.worldbank.org/data-catalog/world-development-indicators (accessed November 10, 2012).

38. Chinese general, January 11, 2005, China, DML, Doc. 334, p. 2.

39. Senior Chinese general, May 24, 1994, Beijing, DML, Doc. 616, p. 2.

40. General Liu Huaqing, May 26, 1994, Diaoyutai State Guest House, Beijing, DML, Doc. 612, p. 3.

41. The inconsistency between this number and the one used in the preceding sentence was in the original DML interview document.

42. Senior Chinese general, May 25, 1994, DML, Doc. 617, p. 2.

43. Ibid, p.3.

44. Senior Chinese general, September 25, 1997, DML, Doc. 407, p. 2.

45. Defense Minister Chi Haotian, March 19, 2001, August 1 Building, Beijing, Notes by Jan Berris, Doc. 774, p. 2.

46. General-grade officer, mid-2011, DML, Doc. 826, p. 2.

47. Chinese general, January 2010, DML, Doc. 679, p. 3.

48. Shaun Tandon, "Clinton Uses Warship to Push Philippines Alliance," *DefenseNews,* November 16, 2011, www.defensenews.com/article/20111116/ DEFSECT04/111160306/Clinton-Uses-Warship-Push-Philippines-Alliance; see also David M. Lampton, "China and the United States: Beyond Balance," *Asia Policy,* no. 14 (July 2012): 40–44.

49. Senior Chinese foreign policy scholar, January 23, 2013, DML, Doc. 883, p. 3.

50. Calculated from the *China Statistical Yearbook* (Beijing: China Statistics Press), 2007–11: table 8–4, "Government Expenditure by Main Item" (yearbook for 2007); table 7–6, "Main Items of National Government Expenditure of Central and Local Governments" (yearbooks for 2008 and 2009); table 8–6, "Main Items of National Government Expenditures of Central and Local Governments" (yearbooks for 2010 and 2011).

51. Former senior U.S. intelligence official, October 2011, DML, Doc. 851, p. 1.

52. One of the last officially reported numbers on "public order disturbance cases" was eighty-seven thousand, and by all qualitative reports that number has continued to rise since. "China Handles 87,000 Public Order Disturbance Cases," *People's Daily Online,* January 20, 2006, http://english.peopledaily. com.cn/200601/20/eng20060120_236813.html. Tsinghua university professor Sun Liping was reported to have asserted that in 2010 the number of protests, riots, and mass incidents was 180,000. Tom Orlik, "Unrest Grows as Economy Booms," *Wall Street Journal,* September 26, 2011, http://online.wsj.com /article/SB10001424053111903703604576587070600504108.html.

53. President Jiang Zemin, May 9, 1992, Beijing, DML, Doc. 403, p. 2.

54. Vice-Premier Zhu Rongji, June 12, 1996, DML, Doc. 395, p. 3.

55. Former senior U.S. intelligence official, October 2011, DML, Doc. 851, p. 1.

56. Senior Chinese individual, January 2013, DML, Doc. 868, p. 3.

57. Senior analyst in foreign policy system, July 24, 2009, China, DML, Doc. 645, p. 4.

58. President Jiang Zemin, March 5, 1999, Diaoyutai State Guest House, Beijing, DML, Doc. 368, p. 4.

59. Senior Chinese scholar, June 10, 2007, China, DML, Doc. 434, p. 1.

60. Senior person in foreign affairs system, May 6, 1999, DML, Doc. 578, p. 1.

61. Senior Chinese security analyst, September 21, 2011, DML, Doc. 847, p. 3.

62. Former senior U.S. intelligence official briefing members of Congress, October 2011, DML, Doc. 851, p. 2. In this briefing by the former senior intelligence official, one member of Congress interjected the comment reported in the text.

63. Senior foreign policy adviser, August 19, 2002, China, DML, Doc. 547, p. 3.

64. Senior Chinese diplomat, September 26, 2002, DML, Doc. 529, p. 1.

65. Senior Chinese scholar, January 3, 2011, China, DML, Doc. 717, p. 2.

66. John Pomfret, "China Tests Stealth Aircraft before Gates, Hu Meet," *Washington Post,* January 11, 2011, www.washingtonpost.com/wp-dyn/content/article/2011/01/11/AR2011011101338_. There is a more benign interpretation of this development than a PLA attempt to embarrass or surprise the visiting American defense secretary. That explanation is that Hu Jintao, of course, knew there was a stealth aircraft program, but knowing the test schedule of an aircraft is more to expect of a national leader than is reasonable. The test schedule was probably worked out at a level sufficiently low in the system that no one connected the dots between the test and the visit of the secretary.

67. Former senior U.S. intelligence official, October 2011, DML, Doc. 851, p. 2.

68. Robert A. Caro, *The Passage of Power* (New York: Alfred A. Knopf, 2012), p. 340.

69. Yang Yi, "China Must Have a Strong Navy," *China Defense Blog,* December 5, 2011, http://china-defense.blogspot.com/2011/12/rear-admiral-yang-yis-latest-oped.html.

7. NEGOTIATION CHINESE STYLE

The first epigraph (from Huang Hua) is from notes by Jan Berris, Doc. 715, pp. 2–3. The second epigraph (from Li Peng) is from Doc. 396 (DML), p. 3. The third epigraph, from an interview of a senior Chinese scholar, is from Doc. 535 (DML), p. 1.

1. Zhou Enlai, "The Past Year's Negotiations and the Prospects" (December 18, 1946), in *Selected Works of Zhou Enlai,* vol. I (Beijing: Foreign Languages Press, 1981), p. 288.

2. Henry Kissinger, *On China* (New York: Penguin Press, 2011), pp. 97–112.

3. Ibid., pp. 101–2.

4. Prominent Chinese businessperson, March 11, 2003, DML, Doc. 514, p. 1.

5. Senior adviser to Chinese leaders, September 20, 1999, Beijing, DML, Doc. 577, p. 1.

6. Lucian Pye, *Chinese Commercial Negotiating Style* (Santa Monica, CA: RAND, January 1982), p. 51.

7. Chinese general, July 16, 2009, DML, Doc. 646, p. 4.

8. David M. Lampton, *The Three Faces of Chinese Power: Might, Money, and Minds* (Berkeley: University of California Press, 2008).

9. Lucian Pye, *Chinese Commercial Negotiating Style* (Santa Monica, CA: RAND Corporation, January 1982), Doc. R-2837; Carolyn Blackman, *Negotiating China: Case Studies and Strategies* (St. Leonards, Australia: Allen and Unwin, 1997); Richard H. Solomon, *Chinese Political Negotiating Behavior, 1967–1984* (Santa Monica: RAND, 1995); and Kenneth T. Young, *Negotiating with the Chinese Communists: The United States Experience, 1953–1967* (New York: McGraw-Hill, 1968).

10. *Peking's Approach to Negotiation: Selected Writings, Compiled by the Subcommittee on National Security and International Operations, Committee*

on Government Operations, United States Senate (Washington, DC: U.S. Government Printing Office, 1969).

11. Fred Charles Ikle, "American Shortcomings in Negotiating with Communist Powers," in *International Negotiation,* memorandum prepared at the request of the Subcommittee on National Security and International Operations, Committee on Government Operations, U.S. Senate (Washington, DC: Government Printing Office, 1970).

12. Sun Tzu, *The Art of War,* trans. and introd. Samuel B. Griffith (London: Oxford University Press, 1963), pp. 63–64.

13. Yan Xuetong, *Ancient Chinese Thought, Modern Chinese Power,* ed. Daniel A. Bell and Sun Zhe, trans. Edmund Ryden (Princeton: Princeton University Press, 2011).

14. Committee of Concerned Asian Scholars [CCAS], "Interview with Chou En-lai" [July 19, 1971], *Bulletin of Concerned Asian Scholars* 3, nos. 3–4 (1971): 48, http://criticalasianstudies.org/assets/files/bcas/v03n03.pdf, abstracted in Doc. 812, pp. 9–10.

15. Jimmy Carter, *Keeping Faith: Memoirs of a President* (Toronto: Bantam Books, 1982), p. 189.

16. Ren Xiao, "The Moral Dimension of Chinese Foreign Policy," in *New Frontiers in China's Foreign Relations,* ed. Allen Carlson and Ren Xiao (Lanham, MD: Lexington Books, 2011), pp. 3–23, esp. pp. 15–20.

17. Ambassador Yu Qingtai, March 20, 2009, Beijing, Foreign Ministry, DML, Doc. 637, p. 2.

18. Sun Tzu, *Art of War,* p. 69.

19. Very senior Foreign Ministry official, January 28, 2005, Beijing, DML, Doc. 342, p. 3.

20. Senior university strategic analyst, July 20, 2009, DML, Doc. 638, p. 3. The same strategic analyst put it as follows sometime later, with Foreign Ministry officials present: "'We are manipulating them.' Taiwan is central. 'China is manipulating the DPRK for its narrow Taiwan core interests.'" June 28, 2011, Beijing, DML, Doc. 833, p. 5.

21. Foreign Minister Huang Hua, October 2, 1977, Beijing, notes by Lucian Pye, Doc. 710, p. 2.

22. Pew Research Center, "Growing Concerns in China about Inequality, Corruption," October 16, 2012, www.pewglobal.org/files/2012/10/Pew-Global-Attitudes-China-Report-FINAL-October-10-2012.pdf, p. 37.

23. Carter, *Keeping Faith,* p. 48.

24. Vice-Premier Li Lanqing, July 21, 1993, Beijing, Purple Pavilion, Zhongnanhai, DML, Doc. 379, pp. 1–2.

25. Very senior foreign affairs official, September 16, 1997, Beijing, Diaoyutai State Guest House, DML, Doc. 410, p. 3.

26. President Jiang Zemin, June 14, 1996, Beijing, Zhongnanhai, island in the Southern Lake, DML, Doc. 394, p. 2.

27. Ibid., p. 1.

28. National Assembly member, March 21, 2006, Hanoi, Vietnam, DML, Doc. 451, p. 1.

29. Lan Lan, "Airline Carbon Tax Talks with EU Stall," *China Daily,* July 23, 2012, p. 1.

30. Senior leader in Taiwan affairs, January 11, 2005, Beijing, DML, Doc. 341, p. 2.

31. Senior Chinese academic, July 17, 2009, Beijing, DML, Doc. 652, p. 4.

32. Minister Fang Yi, June 22, 1979, Beijing, DML, Doc. 426, pp. 1–2.

33. Senior foreign affairs official, August 4, 2011, DML, Doc. 837, p. 3.

34. Defense Minister Chi Haotian, January 12, 1998, Beijing, Ministry of National Defense, Foreign Affairs Office, DML, Doc. 329, p. 2.

35. President William Clinton, "Statement by the President On Most Favored Nation Status for China," Office of the Press Secretary, May 28, 1993, http://china.usc.edu/(S(boflmn2ijuzcks3tmakvrx45)A(nNB4EyowywEkAAAAODZi NWEoMjItMzkoMCooOTMzLTg1OWItYTU2N2I5OTYxOTlhbvg 6UVVONxiw6UYZv5sOCboevw1))/ShowArticle.aspx?articleID=736&AspxA utoDetectCookieSupport=1.

36. Often American flagship companies that produce high-value exports to China (e.g., Boeing for aircraft and Westinghouse for nuclear power plant technology) are mentioned, giving some specificity to their threats.

37. Vice-Minister Zhou Nan, April 1991, notes by Jan Berris, Doc. 767, p. 3.

38. Premier Li Peng, April 3, 1993, Beijing, Great Hall of the People, DML, Doc. 396, p. 4.

39. Foreign Minister Qian Qichen, April 1991, Beijing, notes by Jan Berris, Doc. 765, p. 2.

40. Mayor Han Yulin, July 27, 1993, Zhangzhou, Fujian, DML, Doc. 610, p. 2.

41. Wang Wen and Huang Fei, "Interview with Admiral Yang Yi," *Huanqiu* [Global Times], April 23, 2010, Doc. 852, p. 3.

42. Foreign Minister Qian Qichen, April 1991, notes by Jan Berris, Doc. 765, p. 3.

43. Former Chinese university president, August 26, 1992, DML, Doc. 422, p. 1.

44. Keith Bradsher, "China Is Blocking Minerals, Executives Say," *New York Times,* September 23, 2010, www.nytimes.com/2010/09/24/business/ energy-environment/24mineral.html.

45. Andrew Higgins, "In Philippines, Banana Growers Feel Effect of South China Sea Dispute," *Washington Post,* June 10, 2012, www.washingtonpost. com/world/asia-pacific/in-philippines-banana-growers-feel-effect-of-south-china-sea-dispute/2012/06/10/gJQA47WVTV_story.html.

46. Agence France-Presse, "Japanese Exports to China Drop 14.5pc in November," December 20, 2012, www.scmp.com/business/economy /article/1108586/japanese-exports-china-drop-145pc-november.

47. Senior Chinese general, January 2010, DML, Doc. 679, p. 2.

48. George Bush and Brent Scowcroft, *A World Transformed* (New York: Alfred A. Knopf, 1998), p. 413.

49. Ibid., p. 414 n.

50. Senior information official, January 12, 2005, Beijing, DML, Doc. 339, p. 3.

51. Zhang Wenjin and Ambassador Seignious, January 8, 1980, Beijing, Zhongnanhai, declassified document, DML, Doc. 696.

52. Very senior Taiwan official, June 25, 2008, Taipei, DML, Doc. 389, p. 3.

53. General XX, May 25, 1994, Beijing, DML, Doc. 617, p. 3.

54. Very senior foreign policy leader, June 26, 2011, Beijing, Diaoyutai, DML, Doc. 819, p. 3.

55. Wu Bangguo, August 28, 2007, Beijing, Great Hall of the People, DML, Doc. 430, p. 2.

56. Senior professor, February 24, 2009, Beijing, DML, Doc. 632, p. 2.

57. Chinese strategic analyst, July 20, 2009, DML, Doc. 638, p. 3.

CONCLUSION

The first epigraph (quote by Li Peng) is from Doc. 788 (notes by Jan Berris), p. 4. The second epigraph (quote by the Chinese intelligence analyst) is from Doc. 847 (DML), p. 2. The third epigraph (quote by Xi Jinping) is from Doc. 861 (DML), p. 1.

1. Pollution numbers at this level carry with them the U.S. government warning that "everyone should avoid all physical activity outdoors; people with heart or lung disease, older adults, and children should remain indoors and keep activity levels low."

2. Bruce J. Dickson, *Red Capitalists in China* (Cambridge: Cambridge University Press, 2003); Margaret M. Pearson, *China's New Business Elite: The Political Consequences of Economic Reform* (Berkeley: University of California Press, 1997).

3. Senior Chinese scholar, February 24, 2009, DML, Doc. 632, p. 3.

4. A senior adviser to China's most senior leader, September 28, 2009, Beijing, DML, Doc. 654, p. 2.

5. Two observations illustrate why I believe the Chinese assertion of American decline may be mistaken. First, the United States now is able to exploit shale gas, which holds the promise of reducing dramatically the burden of energy imports to the United States, a reduction that, in turn, will change not only balance-of-trade realities but the cost of manufacturing in America. These developments will, in turn, boost U.S. competitiveness and presumably reduce the need for involvement in conflicts elsewhere. Second, if the United States takes greater advantage of its legacy as a nation able to attract and keep skilled and enterprising immigrants, it will preserve an advantage that virtually no other nation possesses.

6. "Diaoyu: Islands in a Stormy Sea," *China Daily*, September 17, 2012, p. 6.

7. Hu Jintao, "Hu Jintao shibada baogao" [Hu Jintao's report at the Eighteenth Party Congress], section 12, part 7, November 8, 2012, *Zhongguo wangluo dianshitai (China Internet Television Network)* (from People's Daily), http://news.cntv.cn/18da/20121118/100674_12.shtml; see also "Full Text of Hu Jintao's Report at 18th Party Congress," Xinhua, November 17, 2012, http://newsxinhuanet.com/english/special/18cpcnc/2012–11/17/c_131981259_13.htm (accessed December 3, 2012).

8. Xi Jinping, "Zai shiba jie zhonggong zhongyang zhengzhiju di yici jiti" [Xi Jinping at the first session of the Eighteenth CPC Politburo Meeting], Xinhua, November 17, 2012, http://news.xinhuanet.com/2012-11/19/c_123967017. htm# (accessed November 30, 2012); see also Edward Wong, "New Communist Party Chief in China Denounces Corruption in Speech," *New York Times*, November 19, 2012, www.nytimes.com/2012/11/20/world/asia/new-communist-party-chief-in-china-denounces-corruption.html.

9. Robert A. Dahl and Charles E. Lindblom, *Politics, Economics, and Welfare: Planning and Politico-Economic Systems Resolved into Basic Social Processes* (New York: Harper Torchbooks, 1953), pp. 93–126.

10. For the 4 percent estimate, see Minxin Pei, "Will China Become Another Indonesia?," *Foreign Policy*, no. 116 (Fall 1999): 96–100, and Minxin Pei, *China's Trapped Transition* (Cambridge, MA: Harvard University Press, 2005), various discussions of corruption throughout the volume. For the 13.3 to 16.9 percent estimates, see David M. Lampton, *The Three Faces of Chinese Power: Might, Money, and Minds* (Berkeley: University of California Press, 2008), pp. 236–38; see also Wu Jinglian, *Understanding and Interpreting Chinese Economic Reform* (Australia: Thomson, 2005), pp. 391–98, esp. p. 394. For the much higher estimates of other scholars, see Wu Jinglian, *Understanding and Interpreting*, p. 394.

11. Evan Osnos, "Corruption Nation: Why Bo Xilai Matters," *New Yorker*, April 16, 2012, www.newyorker.com/online/blogs/evanosnos/2012/04/chinas-public-servants-why-bo-xilai-matters.html.

12. Cui Liru, "Some Thoughts on China's International Strategy," *Contemporary International Relations* 21, no. 6 (November/December 2011): 1–7.

13. For more on this debate, see Chu Shulong, "Is America Declining?," *Brookings Northeast Asia Commentary*, no. 54 (November 30, 2011).

14. I made this argument in two lectures at the Shanghai Institutes of International Studies in the summer of 2010, lectures simultaneously published in Chinese and English in Dawei Lanpudun [David M. Lampton], "Zhong mei guanxizhong di liliang yu xinren" [Power and trust in U.S.-China relations], *Guoji zhanwang* [Global Review], no. 4 (July-August 2010): 42–58.

15. Conversation with Chinese foreign policy analyst, July 20, 2009, DML, Doc. 648, p. 3.

16. Ren Xiao, "Traditional Chinese Theory and Practice of Foreign Relations: A Reassessment," in *China and International Relations: The Chinese View and the Contribution of Wang Gungwu*, ed. Zheng Yongnian (London: Routledge, 2010), p. 107.

17. Senior adviser to Chinese leadership, September 17, 2012, Beijing, DML, Doc. 863, pp. 2–3.

18. Senior public opinion analyst, November 19, 2012, DML, Doc. 879, p. 3.

APPENDIX

1. Allen Carlson, Mary E. Gallagher, Kenneth Lieberthal, and Melanie Manion, eds., *Contemporary Chinese Politics: New Sources, Methods, and Field Strategies* (New York: Cambridge University Press, 2010), particularly the introduction and chapters by Xi Chen, Victor Shih and colleagues, Peter

Hays Gries, Calvin Chen, Benjamin L. Read, Lily L. Tsai, and Kenneth Lieberthal.

2. Maria Heimer and Stig Thogersen, eds., *Doing Fieldwork in China* (Honolulu: University of Hawaii Press, 2006).

3. Philip Selznick, *TVA and the Grass Roots: A Study in the Sociology of Formal Organization* (Berkeley: University of California Press, 1949).

4. Benjamin L. Read, "More Than an Interview, Less Than Sedaka: Studying Subtle and Hidden Politics with Site-Intensive Methods," in Carlson et al., *Contemporary Chinese Politics*, p. 150.

5. Lily L. Tsai, "Quantitative Research and Issues of Political Sensitivity in Rural China," in Carlson et al., *Contemporary Chinese Politics*, pp. 260–63.

6. Robert A. Scalapino, ed., *Elites in the People's Republic of China* (Seattle: University of Washington Press, 1972); Cheng Li, *China's Leaders: The New Generation* (Lanham, MD: Rowman and Littlefield, 2001), and "The Central Committee, Past and Present: A Method of Quantifying Elite Biographies," in Carlson et al., *Contemporary Chinese Politics*, pp. 51–68; see also www.china leadershipmonitor.org for fine quantitative and qualitative looks at China's elite.

7. These numbers do not always add to 558. Sometimes the number is less because I don't have the necessary data to categorize some respondents; at other times the number is greater than 558 because people occupy more than one category in the coding scheme; and in still other interview settings there is more than one respondent.

8. This category includes scholars, researchers, and think tank personnel, unless they head an institute or university.

9. I did not take down most of my conversations with Chinese ambassadors and their equivalents over time (though the ambassador often had a note taker), generally because they had businesslike purposes, they often were short, and their content was private and understood as such at the time.

10. The nine categories of rank utilized here were Supreme Leader, Rank01; Politburo, Vice-Premier, State Councilor, Central Military Commission Vice-Chairman, Rank02; Provincial First Party Secretary, Governor, Minister, and First Party Secretary or Mayor of a Provincial-Level Municipality, Rank03; Deputy Party Secretaries, Vice-Governors, Vice-Ministers, and Deputy Mayors in the units specified immediately above, Rank04; Bureau Director or equivalent, Dean, Institute or University President, Province-Level Ministry Head, Subprovincial City Vice-Mayor, Prefecture-Level City Mayor, Rank05; Lower-Level "Miscellaneous," a category that includes academics and researchers, Rank06; Ambassador, Rank07; Institute Deputy Director, Deputy Department Director, Rank08; and CEO, Chairman of the Board, Executive Vice President, Rank09. This categorization is not strictly rank in the narrowest hierarchical terms. Ambassadors, for instance, by any fair reckoning, are not literally Rank07, and CEOs of a large, strategic state corporation (e.g., China National Offshore Oil Corporation or CNOOC), are by no means literally Rank09; indeed, they often carry the rank of minister. This categorization of rank simply is intended to provide a parsimonious indicator of the distribution of interviews within the Chinese hierarchy and to take account of the emergence of corporate

leadership in China. Further, any rank categorization schema is incomplete because it cannot take into account informal lines of influence in the system and because people wear multiple "hats," some of which are unseen or unknown to the outsider. Moreover, in many cases I have interviewed the same person over time, so as his or her rank has changed over time, so has their assigned rank for each interview changed when warranted and known.

11. An important exception to this generalization is a substantial set of interviews I conducted in Hubei Province in 1982 on the topic of management and planning in the Yangzi River Valley. This project took me to rural water conservation and construction sites throughout the province. Some of these interviews are in this data set and others are not.

12. Senior Chinese academic, January 23, 2013, DML, Doc. 883, p. 4.

13. For instance, General Liang Guanglie was, in 2011, minister of national defense and state councilor (state posts), member of the Seventeenth Central Committee and the Central Committee's Central Military Commission (party posts), and a general in the military.

14. Cheng Li, in "China's Fifth Generation: Is Diversity a Source of Strength or Weakness?," *Asia Policy,* no. 6 (July 2008): 64, points out that in 2007–8 there were thirty-five non-CCP members then holding vice-ministerial and vice-governor level or above jobs. So things may gradually be changing in this respect.

15. Most notable and informative have been my interactions with the environmental and social organization activist Dai Qing; the Tiananmen-era dissident Liu Binyan (in a joint appearance at the University of Michigan); and the editor of the *World Economic Herald* in Shanghai, Qin Benli, who was fired from his position by Jiang Zemin, providing some of the background to Jiang's rapid rise in Beijing thereafter. I had a minor interaction with Chai Ling in the aftermath of the Tiananmen debacle of 1989.

16. That these statuses are not mutually exclusive with the above three is shown by the fact that, for instance, scholars could be in the military (e.g., at the Academy of Military Sciences), journalists often are in the party, and NGO leaders often have close ties with various state organizations.

17. Cheng Li, "China's Fifth Generation."

18. Cheng Li, in ibid., p. 62, finds that females constitute only 11 percent of Fifth Generation leaders.

19. For a thoughtful discussion of interviewing in China, see Dorothy J. Solinger, "Interviewing Chinese People: From High-Level Officials to the Unemployed," in Heimer and Thogersen, *Doing Fieldwork in China,* pp. 153–67. Solinger's "four fundamental rules" of interviewing are an appropriate place to begin: (1) get appropriate approvals; (2) keep track of people you meet and enlarge your network over time; (3) "be both aware and uninitiated"; and (4) "Keep the subject's safety at the center of your consciousness" (pp. 166–67).

20. Deputy Chief XX, Ministry of Water Conservancy and Electric Power, November 4, 1982, Beijing, China, DML, Doc. 811, pp. 5–6.

21. Former vice-premier Gu Mu, March 31, 1993, Beijing, Diaoyutai State Guest House, Building 15, DML, Doc. 400, p. 1.

Index

Dai Qing, 280n15
debate, 207–11
debt, external, 36
Declaration of Independence (U.S.), 229
deductive strategic perspective, 7
defense. *See* military
defense industry, 133–34, 169, 189
democracy: Chinese claims of, 216; Chinese
views of, 112, 132; experiment in
Shekou, 27; and the middle class,
224–26; and the need for a constitution,
226; in Taiwan, 158–59. *See also*
Democracy Wall movement; Tiananmen
demonstrations
Democracy Wall movement (1979), 21, 25,
64
Democratic People's Republic of Korea. *See*
North Korea
Democratic Progressive Party (DPP,
Taiwan), 64, 157, 158, 159, 166
Deng Pufang, 250n18
Deng Xiaoping: agricultural polices of, 21;
assessments of Pol Pot, 128–29; and the
CCP political monopoly, 24–26; choice
of successors, 58–59, 62; conversation
with Frank Press, 23–24; cooperation
with World Bank, 27–28; "crossing the
river by feeling for stones," 13, 110;
declaration of martial law, 63–64;
devotion to family, 60; and the Diaoyu
Islands, 65; economic policies of, 22, 66,
101, 250n14; emphasis on remunerative
power, 21; energy policies of, 26; era of
Peace and Development, 18–19;
formative experiences of, 140; Four
Cardinal Principles of, 25; interaction
with Robert McNamara, 23, 203–4;
interview with Mike Wallace, 4, 111;
leadership style of, 53, 60, 64–65;
meetings with Americans in the 1970s,
52–53; negotiating style of, 214–15;
nonreliance on think tanks, 67; opening
of China, 1, 66; ouster of, 15, 249n3;
policies on education and technology,
16, 23–24; policies on the military,
19–20, 165, 180; policies on trade, 26,
26–28; policy initiatives before 1977,
247n1; political legitimacy of, 30;
population policies of, 22–23, 52, 64;
pragmatic approach of, 13, 20–21;
praise for capitalism, 24; quoted on
governance, 47; return to power in
1977, 1, 15; revolution of, 4–6, 14–15,
16, 220–21, 247–48n1; role of public
opinion for, 72; Southern Tour of, 13,

66, 178; and split in the party center,
173; state-society balance under, 22;
and statistical systems, 93; strategic
decisions of, 16–18, 18–28, 63–64, 72;
and the student exchange program, 208;
suppression of Democracy Wall
movement, 64; on the Taiwan issue, 64;
and the Tiananmen demonstrations,
63–64, 117, 189; unfinished agenda of,
40, 43–44, 223; Vietnam policy of, 185,
250n7
Diaoyu (Senkaku) Islands, 65, 171, 212,
225
Dickson, Bruce, 224
Ding Guangen, 94
Ding Yuanzhu, 227
diplomacy, 193–94. *See also* negotiations
dissidents, 239, 280n15
domestic politics, 109, 111–21, 136, 164,
184, 232
doufu (beancurd) construction, 154
DPP (Taiwan). *See* Democratic Progressive
Party
DPRK. *See* North Korea
dragon economies, 19, 26
dual-use technology, 208, 213

earthquakes, 155. *See also* Tangshan
earthquake (1976); Wenchuan
earthquake (2008)
economic changes, 33–37. *See also*
economic growth
economic growth, 15, 67, 80, 150–51, 218.
See also economic changes
economic powers, 127, 203, 264n7
economic sanctions, 123, 192, 209–10, 212
education: Deng's policies on, 23–24;
higher, 24, 74–75; inequality in, 163; of
population in 1980, 16, 17; of
population in 2010, 29; role in the
economy, 37; study abroad, 23–24,
74–75, 210–11
Eighteenth Party Congress (2012), 98, 170,
171, 174, 226
Eisenhower, Dwight D., 165, 166
elections, 32, 50; in Taiwan, 158, 159–60
electric power, 113, 244
elite studies, 234
energy, 26, 36, 277n5. *See also* nuclear
power
environmental issues, 35, 149–50, 156
environmental sustainability, 15, 80, 150
European Union, 206
exchange rate policy, 91, 105–6
experimentalism, 4, 20–21, 79, 223

United States *(continued)*
225, 229, 277n5; credit rating of, 125;
"decline" of , 196, 202–3, 225, 229,
277n5; foreign policy of, 109–10;
ideological and cultural institutions,
132; intelligence community, 188;
military sales to Beijing, 213; rebalancing policy to Asia, 73, 182, 183, 191,
211; relationship of military to
government, 190; as threat to China,
128, 134; weapon sales to Taiwan, 75,
178, 211, 218; weapons of, 178, 179.
See also U.S.-China relations
universal values, 131–32, 229
UN Resolution 678, 213–14
untethered pluralization, 3, 55, 55*fig.*
urbanization, 15, 38, 76, 112, 142, 222
U.S.-China relations: action-reaction
dynamics in, 132–35; and the Belgrade
bombing, 117–19, 162; consensus
building and, 115–16; during the Deng
Xiaoping era, 19, 111; future of, 136,
231–32; and the global system, 124–26,
229–31; in the Hu Jintao era, 124–25;
Iran and, 208–9; Jiang Zemin and,
123–24, 125; normalization of, 202;
North Korea and, 196, 202, 275n20;
and the PLA budget, 182; power
relationships and, 196–97, 217–18;
Soviet Union and, 127–28, 202–3;
and space initiatives, 135; succession
and, 114; Taiwan issue, 115, 157,
158, 178, 182, 202, 275n20; and the
US-PRC military aircraft collision over
Hainan, 175. *See also* diplomacy;
negotiations
U.S.-China Strategic and Economic
Dialogue (S & ED), 135
U.S. dollar, 125
U.S. Treasuries, 36, 42, 125

Vietnam: China's foreign policy toward,
128–29, 185; "defensive counterattack"
of 1979, 250n7; Japan and, 200;
mentioned, 192, 203, 204; and South
China Sea claims, 206; U.S. war in, 19
Vogel, Ezra, 44, 64

wages, 21–22
Walker, Richard L., organization chart of
the PRC system, 81, 82*fig.*, 95
Wallace, Mike, 4, 111
Walmart, 147
Wan Li, 151
Wanda Group, 56

Wang Daohan, 57, 61, 66, 78, 186
Wang Hairong, 95, 144–45
Wang Hongwen, 58
Wang Huning, 267n1
Wang Lijun, 99
Wang Shaoguang, 227
Wang Wei, 175
Wang Xuebing, 108
wang dao (kingly way), 57
War and Revolution, era of, 18–19, 83
water, 150
water pollution, 75, 156
weapons: antisatellite, 133, 134, 189;
exports of, to Iran, 208–9; and the
military budget, 178; nuclear, 123, 133,
134, 196, 202; sales of, to Taiwan, 75,
178, 211, 218; and technological
competition, 133–34, 178, 179. *See also*
PLA, technology and weapons
Weber, Max, 61, 62–65
Wei Jingsheng, 25
Weibo, 99. *See also* social media
Wen Jiabao: concern with masses, 50–51,
141; dreams of, 163; on economic
issues, 151; on inequality, 163;
leadership style of, 60, 68; mentioned,
89; on political reform, 62; response to
disasters, 154; on rural problems, 142;
and the SARS crisis, 31; used boat
metaphor for leaders, 58; used data to
respond to assertions, 97; and the
Wenchuan earthquake, 95
Wenchuan earthquake (2008), 30, 95, 153,
155, 213
Westinghouse-Toshiba, 89, 276n36
Whac-A-Mole, governing China compared
to, 50
Whyte, Martin, *Myth of the Social Volcano*,
38
Wildavsky, Aaron, 85
Woodcock, Leonard, 154
workers, 67, 147–49. *See also* unemployment
workplace safety, 35
World Bank: China's role in, 40, 43; Deng's
engagement with, 27–28, 101, 203;
initiative to modernize PRC educational
institutions, 24; lessons from, 252n34;
loans to China, 36. *See also* McNamara,
Robert
World Trade Organization: Doha Round,
213; membership in, 35, 67, 101;
negotiations over China's entry, 102,
120–21, 203; rules of, 78
Wu Bangguo, 60, 130, 217